Silver throughout History

CYRILLE JUBERT

CYRILLE JUBERT

Silver throughout History

All rights reserved © 2013 by Cyrille Jubert

No part of this book may be reproduced or transmitted in any form or by any means, graphic, electronic or mechanical, including photocopying, recording, taping, or by any information storage retrieval system, without the written permission of the publisher.

Published by Omnia Veritas Ltd

OmniaVeritas

contact@omniaveritas.org

www.omniaveritas.org

Silver throughout History

CYRILLE JUBERT

PREAMBLE

For centuries, **Silver** and then Gold, in this order, were means of barter and monetary instruments.

Silver, in the form of bullions or coins, was the basic component of international trade.

Alexander the Great paid his troops in gold, probably because they had to move around a lot and gold occupied very little space in a soldier's haversack in the field.

From then on, gold was exchanged for silver at a fluctuated rate in Europe between a ratio of 1/10 and 1/16, depending on the output at the mines. This ratio was different in Africa and Asia, thus paving the way for a lucrative trafficking business for those who dared to venture beyond the seas. If the discovery and exploitation of the silver mines made the fortune of princes, the latter often hoarded their fortune in gold due to its volume and weight.

China and India produced goods and commodities (silk, tea, spices, precious stones,...), that the West wanted and had to purchase in hard currency. The white metal thus travelled from the West to the East for several centuries, depleting the treasures of princes and bankers of Old Europe. Even today, Asia is still hoarding silver, but, though it is no longer a monetary unit, it is so valuable that it is an indispensable part of our electronic civilization.

Modern day bankers, exploiting the fact that silver is perceived as a safe investment, have created financial products referred to as paper silver, just as there is paper gold. These financial products have served both as a tool for speculating fluctuations in metal prices, as well as substitute for poorly informed investors. According to the financial oligarchy, these stock market products enabled the prices of precious metals to be controlled, thereby controlling the apparent devaluation of fiat currencies, and in particular, the reference money for international trade: the Dollar. The establishment of these purely virtual currencies based on trust was a very long term undertaking, as we shall see in the following pages. The strategy put in place for the implementation of the current system continued for several generations. The best example dates back to the last century:

In 1600, Mexico accounted for three quarters of the world's supply of silver. This white metal was then indispensable, since it was the monetary unit of trade throughout the world: Europe, the Americas, Russia, India, Japan and China.

Mexico's war of independence, an intermittent comedy, fomented by some local idle aristocrats and funded secretly by Anglo-Saxons bankers, put an end to this influx of silver. Spain, in bankruptcy, having granted independence to this very rich colony under pressure from the Anglo-Saxon oligarchy, gave birth to a Mexican Republic. If the war of independence was a sham, then the Mexican Republic was a farce. From 1821 to 1850, Mexico had 50 successive governments. Their respective policies had only one constant factor: They banned the export of silver, the main wealth of the country by accumulating debts. Is this not surprising? Who was interested in destabilizing the universal monetary system at that time? Who was so powerful enough to corrupt 50 successive governments for such a long time? Having failed through diplomacy to convince his successive Mexican representatives to sell this indispensable monetary metal, Napoleon III began the conquest of Mexico by force.

The fact that the English were involved in the previous blockade with the hope of forcing the repayment of Mexican debt, coupled with the fact that the throne was given to the Austrian Archduke Maximilian of Hapsburg, showed how the shortage of silver was a matter of great concern to the political power in place in Europe. Napoleon III's military victory in 1865 was immediately followed by a political defeat. Bankers of the financial oligarchy ordered Napoleon to return to his country which he did without question or battle. The poor Emperor Maximilian of Austria was executed by his subjects.

Bimetallism ensured monetary and political stability. By destabilizing Mexico and the global silver supply, the great dynasties of bankers, secret manipulators, sought to pave the way for widespread use of paper money, which had been tested in Europe with varying degrees of success in the 17th and 18th centuries.

The purpose of this Mexican story is to show you that these "Bank Gentlemen" never work in the same time horizon like you and me. Details of events which later took place on the precious metals market were developed over 20 years ago in a system prior to the abandonment of the "Gold Exchange Standard" by Nixon in 1971. This decision seemed inevitable in itself since the creation of "London Gold Pool" in 1961. The unfolding of history seemed to be controlled like a set of dominoes falling, but with such prescience and intelligence!

Re-read this pamphlet which dates back to 1864: "The Dialogue in Hell between Machiavelli and Montesquieu". A pamphlet that some did not hesitate to compare with Plato's writings including the famous "Myth of the Cave", which is dear to my heart. This should be read over and over again!

Humanity is now at the electronic currency age and the wealth of nations is determined by the number of online accounts, but the NASA helio-physicists are predicting terrible solar magnetic storms that can destroy our electronic civilization at any time within the next three years. One might wonder if the plutocrats, who hoarded precious metals secretly to a near magnetic shock, finally achieved their aims.

On one side, will be the poverty-stricken mass whose bank accounts got depleted overnight, commoners depending on the government's soup kitchen or "food stamps", like the 47 million Americans in June 2012, and on the other side, a rare elite who transformed their capital into gold and silver in time and who will soon gain some value that no hard-working person would ever dream of acquiring.

The rest of the analysis will be quite anecdotal.

The financial oligarchy had plans and a timetable, but in that society just like all others, dissensions broke out and dissidents fought against the supreme authority. This is what we have been experiencing for several years. Some oligarchies want a **unipolar world** whilst others are advocating a **multipolar world**.

The discord ended up in a confrontation which resulted in a financial monetary war, as devastating as a world war in terms of financial costs. Most western banks are currently bankrupt, crippling the economy and plunging states in huge debts that they cannot repay. The world is at the brink of a systemic crash which can occur at any time.

Initial plans and "agendas" of the different factions of this oligarchy, were jostled in recent years and even today, the elites are still negotiating the short term rules between themselves, while scheming some totally unexpected pitfalls. This battle is extremely violent but the masses do not see it, stupefied by the "tittytainment" and permanent misinformation, which has been the norm in the media and politics since Plato's time.

Observers seeking to know the plans of this plutocracy to protect their families can only gather "secret information" from insiders navigating at the periphery of the oligarchy. From this fragmentary information, they are trying to put together the giant puzzle by drawing a global vision relying on their ability to analyze and synthetize. Each observer is scrutinizing the political spectrum based on their personal vision and is gathering clues for support. In order to do this, information and misinformation have to be sort out, since there are some true Orwellian government's administration, whose sole aim is to mislead the scouts towards the wrong path.

The silver metal is one of the Achilles' heels of the system. Though it no longer has monetary value today, it is considered as a precious metal connected to gold. The government's maneuvers to make its monetary status fall faced the reality that as an industrial metal, imbalances of supply over demand could raise the price of silver higher than that of gold.

Today, the world's 3rd and 4th largest banks, HSBC and JPM, are in danger for short selling nearly 7 years of mineral production on the markets positions that they cannot cover. They will one day default on silver. That's for sure.

An increase in the price of silver induces systematic risk. It is possible that China will use this leverage to put pressure on the Anglo American financial oligarchy. The white metal could therefore have strategic geographical importance.

The cash that you invest in coins or silver bullion, is withdrawn from circulation. By doing so, you deprive the bankers of the ammunition to play their destructive mega casino game. It is a form of silent "bank-run", a calm, thoughtful and non-violent revolution. It is an act of good citizenship, rich in true ethics.

At the same time, you are protecting your capital and your family from the risk of the impending monetary and financial chaos.

You will be convinced through the pages of this history book and other stories that silver is definitely the **best investment for the next 15 years**.

The 50F Hercules which was not in circulation was an investment vehicle. This coin weighed 27 grams of pure silver.

The 5 Francs sower below was known to everybody because it was used on a daily basis. It could become an indispensable instrument of barter trade, if the NASA helio-physicists are right that a magnetic storm will destroy the electrical and electronic systems.

It weighed 10.02 grams of pure silver. Its current price could be multiplied by 33 by 2016.

The side of the 5 francs silver coin was engraved with the motto "Liberty, Equality, Fraternity", whilst that of the 50 francs coin was streaked in cupro-nickel.

Silver Throughout History

Ancient Period

CYRILLE JUBERT

GENESIS

Genesis 2

8 And the Lord God planted a garden eastward in Eden; and there he put the man whom he had formed.

9 And out of the ground made the Lord God to grow every tree that is pleasant to the sight and good for food; and the tree of life also in the midst of the garden; and the tree of knowledge of good and evil.

10 And a river went out of Eden to water the garden, and from thence it was parted, and became into four heads.

11 The name of the first is Pishon; that is which compasseth the whole land of Havilah, where there is gold.

12 and the gold of that land is good; there is bdellium and the onyx stone.

The garden of Eden was located in ancient Mesopotamia, from the Greek meso (middle) and Patmos (River). The Bible talks about 4 branches of the river. Two of these branches are Tigris and Euphrates, and the other two have disappeared today, dried in the sands of Arabia.

"The land of Havilah, where there is gold", refers to the mountains of Saudi Arabia between Mecca and Medina to Mahd adh Dhahab. *"Pishon"* would be the Wadi Al Batin which once flowed through Kuwait and showed satellite photos.

Gold, silver and electrum were exploited in the Mahd adh Dhalab mines which employed 10,000 slaves in the olden days. These were probably the famous mines of King Solomon called the "cradle of gold".

These lost mines were rediscovered by the geologist, K.S. Twitchell in 1932. They were exploited from 1939 to 1954, producing 22 tons of gold and 28 tons of silver.

Closed for several decades, geological studies conducted since 1971, updated new veins of extremely richness which have been exploited since 1988.

This was the only region that produced bdellium in the past. The bdellium which is mentioned in Genesis is the resin of trees producing myrrh. It can still be found in Yemen today.

With regards to Onyx, mentioned in the same passage, it was considered as a precious stone in the past and it was also produced in this mountain range.

The garden of Eden was the Happy Arabia of the ancient past. This region was watered by rivers whose dams allowed the irrigation of the plains. The Kingdom of the Queen of Sheba was located there. The eruption of Krakatoa in 416 AD or 535 AD (according to sources) broke the large dam which could never be rebuilt. A long period of extreme drought turned the Garden of Eden into a desert sand, burned by the sun.

That is where the cradle of human history is found.

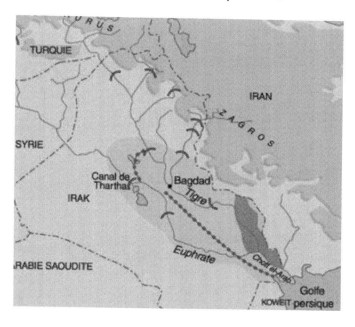

THE CODE OF HAMMURABI

If you take the common book of the three major religions, the Bible, the **Judges** came before the **Kings** in the history of mankind, Hammurabi was one of these Judges who caused justice to reign in Mesopotamia in 1750 B.C.

At the gate of each city in Mesopotamia, he erected a monument which provided a reminder of the Laws so that no one was unaware of them. This was the first code of laws known to mankind. One of these monuments was in Louvre in Paris.

One of these laws set the daily minimum wage of workers expressed in grams of silver.

A laborer was to receive 1.88 and 2.1 grams of silver per day. We shall come back to this in the prospective part of the book.

History is an eternal Cycle.

Around 3400 B.C. appeared in Mesopotamia, the writing in form of a cuneiform script. The text was engraved on fresh clay tablets, before they were hardened through cooking.

With the advent of writing was born journal entry. An administrative system for the management of payables and receivables was developed based on the value of traded goods in terms of known standards: cereals, domestic animals, silver and others. That was the birth of bank money.

A 60 base numbering system, hexadecimal, was used. It was the source of our division of hours, angles and arc, especially for geographic coordinates.

Base 60 has many more divisors (1, 2, 3, 4, 5, 6, 10, 12, 15, 20, 30 et 60) and sixty is the smallest number divisible by 1, 2, 3, 4, 5 and 6.

CYRILLE JUBERT

EGYPT

Around 2900 B.C., Pharaoh Djoser expanded his kingdom by taking control of territories rich in copper and gold, especially near Wadi Maghara. Ramses II and his descendants conquered new gold territories in Nubia and all deserts in the East.

Stones extracted from gold-bearing quartz veins were heated in fire to make them brittle. They were then crushed in mortars before they were washed on tables of fine grooved basalt. The heavier gold accumulated in the grooves.

The River Nile bed was rich in gold dust which the prospectors in the service of Pharaoh could extract with the simple panning technique.

In Egypt, gold was long reserved for the temples of the gods. In those early days, the fear of divine anger was sufficient to temper the lust of mere mortals.

The monetary unit in Egypt around 2000 B.C. was the Sha. It was associated with a unit of weight, the *Deben*.

A Deben of gold was worth 12 *Shas*.
A Deben of silver was worth 6 *Shas*.
A Deben of lead was worth 3 *Shas*.

The *Sha* was worth 7.5 grams of gold or 15 grams of silver or 75 grams of bronze.

Under another dynasty, the gold/silver ratio was slightly changed. 5 *Shas* of silver was equivalent to 3 *Shas* of gold.

Egypt was always poor in silver, which accounted for the extremely high ratio. When trade was established with Athens, silver started pouring into Egypt and its relative value fell compared to that of gold.

It appears that ancient Egypt did not mint coins till very late. Some gold coins were found as far back as 404 and 341 B.C., when Pharaoh had to pay foreign mercenaries, first to free themselves from the Persians, and then to resist the return of their soldiers.

Gold coins had already been associated with warriors.

THE HITTITES

Around 1500 B.C., the Hittites, Indo-European people of Central Anatolia invaded Mesopotamia and exploited their silver mines which were coveted by the rival armies of Sumer, Assyria and Persia.

They used the proceeds from these mines to make calibrated and standardized means of payments.

- "Shekel"   8.41 grams of silver
- "Stater"   16.82 grams of silver or two shekels
- "Mina"   500 grams of silver
- "Talent"   30 kilograms of silver or 60 minas

Hittite merchants battered silver against the goods they wanted to acquire: tin from Iran, fabrics, corn from Egypt, etc. Just like the way Iran today is swapping its oil and gas against gold in its trade with India. Mesopotamians, Hittites, Persians, Iranians; a long cycle of history takes us back to the same matrix of civilization.

CYRILLE JUBERT

CROESUS AND THE GOLDEN FLEECES

In the 7th Century B.C., small oval nuggets made from natural gold and silver alloys were discovered in the famous river Pactolus, in the kingdom of Lydia, modern Turkey. Plutarch specified that the river was called **Chrysorrhoas,** which in Greek signifies "which carries gold".

King Gyges panned for gold in this torrential river, leaving his sheep fleeces in the bed of the river. The latter trapped the nuggets and that was enough to recover them. This practice was also used in all the torrents of Colchis, current Georgia.

Gyges circulated these electrum nuggets throughout the East, which when weighed and stamped became coins. These are the very first coins listed.

A century later, the famous King Croesus improved the smelting technique of his predecessor by separating gold and silver from the electrum, before creating the first bimetallic system of coins: 1 gold stater weighed 8.17 grams of pure gold.

It was worth ten staters of silver, representing 10.89 grams of silver. This was equivalent to a gold/silver ratio of 13.3.

The Lydian system gradually extended throughout the East, then to Greece and, from there, to the whole of Mediterranean Europe, thanks to the development of trade. Pactolus resources had already been exhausted before the 1st century according to the testimony of the Greek geographer, Strabon (1st Century A.D.).

SILVER & THE PHOENICIANS

In 3000 B.C., the kingdom of Phoenicia, was situated on the eastern shores of the Mediterranean today including Palestine, Lebanon and Southern Syria. Its powerful neighbors, Egypt and Mesopotamia, limited the possibility of expanding the kingdom to the interior and the boisterous nomadic people of Asia Minor were a constant threat. This is what drove the Phoenicians to sea, caulking their boats, thanks to the bitumen which gave them an advantage over all the other people in the Mediterranean, because it allowed them to move from mere coasting from port to port to ocean navigation. The Phoenicians quickly dominated the Mediterranean trade and created trading posts to facilitate trading with local people. Unlike the Greeks, who founded colonies in the cereal plains, the Phoenicians created ports to help them remain focused on trade. It was through this that they founded Gadir, now Cadiz, and Carthage.

Diodorus Siculus, Greek historian of the 1st Century B.C., author of one of the largest historical encyclopedia in antiquity, referred to this subject: *"The country of the Iberians contains the most numerous and the most beautiful silver mines ever known. The natives were ignorant of its use, but the Phoenicians who came to trade, bought the silver in exchange for a small quantity of goods. They carried it to Greece, Asia and other countries and acquired great wealth as a result."* "the Carthaginians found so much gold and silver in the Pyrenees that they used it to anchor their ships."

Aristotle wrote that the Phoenicians, who landed in Tartessos, found so much silver that their ships could not contain it. They used this metal for their utensils. Andalucía became the hub of trade in copper, silver, gold, lead and tin ores.

Polybius, born in 208 B.C., Greek General, statesman and political theorist was probably the greatest Greek historian in his time. Head of the Greek cavalry in the war between Rome and Macedonia, he was captured and sent to Rome. He became Tutor of the children of Scorpio, (referred to as the second African). Released after 17 years, Rome used his talents as a General to attack and raze down Carthage, capital of the Phoenician Empire Polybius, in his work, mentioned the silver mines of Betis, current Guadalquivir, where forty thousand men were employed. The Romans called these the Silver Mountains. Mons Argentarius, produced 25,000 silver drachmas.

Since Polybius participated in the destruction of Carthage, he mentioned the Phoenician drachmas. The latter weighed approximately 3.54 grams of silver. These mines produced nearly 32 tons of silver or 1 million one hundred and twenty eight thousand ounces per year at that time.

GREECE

Athens could only develop its civilization thanks to silver-lead veins running south of the city in Laurium region ending at Cape Sounion, at the temple of Neptune. The numerous mines dug over the centuries since the Bronze Age, left many remains, tunnels, wells or workshops. The first mines exploited the surface veins where the ore came into contact with shale and limestone. From the 5th and 6th Centuries B.C., the Athenians developed the large scale mining industry and ore refining techniques. This helped them to get a strong currency that was recognized throughout the Mediterranean basin, where sailors, traders and settlers managed to develop trading posts.

Athenian drachma was struck with an owl,
symbol of goddess Athena.

In 465 B.C., Athens sought to conquer the Pangaea region, in the north-east of current Greece whose mountains were known for their silver and gold mines. However, this expedition was a disaster ; the whole team was massacred by the Thracians, the

Bulgarians of today.

Athens was able to impose its model of society in the ancient world due to the prosperity of its mines, which were exploited by slaves. The city invested in majestic public buildings, whose remains are still the glory of the city today.

One of the neighboring cities, Sparta, had an entirely different political philosophy which favored the community to the disadvantage of the individual. Sparta's social services were well developed with a strong and powerful army because they were closely knit together. These two Greek cities showed perhaps the opposition between capitalism and socialism prematurely.

Athens, with strong monetary and commercial power was very belligerent. The Peloponnesian War, triggered in 429 B.C. by Athens, was sponsored with the city funds, but Pericles and his peers did not anticipate that it would last 27 years. The conquered armies were used as garrisons to preserve the "pacified" territories and this cost them dearly. In 407 B.C., the Athenian treasury was almost empty of gold and silver; the currency had to be devalued by adding copper to the metal. The face value was far from its fine metal content.

A further devaluation in 405 B.C. led the government to put copper coins as well as the old gold and silver currencies in circulation at the same time.

Athens finally lost the war. The garrisons could no longer buy goods from the populations they occupied so they had to retreat.

The worthless copper coins that the state minted continuously had legal tender in Athens and its region as fiat money.

But while Athenian civilization cast its pearls before the swine with men who made history like Demosthenes, Socrates, Plato and Aristotle, the barbarians in the empire became increasingly boisterous.

Philip of Macedonia who was rich thanks to his gold mines raised an army and expanded his kingdom at the expense of Athens.

In 338 B.C., Philip II of Macedonia sought to unify the Greek cities to better defend the region against repeated Persian incursions. Unable to do so verbally, he did it by force. After his assassination, his son Alexander took over from him and developed his plans for conquest.

His plan was to conquer Byzantium, (now Turkey), Troy, Syria, Lebanon, Palestine and Egypt, before taking Mesopotamia (Iraq, Persia (Iran), and northern India (Pakistan and Afghanistan). Not allowing anything to stop him except the Himalayas mountains.

Thanks to the mines of Pangaea, bordering Macedonia to the north, Alexander created a strong currency which unified his empire.

Alexander's silver tetra drachm, represented by Heracles head covered with skin of the Nemean lion.

This coin, which was the most popular in ancient times, weighed 17 grams of silver.

The king was equal to the Minister of Finance, managing the revenue of the Macedonian Kingdom. Levies (taxes) owed by the people conquered went back to the people and not the king who was sometimes called upon to give account.

During Alexander's great conquests, articles in gold and silver taken from the conquered people were melted into coins and bars and sent to Macedonia. This influx was very significant during the home coming of veterans, exhausted after endless conquests around 323 B.C..

At the beginning of his conquest, Alexander was not interested in the money issue, but an army in the field being very expensive, he was obliged to look closely at his accounts.

After the battle of Issus, where he laid his hands on a large booty of silver and especially after the capture of Tyre in Lebanon, where the gold treasure was significant, Alexander considered himself as "king of Asia" and minted coins bearing his effigy.

The Tarsus workshop, after the capture of city by Philip II in 333 B.C., was the first to exchange for what later became the Macedonian Empire.

The Pella and Amphipolis workshops, the most active during Alexander's reign minted 13 million tetra drachmas of silver or 221 tons of silver in 18 years.

The gold/silver ratio was 1/15.
The stater was worth 20 drachmas and weighed about 8.5 grams of gold.

A gold stater was the monthly wage of a Macedonian soldier. A delegate of the 4th Century B.C. received 6 obols or one drachma per work day in Parliament.

Obol weighing 1 gram of silver

The Greeks discovered the currency manipulations used to stimulate an economy exhausted by war. The collapse of the currency led to the decline of the economy which in turn caused the fall of the Empire.

CYRILLE JUBERT

SILVER & ROME

The Republic of Rome gradually dominated the neighboring cities.

In the 4th Century B.C., the Gallic Chief Brennus, after conquering the south of France and north of Italy, advanced towards the south to capture Rome and plunder it.

To guard against new invasions, Rome implemented a "defensive imperialism" and gradually imposed its suzerainty over the neighboring peoples, Etruscans, Latin people, etc. till they subjugated most of Italy except the north. These areas were rich agricultural regions but they were poor in metals. Gallic territories were metal-rich areas. Rome first captured Cisalpine Gaul, now Northern Italy which was annexed. At the end of the 2nd Century, Rome conquered current Southern France and Rhone Valley which became previously defeated "provinces of Rome", from the Latin "provincia". The name province came from that.

It was not until the middle of the 1st Century that the rest of Gaul was conquered (Spain, Aquitaine, Brittany, Normandy, Belgium, Switzerland...) The Provinces paid taxes to enrich the Roman Treasury.

Silver throughout History

After the 3 Punic wars against Carthage, the conquest of the Iberian Peninsula was not yet complete. The Mediterranean border was under the control of Rome but the belligerent people of the West, Lusitanos, Cantabers and Asturians opposed a fierce resistance to the invasion in the First Century B.C.. It took the war of Cantabira in 29-19 B.C. for Augustus to enslave the rebels and annex these territories in Rome. Some lead and silver mines were exploited in Galicia, Beltic, Lusitania and Asturias. The copper mines were equally renowned and some of them are still being exploited today like Rothschild's RIO TINTO which was sold recently.

Hispania was known since ancient times for its mineral wealth. Diodorus Siculus, Greek historian of the 1st Century B.C. said that *"the forest fires in these lands poured streams of silver"*.

This sentence by Diodorus seems like a tall story, an obvious exaggeration of a Southerner in the manner of Tartarin but it has an element of truth. To understand this, we must briefly take a closer look at the mining techniques.

If at some mines, the tunnels were carved and chiseled out of solid steatite, one of the most commonly used techniques before the invention of gunpowder was the fire technique, which was used to blast the hardest rocks. Logs of wood were stacked against the wall, where a silver-lead vein appeared. By firing, the rock burst into a myriad of small pieces of ore that were quickly turned into powder. After washing, they were first placed in kilns that turned the ore into metal.

It was possible, especially in places where there were rich silver-lead veins to see metal castings in the course of a raging fire because the lead melted easily and did not require very high temperature.

The tunnels in the mine were dug by fire over several kilometers, as was the case of the Melle mines in Poitou which can be visited today. Obviously they needed smoke removal ducts that the ancients controlled perfectly.

The Cantabrian Wars allowed Rome to place their hands on the rich gold mines in Las Medulas. To ensure the safety of the area and transportation of the gold extracted in Las Medulas, Rome subsequently installed permanent troops. It was through this that was born the city of Leon whose current name is derived from the

Latin "legio": the city was founded around the camp of the 7th Roman Legion called "Gemina".

The testimony of Pliny the Elder

Chapter 33 of "Natural History", title of the vast encyclopedia of Pliny the Elder, born in 23 B.C., was entirely devoted to metals. Besides his literary work, Pliny the Elder was a devoted servant of the Empire. During the reign of Vespasian, he was a procurator in Narbonnese Gaul in Hispania (73 A.D.). It was on this occasion that he became familiar with mining techniques.

Aureus the Vespasian

Pliny listed the various ways to mine gold: he mentioned panning, that is extracting gold from the sand of rivers, digging wells to track gold veins and the "ruina montium" technique, that is the destruction of mountains through the force of water or the strength of miners. Dams, Acqueducts and water conveying tunnels were built across mountains and valleys to transport water to the mine. In Las Medulas, these aqueducts covered 147 kilometers. The water force disintegrated the gold mountain and the debris were washed down into wooden canals lined with heather; then the dried heather was burned. After washing the ashes, the precious metal appeared.

The last method involved the digging of tunnels until parts of the mountain walls removed. Once the sapping tunnels were well advanced, the miners blew up the pillars until the mountain collapsed. A guard placed on top of the mountain trusted his instincts to seize the moment of collapse; when he sensed this coming, he sent a signal to gather the workers before he put himself to safety.

More than six tons of gold per year!

According to Pliny the Elder, these mining methods used in various places in Asturias, Galicia and Lusitania allowed the extraction of 20,000 pounds of gold (or 6.5 tons) annually. This lasted until at least the 4th Century A.D.

DEVALUATION OF THE ROMAN CURRENCY

The denier was the basic unit of the currency of Rome, at the inception of the Republic in the 5th Century B.C..

Denier comes from "denarius", which means ten, since that currency weighed 10 Aces. This coin weighed 4 grams of silver at the beginning but increased to 3 grams in a relatively stable manner until the assassination of Julius Caesar, which marked the end of the Roman Republic.

At the time of the Republic, 50 deniers, or 5 ounces of silver was enough to purchase the total annual family cereal needs. During the era of the empire and the mismanagement of the army and civil servants in 300 AD, one needed 6,000 deniers to enjoy the same lifestyle.

Under Julius Caesar and Emperor Augustus, bonuses of legionnaires were paid with gold coins, the "Aureus". This was only a wartime bonus which became the standard expected by the military and it was endorsed as ordinary income by Tiberius.

Praetorian troops, bodyguards of emperors, at the latter's accession to the throne, received 10 Aurei per guard; soldiers of the regular city police received only half of that and an ordinary army legionnaire received only 3.

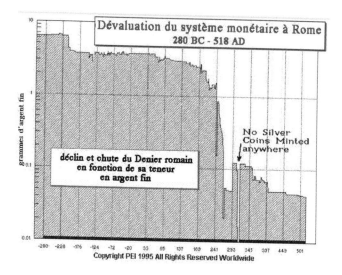

After the assassination of Caligula, Claudius paid 150 aurei per head for his Praetorian guard. This costs 35 million deniers and additional 50 million for the rest of the army. This is what cost the empire to ensure political stability after the death of Caligula.

Nero paid the same thing at his accession to the throne and after his death, his successor, Vitellius promised his Praetorian guard a premium equal to 88.8 million deniers.

Between 96 and 192 AD, there were 44 different allowances representing 567 million deniers or 22 million aurei.

Note the gold/silver ratio of 25.

After the assassination of Emperor Commodus in 192, the Praetorian guard had become so corrupt that she put the throne in the hands of the highest bidder at the auction. Didius Julianus offered 6,250 deniers or 250 aurei per head. To enable him to pay this amount, he recast the silver coins by lowering their fine metal content from 2.75 to 2.4 grams. He reigned for only 5 months.

Fear of civil and military unrest became increasingly expensive for the empire.

Thus, costs of government employees and pensions were increasingly raised in the state budget which forced him to reduce the real value of the currency to pay his debts.

Silver throughout History

The silver content of coins was divided by 54.

\multicolumn{4}{c}{DEVALUATION OF THE ROMAN CURRENCIES}				
Year	Emperor	Weight of Coin	Weight of Silver	
158 - 167	Nero	13.22	2.19	
167 - 170	Marcus Aurelius	12.68	1.57	
191 - 192	Commode	11.90	0.92	
193 - 211	Septimius Severus	11.55	1.16	
212 - 217	Caracalla	12.62	0.88	
218 - 222	Elagabalus	12.28	0.88	
224 - 227	Alexander Severus	12.75	0.74	
235 - 238	Maximanus I	12.41	0.74	
238 - 244	Gordian	12.38	0.61	
244 - 249	Phillip	12.20	0.87	
249 - 251	Trajan	12.56		
251 - 253	Trebonianus Gallus	10.59		
253 - 260	Valerian	10.52		
260 - 261	Macrianus	10.49		
261 - 268	Gallian	9.97	0.40	
268 - 270	Claude	9.71	0.26	
270 - 275	Aurelian	7.99		Menthalo
275 - 276	Tacit	8.05		
276 - 282	Probus	7.77		
282 - 284	Carmus	7.47	0.04	
284 - 296	Diocletian			

CYRILLE JUBERT

THE 30 DENARII OF JUDAS

Judas Iscariot has gone down in history for having delivered Jesus against hard cash. For what amount did this accursed of the church sell his soul to the devil?

From the Latin, denarius, the denier was one of the basic currencies of the Roman Empire. It had legal tender in most parts of Europe, the whole of North Africa and the Middle East and lasted until the Middle Ages in the kingdoms of the West and many Arab countries under the name of dinar. This silver coin was created in 212 B.C. to fund the Second Punic War between Rome and Carthage. In the bimetallic monetary system established at that time, the denier which proved to be 950% of silver, was minted alongside other more classical copper coins. At its creation, it weighed 4.51 grams but monetary inflation caused it to be devalued in 140 B.C. to weigh only 3.96 grams of silver.

In the light of this information, Judas Iscariot betrayed Christ for 118.8 grams of silver or nearly 3.82 ounces. As we approached the Passover, the night when Jesus was arrested, the value of this betrayal to the current rate of COMEX seems pretty ridiculous since an ounce of white metal is now worth about 24 euros.

Was the head of Jesus pegged at a price of 92 euros?
No, I can assure you. The current rate of silver is exceptionally low.

Under the Roman Empire, the gold/silver ratio was 12 against 75 now. The price of gold today, taking the ratio of 12, an ounce of silver cost 103.8 euros so the denier cost 6.82 euros assuming that there was no premium for the purchase of this coin. This pegs the price of betrayal at 396 euros and 50 cents. But this assessment is not realistic.

A soldier in the Roman Empire received a very comfortable wage amounting to 40 deniers per month, excluding field allowances as well those for expatriation, daily meals, discounts on wine, meat and other benefits in kind.

These 30 deniers therefore was equivalent to one month's average salary today, or nearly 1,650 euros (average salary in 2011 or 1.5 times of the net minimum wage).

You could conclude two things:

Firstly, in terms of benefit, Judas's friendship was not worth much...

Secondly, silver is significantly undervalued at the moment. To restore the same purchasing power to silver as in Herod's time, an ounce of silver should be worth approximately 450 euros, or 18 times more than the current price.

<u>Please Note</u>:
There is controversy about the monetary unit of this expression "Judas' 30 silver coins".
St John's gospel mentions 30 silver coins whilst Mathew talks about 30 shekels of silver.

The shekel was originally a unit of weight and currency used in Mesopotamia from the 3rd Millennium B.C. until the 1st Century AD. It was also the unit of weight used by the Hebrews. The biblical shekel weighed 6 grams of silver. The double shekel weighed twelve, 11.9g to be precise.

The shekel, 'hadash (in Hebrew: שקל חדש, meaning *new* shekel, shortened to ח"ש in everyday language), or *shekalim* in plural (pronounced shkalim), is the national currency of the state of Israel today. The shekel was divided into 100 agorot, plural agorah, which comes from the Akkadian word (Mesopotamia), meaning, seed.

This shekel, dating from 66 A.D., was known only in duplicate. It was awarded for 1 million dollars. Aware that it weighed 6g of silver, that makes one ounce of silver about 51 million dollars.

BARBARIAN INVASIONS FORGOTTEN MINES & TECHNIQUES

Climate change resulted in the migration of the tribes from the ramps of Central Asia and Asia Minor to move from east to west, to areas less affected by climate disruption. Each wave of migrants pushed the previous one further to the west, causing the fall of the Roman Empire.

Alans, Vandals, Huns, Goths Ostrogoth devastated the limes of the Empire before breaking out to Gaul and then to Rome to devastate it.

In these times of unrest, slaves working in the mines fled and dispersed. People went into hiding and sought to survive the lootings, fires and massacres. For the survivors, the primary concern was to find food and shelter. It took many years to rebuild communities and the economy took a downward trend because there were fewer qualified manpower.

As incredible as this may seem, the gold and silver mines were abandoned, lost or forgotten in these times of unrest. Worst still, mining techniques and know-how in metallurgy often disappeared with men who passed on their knowledge as a secret.

This phenomenon was repeated several times in history, especially during the Great Famine of 1425 and the ensuing Great Plaque.

CYRILLE JUBERT

Silver Throughout History
Medieval Period

CYRILLE JUBERT

CHARLEMAGNE – CHARLES THE GREAT

Skimming through history, it is difficult to ignore this "Good Old Charlemagne", not because he "invented the school", as France Gall sung gaily in 1964, but because he made a monetary change in European history, a system that will last for thousand years.

At the death of his brother in 771, Charlemagne became king of Gaul and part of Germania. He expanded his kingdom to the north by defeating the Saxons and converting them to Christianity. Then he went on to defeat the Avars in the east, people of Austria today, before taking Lombardy, Northern Italy. Without forgetting the Saracens that he repelled beyond the Pyrenees: remember Roland burst the veins in his neck in the battle against Roncesvalles, in your history books.

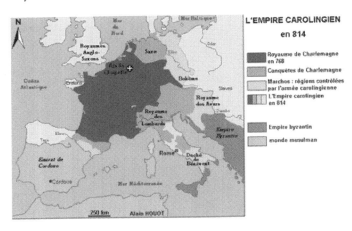

Abandonment of the Roman Monetary System

To unify his kingdom and facilitate trade, Charlemagne decided in 781 to replace the old worthless currency with a new one. This currency was strictly minted in silver, the only precious metal relatively abundant among the Franks.

The basic unit was the Roman denarius, weighing 1.70g. The obol was worth half a denarius.

The penny, which was popular, was worth 12 denarii. Charlemagne created **the pound** which was worth 240 denarii.

1 pound = 20 pennies of 12 denarii = 240 denarii

From 812, after the recognition of his imperial title by the Eastern Emperor, Michael I, Charlemagne minted denarii with his image, draped with laurel wreath as the Roman coins, with the legend IMP. AVG. KAROLUS.

At the end of Charlemagne's reign, the emperor's portrait disappeared from the face of all currencies. It was not until the 16th Century that it was restored.

This monometallism lasted for 4 centuries until the minting after 1250 of Louis d'or of France, Ducat of Venice and florin of Florence, as we shall see later.

THE CAROLINGIAN MINES

It should be recalled that the Franks who gave their name to France were Germanic people, who had conquered our territory and taken ownership of it under Clovis. Charlemagne, descendant of this line, had his capital in Aix-la-Chapelle, Aachen in German, between the far North-Eastern Belgium, Western Germany, Eastern Netherlands and Northern Luxembourg.

Germanic mythology focused a lot on metallurgy and war. God Thor, the god of lightning and powerful warrior was very venerated. Reading these ancient stories, one gets the impression of reading books of science fiction, talking about aliens. Thor's residence was called "Glittering Radiance", his kingdom, "force fields", (made me think about Nicolas Tesla's electromagnetic domes). His hammer launched lightening like a laser. He had a magic belt, iron gloves and crossed the sky in his flying chariot wheel…

Picture showing Thor's belt painted in 1872 by Martin Winge

Siegfried, the legendary Germanic hero, was trained by the king's chief blacksmith. Without going into details with these magnificent legends, my goal is to emphasize that at the beginning of time, as in the Middle Ages or today, the Germans were known for their expertise in mining and metallurgy. Therefore, our Germanic cousins set up and exploited mines, especially silver mines throughout Central Europe, thus ensuring the regular income of the white metal, essential for currency and commercial exchanges. These masters and craftsmen migrated easily when a mine was exhausted or when they heard about richer veins elsewhere.

Lower Saxony, and in particular the massive Hartz mountains in the center north of the country, show the most turbulent relief in Germany. The region has been exploited for its silver mines since 968 AD. The ore was very rich in silver and gold and they made the fortunes of Princes and Lords who exploited them.

THE TEUTONIC KNIGHTS

The migration of the population was not due to chance.

The Holy Germanic Roman Emperor, Frederick II of Hohenstaufen, unable to expand his territory to the west, initiated the **"Movement towards the east"** at the beginning of the 13th century. The goal was to colonize the east through the establishment of Catholic settlements in the Baltic and Slavic Orthodox or pagan territories. This colonization was protected by the knights and monk soldiers from the Order of the Teutonic Knights.

This order was created in Saint-Jean-d'Acre by German pilgrims and crusaders during the 1190 crusades. Purely hospitaller initially, the order became military and hospitaller and recognized by the Pope, in the same way as the Order of Malta and the Templar Knights. While these two orders welcomed the nobility throughout Europe, the Teutonic Knights were reserved solely for the German nobility, who quickly obeyed only their Great Master and the Emperor. Barely 13 years after its creation, the order became detached from its original mission to defend the Holy Land, to found the fortified town of Kronstadt in Transylvania before serving in the expansion of the empire. They first "converted" the people around the Baltic Sea, before turning to the "Movement towards the East", an expression to be taken in the sense of "oriental threshold" of the Germanic Empire.

The Order was a powerful war machine with formidable efficiency and within a century, they conquered a large part of the Baltic, Courland (Latvia) Livonia (Estonia). As they made conquests, they created fortresses to keep their territories.

The movement towards the East was triumphant from 1211 and during the next two centuries. That was how Prussia was created. The Teutonic Knights converted the people by the sword and protected their German settlers, farmers, miners, artisans or merchants, who came to live in and populate the immense territories won in the east and north east.

In 1168, it was at Meissen, near Dresden in the east of the country, near the border of the current Czech Republic, that a rich and extraordinary silver vein was discovered.

Once again, the German miners and metallurgy specialists came to settle, at the request of the local nobility who could only be enriched by an industry synonymous with prosperity.

From the early years of its exploitation, the mine produced 4 tons of silver yearly, under the leadership of a Margrave who was soon renamed "Otto the Rich".

The title margrave, Markgraf in German, literally means Count of the March in the former Carolingian empire. In France, we always have "Poitou's March", "Brittany's March" and "Count of the March" in Limousin. This dates back to the same era. The title, Marquis, came from these March, a territory on the frontier, like a door-step.

The grandson of Otto the Rich, Henry the illustrious, ruled

Meissen from 1195 to 1255. In a famous tournament that he organized, he sat at the foot of a finely carved silver tree, whose leaves were made of gold and silver. The knights who broke a spear on the body of their opponents won a silver leaf; those who managed to throw and knock down their opponents received a gold leaf. Henry built the citadel of Dresden after the Meissen fire.

Almost at the same time in the late 12th Century, in the South Eastern part of St Germanic Roman Empire in the Eastern Alps, new extremely prolific silver veins were found in the territory of Prince Bishop of Salzburg. The Fiesach mine was the wealth of the city for some time. Thanks to new techniques developed two centuries later, from 1526 to 1535, the annual production peaked at 80,000 marks, or 19 tons.

Silver-bearing mountains were then discovered in Tuscany. Tuscany was part of the Carolingian Empire in 774, some years before Charlemagne was crowned Emperor. Erected in marquisate, the last heir bequeathed his estates to the papacy in 1115. Legacy that was disputed by the Germanic Roman Emperor who in an open conflict with Rome, freed himself from the Pope. From the 12th to the 15th Century, recurrent conflicts between the Emperor and Rome and the wealth generated from the mines in the region enabled Siena, Pisa and Florence to become independent cities.

In 1220, at the border of Austria and Moravia, a new major mine was discovered at Inglau.

Meissen and Salzburg miners always rushed there in search of the most dense veins to make their wealth. Each time they left one site in search of another, it weakened the already declining mining production even further. Inglau produced 4 tons of silver yearly from 1253 to 1274 during the reign of Ottokar II, King of Bohemia.

The German expansion resumed generation after generation, century after century, around the myth of Europe from Brest to Vladivostok. Isn't the alliance between Merkel and Putin still top news today?

The Second World War was triggered because Germany wanted to keep the Danzig corridor linking Bohemia and Moravia in Czechoslovakia (created in 1919), where the dominant minority for centuries were German. This population was made up of the descendants of settlers of the 12th and 13th Centuries who settled and were defended by the Teutonic knights.

The Cross of the Teutonic Knights declined over the centuries as a badge or medal for the German army.

History of Silver Production

Mining production in billions of ounces

It took humanity 4,500 years to produce 236,000 tons of silver, then 437 years to produce twice as much white metal.

The last 80 years were sufficient to produce 777,000 tons.

The discovery of the Americas and improved techniques allowed the geometric acceleration of silver mining production. Growth in money supply and the development of international trade necessitated the development of the banking system, the creation of "bills of exchange", starting point of fiat money.

Today, money supply is not commensurate with the mass of silver metal produced, and without any link, silver, having been demonetized a long time ago, is supposed to be only a metal for industrial use.

Let's study the past before to analyze the present, or look into to the future.

The late Middle Ages were a pivotal period in the history of mankind when people experienced economic, political and social collapse due to speculation.

In the Middle Ages, the Templars acted as bankers among their various strongholds in both the East and the West. They developed a sophisticated system of deposit and investment banks. Their bills of exchange were worth our checks of today and already enabled them to move from one place to the other without carrying their treasures along.

We must keep in mind that loans with interest or usury were condemned by the Church and the Koran, prompting traders and money changers to hide their practices through double accounting and other tricks.

Luther's reformation (1521) and Calvin's soon after, were adopted by most of northern Europe and especially the Dutch provinces that enabled the development of the Protestant Bank (Netherlands, Great Britain, Switzerland, Germany).

It was not until the 17th Century that these banking techniques became widespread. Trade between the different continents and civilizations led to the development of the monetary systems. The banking system was refined and structured after many experiments and adjustments.

VENICE

Venice was founded in the 6th Century on an archipelago of islets in the middle of a dangerous lagoon, to protect the people against the invasions of the Goths and Huns. Its location made it a protected harbor from both land and sea attacks. Indeed, foreign ships with no native captains who knew very well the channels in the marsh, risked sinking. This port city could then thrive and develop a successful trade between the East and the West. The Venetian merchants dominated trade with the ports of the Eastern Mediterranean where all the caravans loaded with silk on one hand, and those with spices from India, on the other, converged.

The oriental goods could be paid for with only silver coins. Since silver was produced mainly in the Roman German Empire, Northern and Central Europe became the major consumers of spices and other luxury goods from the East. The white metal and gold were above all, the most important elements of barter for the Venetian merchants. **The Bankers of Venice speculating on gold and silver** led to the systemic crash in 1345.

The Venetian Patricians were less interested in the profits they derived from the industry than those from the trade between the regions where gold and silver prices were different.

Between 1250 and 1350, Venetian financiers put up a structure for global speculation on currencies and precious metals, reminiscent in some aspects, to our modern casino of today "derivatives". The dimensions of this phenomenon exceeded by far the most modest speculation on debt, goods and trade of the then

Florentine banks.

Through this, the Venetian bankers managed to remove the monopoly that the monarchs had relating to the issuance of money. But, instead of jumping to conclusion, let's go back to history in a chronological order.

Twice a year, a "convoy of bullions" left Venice, with 23 galleys, armed and escorted at great expense, sailed to the Eastern Mediterranean or Egypt. Loaded mainly with silver, the ships returned to Venice, carrying gold in all its forms: coins, bullions, bars or leaves.

The profits gained from this trade were far greater than those from usury in Europe, even though the Venetians did not hesitate to take advantage of the second activity.

In Asia, from the second half of the 12th Century, the Mongol hordes plundered gold from China and India, whose economies were then the richest in the world. In Europe, gold came from the mines in Sudan and Mali, where it was sold to Venetian merchants in exchange for European white metal which was highly sought after in Africa.

This silver came from the mines in Germany, Bohemia and Hungary. It was sold more exclusively to Venitians, who used to pay in gold. Therefore, the non-Venetian coins began to disappear, first in the Byzantine Empire in the 12th Century, then in Mongolian areas and finally in Europe in the 14th Century.

The amount of European white metal exported in the East by Venice between 1325 and 1350, was 25% of all the silver exploited in the European mines. This precious metal was used as currency by the St Germanic Roman Empire and England since the time of Charlemagne. The Venetian export to the East destabilized the balance of payment in England and Flanders, and created serious problems with trade settlement. As a result, France was stripped of silver coins. The Director of Mint of King Philip VI of Valois calculated that at least 100 tons of white metal were exported to the land of the Saracens, business partners of Venice.

As a result of this, the production and exchange of goods manufactured in Europe was weakened and the circulation of money was disorganized because of the Venetian banks.

The first **sequins** were minted in Venice in the late 13th Century, under the name of *ducato* (ducat). The word "sequin" comes from Zecca, name of the Mint in Venice. The Zecca was not removed until 1870, during the unification of Italy. The sequin was first called "**Ducat**". In 1283 it weighed 3.60g including 3.495g of fine gold in 20mm in diameter.

On the reverse side of the coin, Saint Marc, holy patron of the city, presented the Doge of Venice with the standard cross and bearing. On the reverse side was the legend: "May you be given, Christ, this duchy that you govern."

From 1275 to 1325, the Venetian bankers gradually imposed an exchange rate for gold and controlled its influx. If in 1275, 8 silver coins were needed to buy a gold coin, in 1325, the **gold and silver ratio** rose to **15**.

Venice, in its trading relations with the Mongols and Africa, on one hand and its near monopoly on the sources of gold, on the other, forced Europe to adopt **a monetary system based on gold.**

From 1320, Venice bankers began large financial maneuvers which upset the monetary balance in Europe for a little over century.

In 1324, the emperor of Mali, Moussa Kankou, undertook a pilgrimage to Mecca. His suite was composed of 60,000 men, 12,000 slaves and the holy pilgrimage. He provided food for this huge caravan. He travelled with a treasure of eight tons of gold dust carried by 80 camels. In every city he went through, Moussa paid generously with gold to the needs of his followers or to build mosques. This influx of gold throughout its passage, as in Cairo as in Arabia, brought down the value of this rare metal and generated a very high inflation.

This phenomenon impacted quickly the whole Mediterranean world. The bankers of Venice, who traded annually with Cairo and Arabia amplified this phenomenon. From 1325 to 1345, Venice bankers orchestrated a reverse financial manipulation. As their coffers were full of silver and their competing banks had just moved to a gold standard, **Venice brought down the gold/silver ratio from 15 to 9, raising the value of silver significantly.**

Florentine bankers who issued a currency called "guilder", controlled international finance before the Venice maneuver. They raised the gold standard belatedly and reluctantly and were totally ruined by the Venetian manipulation of the gold/silver ratio. Their fortune, initially mainly in silver, was almost slashed by half, when Venice raised the gold/silver ratio from 8 to 15. This new Venetian bankers maneuver made them lose 3/5 of what remained. Since bankers always lent out more money than they had actually deposited, they found themselves ruined.

In 1345, the collapse of the great Florentine banks of Bardi and Peruzzi led to a real financial meltdown. One can read from the chronicles of the time that ***"all the money vanished at the same time."***

CYRILLE JUBERT

SYSTEMIC CRASH OF 1345

The systematic crash led to a very high inflation in the prices of essential commodities, bringing general famine and extreme poverty of the masses. Famine normally weakens the immune system of the human body and paves the way for great epidemics. This is what happened in 1347.

The black plague which first struck Constantinople and killed 8/9th of the population spread in the whole of Europe through the Mediterranean ports. It totally destroyed between 30 and 50% of the population in just five years.

- Labor became scarce and led to an increase in its cost, especially in agriculture. Many villages were abandoned, the poorer lands became fallow and the forests redeveloped;
- Landowners were obliged to abolish serfdom to try to keep the labor force;
- The cities, which were more affected than the countryside, became depopulated one after the other. Medicine at that time did not have adequate knowledge to curb the epidemics;
- Land revenue collapsed due to the decline in the rate of royalties and the increase in wages;

The *"Italian"* bankers, Jews, Gypsies and other nomads, were massacred or driven out of the kingdoms of Aragon, England, Flanders and France. In Germany and Central Europe, they experienced pogroms.

The 1345 Crash and the Black Plague which followed rolled back civilization for nearly one century.

A CENTURY OF SILVER SHORTAGE & ECONOMIC RECESSION

It was during this troubled period that the conflict between two dynasties, the Plantagenet and the Capetian House of Valois, called "the hundred years war" took place on the French soil. The war lasted for 116 years from 1337 to 1453 and officially ended in 1475 after the signing of the treaty of Picquigny.

Most of the Western silver mines were exhausted.

Kutna Hora, the largest mine in the world at that time, situated in Kingdom of Bohemia, experienced the Hussites War. The protestants-before-its-time revolted against the authority of the church of Rome. The city was burned, Mints were lost and the mines were severely damaged. New mines were dug after the Hussites Crusade but the decadence of the city increased and the veins were depleted around 1550.

The shortage of new metal caused the authorities to devalue the currency by reducing the silver content of coins. Individuals hoarded the old coins thus making the shortage even worse.

According to some American analysts, the highest price of silver in history was between 1450 and 1489.

This means disregarding Ancient Egypt, India and China in the 16th Century but especially Mesopotamia at the beginning of times, as we shall see further.

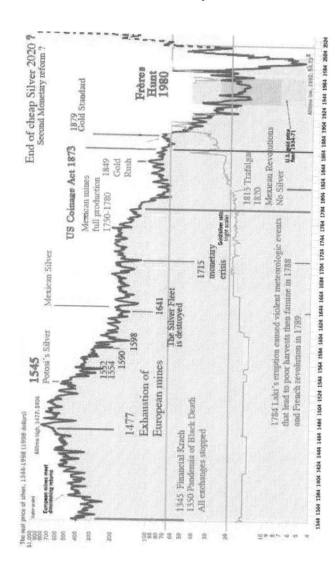

JEWS EXPELLED FROM SPAIN

In the 13th Century, the church expressed a desire to Christianize the Spanish. Founded in 1216, the order of the Dominicans had a mission to convert heretics, Jews and Muslims to Catholicism. After the 1345 monetary and economic crash, wars and civil wars in Europe worsened the living conditions of the Jews. Spain was at the forefront of the persecution of both Jews and Marranos, the newly converted. In 1408, they were banned from the administration, confined to ghettos and forced to wear codified clothes, particularly those marked by a badge, a small wheel sewn on a yellow fabric.

On the 2nd of August 1492, at the anniversary of the destruction of the First and Second Temples in Jerusalem, King Ferdinand and Isabella the Catholic expelled the Jews from the Spanish Kingdom. According to historians, between 50,000 and 300,000 people took the path of exile, and fled from the pyres of Torquemada.

The majority were welcomed into the Ottoman Empire, where the Sultan Beyazid II, who opened their doors to them, scoffed at the Spanish Monarch saying: *"You call Ferdinand a wise Monarch when he impoverished his kingdom to enrich mine."* A quarter of this diaspora settled in North Africa and a quarter went to the Anglo-Saxon countries. (Holland, England, Hamburg and the Baltic ports.)

The last quarter probably contributed to the irresistible expansion of the international trade and finance of these countries in the coming centuries.

CYRILLE JUBERT

Silver Throughout History

The Renaissance

CYRILLE JUBERT

The systemic crash in the west, shortage of silver, famine and pandemia caused a long economic hardship which led to the capture of Constantinople by the Turkish hordes from the East. The fall of the Eastern Christian Empire marked the end of an era and the transition to another.

The Renaissance began at the end of the Quattrocento in Italy.

The emergence of navigational instruments like the compass, sextant, log or astrolabe in Europe enabled the navigators to discover new horizons and to create maps. The Portuguese explored the coasts of Africa, India and Asia. During the same period, the Conquistadors discovered and explored America.

From **1451**, the discovery of new technical methods for extracting silver by adding mercury, salt and copper sulfate stimulated the production of silver in Central Europe, in particular, the Bohemian mines. **The re-usage allowed double extraction of silver from the copper and silver ores.** The Fugger's merchants and financiers invested massively in this mining industry, by implementing new hydraulic processes to extract water from the tunnels in the mines, work which required hundreds of workers at that time. They transformed this sector into a real industry by including mining and refining, while a commercial structure was being developed throughout Europe. A significant amount of the copper was sold in Antwerp at the Casa da India founded by the Portuguese, who sold the metal in India against spices.

The scarcity of the white metal gradually reduced, allowing the stabilization of the monetary systems and a "renaissance" of trade as well as the economy.

CYRILLE JUBERT

THE KINGDOM OF ENGLAND

The shortage of silver brought a monetary crisis in England which was called "the Great Debasement", or the great devaluation.

In 1509, Henri VIII ascended the throne in England. His reign was chaotic involving alliances and treason with Spain, Rome, Charles V or François 1st. He is remembered as Bluebeard who married 6 women and beheaded 2 of them. It was because Rome did not want to end his marriage with Catherine of Aragon, that Henry VIII seceded with Rome and established the Church of England.

In 1543, the English coins contained 11.2/12th of silver metal or the equivalent of 950/1000th.

In 1551, the silver coins were melted and then reminted with less and less silver in the coin alloy. The initial proportions were divided by 4 so the new coins were 250/1000th. A 75% depreciation resulted in higher inflation.

It was not until the reign of Elisabeth the First, who ascended the throne in 1560*, and especially with the advice of Financier Gresham, that the British currency regained its previous value. This advisor is known for his **"Gresham's Law"**: **"Bad money drives out good"**.

When two currencies circulate concurrently, one gold and the other silver, the one that inspires the least confidence is used to make payments while the best is hoarded. Good money ends up disappearing from circulation and hoarded by those who think it will not be devalued. Finding itself replaced in current trade by the bad one as people want to get rid of it as soon as possible before it is devalued.

*1560 corresponds to the beginning of the arrival of silver from the Americas.

It is also interesting to note that the **right of seigniorage**, the right to coin money, was considered by the princes as a source of income. Thus, a freshly minted currency was overvalued by nearly 20% compared to its fine metal weight just like the silver coins of Paris today which is sold including 20% VAT. This is why we used worn or poor quality coins for current usage and hoarded the best ones.

International traders, in turn, issued valid bills of exchange in other centers to keep the most beautiful silver coins, playing for differences in price and quality of the currencies from one financial center to another, confirming Gresham's Law.

Each new minting resulted in inflation or confirmed the latter.

In 1550, Antwerp was one of the dominant financial centers in Europe, with Genoa, Florence, Seville and Venice just to mention the most important ones. The bankers of Lombard Street in London totally depended on Antwerp at that time, to negotiate their bills of exchange in European trade.

The fall of Antwerp on the international market dates back to

1568, when **Elizabeth of England** seized treasure on board of Spanish galleys who had to take refuge from a storm at the port of Plymouth. This robbery deprived the Duke of Alba the silver to pay his troops, while the Flemish Provinces revolted for freedom of religion considered by the then Spanish Crown as a crime of lese-majesty.

The silver plundered from the Spanish allowed the British Crown to mint better quality coins at a time when the pound sterling was experiencing a serious crisis of confidence among the European changers.

After this act of piracy by England, the Channel was considered as a dangerous zone, transportation of precious metals was redirected to Genoa and the Mediterranean, depriving **Antwerp** of a large part of its market and monetary importance.

This painting of Boyermans shows the fall of the powerful city of Antwerp. Very rich in esoteric symbols it describes the time and knowledge spiral, and it brings to mind the golden section and the Fibonacci sequence.

At the center of this picture, a gilt bronze cherub, like an Atlas carrying the vault of heaven is holding a nautilus at arm's length. The nautilus is a marine cephalopod mollusk whose shell is wrapped in a spiral as you will see across the picture. At the beginning of time, the Atlanteans, according to the mythology, rebelled against the gods but they were defeated. Atlas was condemned to carry the vault of heaven for ever. To the right of Atlas, carrying the nautilus or the time spiral, you have Heracles. This demi god son of Zeus and a mortal woman, is known to us under the name of Hercules. It is represented on many silver coins. In the time spiral, after the reign of the Atlanteans and the era of the demi gods, the human civilization blossomed through writing, drawing, astronomy and philosophy, represented here by the bust of Socrates and Plato. In the shade, the hammer and the anvil speak about the art of fire and war whilst in the light, the music talks about peace and harmony. The picture on the easel shows a tender nursing mother and a dark and jealous man in his armor of war to remind us that the women come from Venus and the men, Mars. The goddess of love is holding the god of war while the careless cherubim are dancing and playing music.

The floor is littered with instruments reminiscent of geometry, calculation, astronomy, writing, humanities and sciences, while the statue without head draped with marble is reminding us that "science without conscience is but a ruin of the soul."

To the right, in the shade beyond the whirlwind of life, and the acceleration of time behind the flamboyant curtain is the secret ladder which talks about ascension, elevation and interior journey. These are the twelve steps for initiation into zodiac or the twelve degrees of humility, the path that leads to truth and knowledge…

If you step back, the orchestra is silent. Musicians throw their instruments on the ground. The party is over. Man is overwhelmed by evil. The latter is represented by the statue made of black marble which is dominating the scene.

The tree's perspective mark the boundary between heaven and earth, shade and light. This "Fool's diagonal" leads directly to the heart of the nautilus spiral.

The man who has fallen is holding a shovel. Does this mean that man has the tendency to dig his own grave?
Certainly not, don't worry! Down from heaven comes a shining light and an angel comes to save him. He invites him to get up and stand up straight.

If you go into details, the human skin is tanned by the sun, and that of the angel is white. The painter that I am could explain the number of sub-layers in white silver paint necessary to get this effect.

Among the Incas, gold symbolizes the sun's sweat and silver, **"the tears of the moon"**. The woman is lunar and the man is solar. Water and fire. Hot and cold. Which will lead us to Yin and Yan and the middle course.

But let's forget Antwerp, the painting, philosophy and knowledge to return to the history of silver through civilizations.

THE VAST PORTUGUESE EMPIRE

Christopher Columbus discovered America when he was looking for a new route to India, paradise of spices. The Portuguese had preceded him by opening the southern route. Soon after they were freed by the Moors, the rulers started a re-conquest phase (1250), seeking to expand their kingdom to the south through the Atlantic coast of Africa. Their successive conquests made them cross the boundaries of the mythical land of the ancients and discovered Madeira, Azores, Mauritania, Cape Verde, Senegal, Gulf of Guinea, Congo and finally the Cape of Good Hope in 1499. In 1479, Portugal received possession of the discovered lands and monopoly of trade and navigation in the new waters through a Treaty.

After the fall of the Eastern Roman Empire and the conquest of Constantinople in 1453, due to the weakening of the Empire after the Financial Crash and Black Plague, the traditional route to India was cut off. The Portuguese who were excellent navigators looked for new routes. This was done when they passed the Cape of Good Hope. They discovered and secured control of the Indian Ocean. Francisco de Almeida, first viceroy of Portuguese India, established trading posts and imposed the presence of the Portuguese in the trading channels previously dominated by Muslims.

His successor built fortresses in the straits that controlled the Indian Ocean:
- The strait of Hormuz at the entrance of the Persian Gulf
- Goa which controlled the Malabar coast in South East India
- Malacca in Indonesia, which controlled traffic to China and Japan

In 1500, the Portuguese discovered Brazil. In 1513, they were the first Europeans to open an embassy in China and had the right to open a trading post at Macao in 1557. They reached Japan in 1543.

Very soon, the Crown established a central administration, Casa de Ceuta, which became the Casa da Guiné then Casa da India in 1501. As forerunners of the East India Company, they ensured the royal monopoly of trade with the new colonies and trading posts. The Casa da India monitored the customs duties and the exclusive royal monopoly of the spice trade. The King of France, François 1st made fun of the Portuguese sovereign by calling him the spice king. In French, spice is "épice" and the "épicier" is a grocer. So "King of the grocers".

Portugal, for a century and a half, dominated trade between India, Asia and Europe. Pepper, cinnamon, cloves, vanilla, cinnamon, cotton, fine porcelain... abundant wealth flowing to this small European kingdom.

But Portugal had only one million inhabitants and could not manage such a vast empire.

The Battle of the three Kings

In 1578, Sebastian I gathered a strong Christian army of seventeen thousand men in the small port of Lagos to conquer Morocco. He could count on the alliance of a Moroccan prince of the Saadian dynasty, Muhammad al-Mutawakkil, who was ousted by his uncle and hoped to return through the support of the Portuguese. The Portuguese settled long ago in several coastal fortified towns: Ceuta, Tangier, Mazagan.

He left Lisbon on the 24th of June 1578 and landed in Asilah. Sebastian's army penetrated inland to meet their opponent, Moulay Abu Marwan Abd al-Malik.

The battle took place on the 4th of August near river Oued Makhzen.

Having believed in victory for some time, 23,000 Portuguese were routed by 40,000 Moroccans and, probably the first time in history, all the three kings engaged in this battle died.

In 1578, King Sebastian 1st of Portugal died in the *"Battle of the Three Kings."*

On that day, Portugal lost its king, nobility, army, independence and global position. The country and its vast empire were annexed to the Spanish Crown.

CYRILLE JUBERT

CHARLES V

It is difficult to understand the power of Spain in the early 16th Century, if you do not remember that Charles of Habsburg, better known by the name of Charles V, inherited various grandparents of the vast kingdoms. He was the Archduke of Austria, Duke of Burgundy, king of Spain, King of Naples and Sicily. He also reigned in Flanders and Franche Comté.

Born in 1500, he was crowned emperor at the age of 19 and four years later when he turned 21, he became King of France after **Francis I** in 1515.

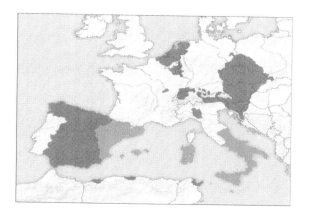

Charles V and the Fugger Bankers

The Fugger's came from a lineage of merchants who traded with the Levant and the Baltic states before they became bankers of the Holy Roman Empire. Jacob I, who died in 1469, was from the Fugger of the Lily's branch. He established the most prestigious bank which was developed by his 3 sons, Ulrich (1441-1510), Georg(1453-1506) and Jacob II the rich (1459-1525). The latter was the

Owner of the silver and copper mines in Hungary, Tyrol and Spain. He eventually obtained a quasi-monopoly of the mines in Europe. Therefore, the Fugger's dominated European finance at the end of the Middle Ages and during the Renaissance. Jacob II was reputed to be the richest man in his time. This branch of the Fuggers was ennobled by Emperor Maximilian II for services rendered; the rich Jacob II, was elevated to the dignity of the Count of the Holy Roman Empire in 1514, in recognition of the loans granted to the future Charles V. The loans (800,000 guilders) were used to buy the seven prince electors who received bills of exchange payable *"after the election of Charles of Spain"*. Charles of Spain's opponent to the title of Emperor, was the King of France, François I.

A few years later, this did not prevent the Minister of Finance of the Holy Roman Empire, from attacking the Fuggers, accusing them of establishing a monopolistic banking position.

Prince Albert, Archbishop of Magdeburg, borrowed from this same Jacob Fugger to win the favor of Pope Leo X and obtain the Archbishopric of Mainz. To enable him repay the loan, the Prince Archbishop begun to sell "indulgences", imitating Leo X, who sold indulgences to build Saint Peter's Basilica in Rome. This practice was denounced by Martin Luther who flooded Germany with his pamphlets against the church of Rome. His Protestant Reformation sent him into exile but he was supported by the German Princes thus creating a German unit. The Fugger Bank became bankrupt on November 9th 1607, year of the Halley's comet passing after the third bankruptcy of the Spanish state.

The Fugger dynasty grew and thrived. The Fugger de Babenhaussen branch was elevated to the title of Prince in 1803 and the Fugger von Glött was made Prince in 1913.

Honoré de Balzac cited this dynasty in his book, *"The Nuncingen House"*: *"To survive, the banker must become noble, found a dynasty like the moneylenders of Charles V, the Fugger's, created Princes of Babenhausen who still exist in the Gotha's Almanac."*

The discovery of the Americas further enriched Charles V's empire and brought silver into the different kingdoms. Flanders (Bruges, Ghent) were world trade and financial centers at that time. These provinces were transferred in 1581 under the reign of his son Philippe II. It was restored to the Crown of Portugal and its vast empire in 1580.

Improved navigation techniques enabled the Europeans to discover the route to India and China without going through the old silk route and its numerous middlemen who demanded tribute from caravans that passed. The silver of the Americas facilitated the development of international trade as we will see in the next chapter.

However, the silver mines of the Americas, exploited by indigenous slaves, marked a turning point in the mineral wealth of the Fugger's. It was more expensive to exploit silver in the European mines and the continuous flow lowered its relative value.

Silver Throughout History

16th Century

Treasure of the Americas

CYRILLE JUBERT

SILVER OF THE CONQUISTADORS

If in 1492, Christopher Columbus discovered the West Indies and the Caribbean while looking for a new route to India, it took almost 50 years for the Spanish conquistadors to conquer the New World before they started exploiting its mineral wealth.

During the early decades, the conquistadors brought back mainly gold, plundered from the treasures of the people they conquered in South America. From 1500 to 1595, 330 tons of gold were shipped from the Americas to Spain. As early as the middle of the century, this influx of wealth decreased at the very moment when the conquerors discovered silver mines with unprecedented wealth.

The arrival of silver from the Americas started in 1550 with 177 tons, then it increased to 942 tons in 1570 to peak at 2,000 tons in 1595 Around 1625, the import of silver from the Americas to Spain started declining and this continued until 1660.

CYRILLE JUBERT

The Potosi mines

Discovered in 1545, the Potosi mines in the Andes cordillera proved to be a mountain with very pure silver ore deposits, which produced 60 tons during the first 20 years, then 240 tons yearly until 1680.

Silver production in Potosi experienced a drastic decline from 1680. Once the very rich surface veins were exploited, the density of the ore reduced gradually as the mines sank into the ground. The expression "it's worth a Potosi", used by Don Quixote, is still used in Spanish, translated as "this is Peru" in French.

The Potosi mines produced 4,800 tons or 170 million ounces of silver. The exceptional production volume of the Potosi mine discouraged research and exploitation of other mineral sources, especially gold. As a result, the Spanish were unable to extract sufficient quantities, contrary to hopes raised by the discovery of the "gold of the Incas".

The Mines of Mexico, discovered after the Potosi mine, took the lead in 1650 and quickly exceeded the production of Peru. Mexico reached its peak production in 1780 with 24 million pesos representing nearly 650 tons of silver or 22 million ounces.

New techniques developed in the 20th Century enabled better prospection, extraction and more efficient refining, which explains why Mexico now produces 128 million ounces per year.

For the record, the improvement in technology resulted in the production of more silver between 1930 and 2012 than the 5,000 preceding years.

During the reign of Charles V and his successors, the Spanish Imperial Crown owned the mines. As such, it received the "royal fifth", that is 20% of bullions or gold or silver coins extracted from ground. To this heavy tax was added the seigniorage (tax for producing money). The Spanish Crown also had monopoly over the production of mercury, powders and explosives produced in Almadén, essential products for miners from which it derived substantial profits.

Too many taxes soon led to considerable tax evasion through smuggling and capital flight to Asia. It took Spain 200 years before reacting to this and limiting the "royal fifth" to 10%.

CYRILLE JUBERT

The Peso

A **peso**, the famous **coin of 8** in the pirates' stories, also called "piaster" was worth 8 Reals.

A peso weighed 27.07 grams of silver in 900/1000th

It had a market value equivalent to the Thaler produced in Bohemia and it was equivalent to a dollar in colonial America. Is it necessary to say that Dollar comes from Thaler?

3.2 billion pesos were minted in Mexico from 1537 to 1892, representing **86,000 tons of silver.**

Table 1: Annual Average Strikes of Mints in the West Indies (Late 18th Century)

Mints	Annual Average Strikes 1790 - 1796
Mexico	24 000 000 pesos plata (Silver piasters)
Lima	6 000 000
Potosi	4 600 000
Santa Fe de Bogota	1 200 000
Santiago du Chili	1 000 000
Popayan	1 000 000
Guatemala	200 000

FORTUNE OF THE SEA

The influx of precious metals from the Americas in 1503 resulted in the creation of the *House of Trade,* royal body responsible for the regulation of maritime traffic between the port of Cadiz and what is still referred to as the West Indies. To guard against insecurity at sea the "House" organized an annual convoy of galleons, nicknamed silver fleet, "plata flota," because gold represented at best only 10% of the cargo. This convoy carried along the needed Spanish products to the settlers and miners on the outward journey, and returned with the booty that the conquistadores took from the indigenous people, especially products from the mines. Before it left Spain, the silver fleet consisted of between 30 and 40 galleons and "armed" merchant vessels. These boats were accompanied by about a dozen lighter boats to transport mails and low-value goods. Throughout the journey, the convoy was subject to the Law of the slowest ship. The least damage to any one of the boats delayed all the others.

Berthing in spring, this convoy was split into two fleets beyond Santo Domingo in the Caribbean. The New Spain fleet headed for Cuba, then Veracruz in Mexico and the Cartagena Main Land, in current Venezuela.

From Calao, on the Peruvian Pacific Coast, a flotilla transported the treasures of the Andes to the Isthmus of Panama, where a convoy of trucks loaded with mules crossed the lands towards the Atlantic Coast. The silver from Potosi waited there for the "silver fleet" to be loaded.

The two fleets then converged in Cuba, where the returning maritime convoy set off again and came back to Cadiz at the end of the year.

If these convoys appeared to be efficient in fighting against the common pirates, by contract, the losses were terrible when a fleet was captured by hurricanes in the Tropics. A miscalculation of the flagship could have disastrous consequences in the Caribbean.

In 1641, the Spanish Admiral in charge of the fleet loaded all the gold and silver onto only two galleons in bad condition. One sank off Santo Domingo after escaping a cyclone, which had already sank eight other ships during the same expedition. The second continued with the crossing but sank into the Spanish coast.

During a storm in 1563, seven galleons sank in the Nombre de Dios Port in current Panama because the port offered only a temporary protection. Five other ships in the same fleet smashed against the reefs of the Gulf of Campeche during the same storm.

In 1567, a hurricane came down on convoy off the West Indies. The majority of the galleons sank or were thrown onto the coast of the Dominican Island.

In 1590, fifteen galleons sank in the port of Veracruz during a cyclone.

When the "silver fleet" managed to cross the Atlantic, their ordeal was not yet over.

In 1591, sixteen ships sank in the Azores. In 1715, the entire silver fleet sank into a hurricane in the Caribbean, causing monetary crisis throughout Europe.

Imports of Spanish Gold and Silver

Period	Silver	Gold
1503-1510	......	4 965
1511-1520	......	9 153
1521-1530	148	4 889
1531-1540	86 193	14 446
1541-1550	177 573	24 957
1551-1560	303 121	42 620
1561-1570	942 858	11 530
1571-1580	1 118 591	9 429
1581-1590	2 103 027	12 101
1591-1600	2 707 626	19 451
1601-1610	2 213 631	11 764
1611-1620	2 192 255	8 855
1621-1630	2 145 339	3 889
1631-1640	1 396 759	1 240
1641-1650	1 056 430	1 159
1651-1660	443 256	469
Total 1503-1660	16 886 807	181 327

(in kilos of fine metal)

According to E.J Hamilton (1934)
«American treasure and the price revolution in Spain»

During the first twelve years, the "House" kept statistics: Out of the 391 vessels sent, only 269 returned.

In the 16th Century, the losses were over 30%.

The situation did not improve in the following century, due to piracy and the "naval war*", organized by Holland, England and France.

(*) A "letter of marque" or "letter of reprisal" was a royal license given to attack and plunder ships and territorial enemies. This is what made the difference between privateers and pirates.

CYRILLE JUBERT

PIRATES OF THE CARIBBEAN

Sir Henry Morgan

Two phenomena disrupted the monetary circuit of Spanish silver: privateers and smuggling.

Instead of 7 to 8 million pesos crossing the Atlantic to Cadiz each year, soon, only 2 million pesos arrived in Spain. A terrible hemorrhage of Spanish public finances.

The Turtle Island which was quickly abandoned by the Spanish was colonized by the French, buccaneers engaged in smoked meat trade. They sold their products to transient vessels. As the Island was near the maritime routes used by the Spanish galleons, it became the regional capital of the "filibusters" and a haven for the "Republic of the Brethren of the Coast" throughout the 17th Century.

In 1552, the French Pirate, François Leclerc, called "Wooden Leg" plundered Porto Santo Island before ravaging Santo Domingo and the current "Port-au-Prince" the following year. In 1554, he captured Santiago de Cuba, capital of the then Cuba and main port for transferring silver from the Americas to the Spanish. The city was so destroyed after the passage that Spain transferred the capital to Havana.

In 1555, the French privateer, Jacques de Sores led 200 sailors who captured the city of Havana, plundered and burned it. The Spanish then built impressive fortifications to protect the bay and the harbor, essential to the galleons transporting silver to the Americas.

In 1655, the English took Jamaica from the Spanish. Henry Morgan was sent to Cuba by order of the Jamaican Governor. With 10 ships and 500 men, he plundered the major cities of Cuba before attacking Puerto Bello in Panama, a major center for gathering precious metals for the Spanish. Henry Morgan was a poor sailor, who often wrecked, but he was a very great General for ground attacks. Fearing neither God nor man, his legendary cruelty did not put off the British Admiralty, who appointed him Admiral of the fleet from Jamaica, with a mission to plunder the Spanish colonies. On order, he recaptured Cuba and Panama. During the second plundering of Panama, the booty of the pirates was valued at 100,000 pound sterling, or 45 tons of silver.

Spain protested vehemently and Henry Morgan was imprisoned and sent to England in 1672 to be tried for piracy, even though he had "letters of marque", authorizing him to attack enemy ships and ports of England at war at that time. Through further shift in international policy, instead of being hanged, Henry Morgan was made a knight in 1674 in recognition of services rendered to England. He received two important sugar cane plantations in Jamaica from the Crown and was later appointed Governor General over them.

The kingdom of France also gave "letters of marque" to French amateurs to go and plunder the wealth of Spain.

In the 16th Century, the monarchs demanded 10 to 20% of plunders from their privateers. In the 17th Century, the state was satisfied with just the registration fees, a kind of license allowing them to plunder the seas to make the enemy kingdoms financially weak.

The booty was then divided into 3 shares: 2/3 for the ship-owner, 1/3 for the crew. The last third was divided into shares. A sailor had one share, a cabin boy, ½, a captain and doctor 25 shares, etc. All in accordance with established boarding code.

From 1678, the French governors of the Turtle Island gradually disarmed the filibusters, though a bit too rowdy, to develop sugar cane production, rare and expensive commodity at that time. This source of great wealth led to the development of slavery and the triangular trade with Africa.

The pirates then went to plunder the Southern, Pacific and Indian Oceans.

In the 1680's, it was the French buccaneers of Rendez-vous de l'Ile d'or, along the Isthmus of Panama, then the French pirates who at that time attacked the Pacific Coast. They took part in a joint expedition to plunder Cartagena in 1697.

On the European coasts, the ships that were separated from their convoy by a storm became prey to any assigned privateers and pirates who waited near the coasts of Spain on the way back.. Some were taken almost off Cadiz.

In 1697, the Treaty of Ryswick between France, the United Provinces, England, Spain and later Holy Germanic Empire put an end to the naval war which was the only one of its kind.

In 1702, despite the treaty, seventeen galleons were attacked by an Anglo-Dutch force. The fleet took refuge in the Bay of Vigo in Spain where it attempted to sink itself.

The privateers of Saint-Malo passed Cape Horn in 1700 to plunder the coasts of Chile and Peru.

SMUGGLING

Indeed, the pirates and privateers were not solely responsible for this considerable decrease in the flow of silver from the Americas to the Spanish ports. Smuggling played a major role.

135 to 159 tons of silver production from the U.S. was diverted and therefore did not arrive in Spain. This represented nearly half of Peru's mineral production. Merchant vessels from the ports of Buenos Aires or Sacramento carried cargoes of silver to the Indian Ocean, to go and negotiate directly with Arabia, India and China.

On arrival at the home ports, the merchant vessels and the buildings of the privateers had to wait for inspection by the Admiralty authorities who had to assess the cargo. Literature including the saga of Bernard Simiot **"These Gentlemen of Saint-Malo"** told us how the bulk of the cargo was unloaded into secret coves for smuggling to avoid payment of taxes to the state, before the ship officially made its entry into port.

Pirates, privateers and merchants represented a parallel economy which was nearly three times the size of the official economy. Silver was mostly hoarded and gradually withdrawn from the real economy. The fortunes thus accrued were probably used later on to fund the rapid development of the industrial revolution.

To measure the value of the embezzled funds, **50 tons of silver in 1600 represented:**
- The total annual official trade from Portugal, Holland and the new English East Indian company to Asia.
- The total trade to Northern Europe through the Baltic Sea and from there to Central Europe, Germany, Poland, Russia.

CYRILLE JUBERT

THE BANKRUPTCIES OF SPAIN

When Charles V's son Philippe II succeeded his father in 1556, Spain was apparently the largest European power, but that was only an illusion. The empire was poorly managed.

Philippe II found it difficult to finance the construction of his sumptuous palaces, maintenance of Spanish grandees and incessant wars against France, Turks or England at the same time. During that period, the Flemings revolted and demanded their independence and religious freedom. Spain imported all their manufactured products from Europe and exported only raw materials, thus creating an imbalance in the balance of payment.

When the state coffers were empty, the King borrowed from foreign lenders, like the German Fugger's or Genoese bankers. These bankers accumulated debts, hoping to be reimbursed with the silver from the Americas. They knew that if they stopped lending they risked losing everything.

However, the arrival of precious metals was occasional: Silver from the mines of Potosi and Mexico had to be sent to the Atlantic ports, loaded onto galleons, which then had to face the storms and the English, Dutch and French privateers.

In addition, too heavy taxes imposed by Philippe II and his successors on the precious metals from "Mexico" was the cause of their loss, creating a hemorrhage of government revenue through smuggling.

On three occasions, in 1557, 1575 and 1598, Philippe II could not honor his debts, like his successors, Philippe III and Philippe IV, in 1607, 1627 and 1647. These repeated bankruptcies ruined those who had confidence in the Spanish government and this limited the possibilities of financing the real economy.

The bankruptcy of the 9th November of 1607 which led to the bankruptcy of the Bank of Fugger, was the result of the first battle of Trafalgar. On April 25, a Dutch fleet surprised the silver fleet returning from Cuba and destroyed it, looting the entire cargo of precious metals. Moreover, the War of Succession between Mathias and Rudolph of Habsburg led to the dismissal of the Emperor who was declared insane. This cost his bankers a fortune.

Spain's repeated bankruptcies by defaulting on its debts in the 16th and 17th Centuries have remained like indelible stains that no financier will ever forget.

For failing to stimulate domestic production, the 16th Century Spain sank into a crisis, and in the following century, it was overtaken by Northern Europe in crafts and more dynamic trade. Spain had the means to monopolize trade with Asia but it allowed that chance to slip. Unable to develop its rich home-made fabric, it could not follow the industrial revolution in the 19th Century and remained one of the poor nation of Europe in the 19th Century.

CYRILLE JUBERT

MONETARY INFLATION

The stock of precious metals in Europe in 1500 prior to the discovery of America was estimated by the historian Hume at 600 million pesos, representing 16,200 tons of silver or 571 million ounces. In 1800, the stock was 3 billion pesos or 81,000 tons.

But the price of precious metals dropped during these last three centuries. According to the study, "History of Prices", by the historian Earl Hamilton, you could buy more wheat in 1500 with 600 million pesos than in 1800 with 3 billion. All these studies showed a strong price inflation. Until the middle of the 16th Century, the increase was insignificant and affected only food products. From 1550 until the early 17th Century, the price increase became an intense universal phenomenon. According to Stanislas Hoszowski, the rise in the prices of food products reached its peak during the second half of the 16th Century but that of wage increases remained lower than prices of food products throughout that period.

We find a similar phenomenon occurring at different times in India and China. The sudden abundance of precious metals and hence the sudden increase in money supply created a very strong wave of price inflation in the world.

"Profit Inflation"

The "price revolution" coupled with the delay in wage increases created "profit inflation". The latter was a boost for businesses and capital investment. The development of small business sectors, rapid urban development and the creation of a bourgeoisie allowed the formation of a capitalist economic structure with new forms of small businesses and extensive development of maritime trade.

The nobility who were the landowners did not allow the farmers to benefit from the higher agricultural prices by reserving the right to negotiate the grain market to themselves. "Profit inflation" enabled some of the nobility to get sufficient money to invest in factories. The latter made it possible to develop the manufacturing of industrial products. The first step in the next industrial revolution.

Silver Throughout History

Development of International Trade

Creation of Central Banks

CYRILLE JUBERT

COMPANIES OF THE WEST INDIES

In the 17th Century, different companies of the Indies were born in Europe : English (1600), Dutch (1602), Portuguese (1628) or French (1664).

The Dutch, newly independent from the Spanish Crown, engaged in international trade with determination. At **Amsterdam**, the Ship-owners Guild, encouraged by the new power in place, sought to avoid any counter-productive competition. To unite their efforts, ship-owners and merchants created the "United East India Company of Amsterdam" in 1600. Other companies were created at the same time in the other cities of the "United Provinces", but in 1602, the new government put pressure on them to merge into the "Dutch East India Company". The Dutch quickly conquered many Portuguese colonies for their own business.

The United Provinces increased their weight in international trade to become the "International Trade Intermediaries" according to the historian, Blanqui. Merchants first built trade posts along the coasts, turned them into fortresses, before colonizing the interior: Africa, America or Asia.

These trading companies chalked different levels of success, depending on whether they were private or state-owned enterprises. The Spanish East India Company went bankrupt very quickly. The East India Company under John Law in the Regency period marked a resounding failure as we shall detail later.

CYRILLE JUBERT

THE RUPEE OF THE MONGOL EMPIRE

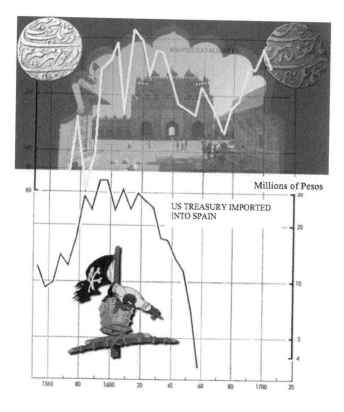

Ten years later when the silver from the Americas arrived in in Europe, the money stock ended up in India.

On this graph, we see that the pirates were effective in cutting the maritime routes to Spain. The silver took other routes, particularly those of Holland and England, and still arrived in India 20 years later, as seen in the top of this graph.

When the Mexican pesos arrived in India as payment for trade, they were immediately reminted to become rupees. The Mughal emperor's coins were almost pure silver, whose content and weight did not change for many centuries. The rupee often had more value than the value of the metal it contained. As there was freedom of minting throughout the empire, it was more profitable, for both individuals and trading companies to transform their metal bars into rupees at that time.

Silver throughout History

India did not produce precious metals but since the time of Alexander the Great, Europe valued their spices and paid them at the gold price. These products arrived from southern India by caravan, who had to pay tribute or tolls to each small kinglet along the route. When they arrived in Europe, the spices cost at least 100 times their purchase price.

In 1519, Magellan discovered Moluccas. His ship returned in 1522 with 26 tons of cloves in their hold. They were resold 10,000 times their purchase price.

Such a prospect for profit motivated all the European ship-owners to engage in maritime trade with the Indies.

Ginger, pepper, chili, curry, cinnamon, cloves, cardamom, coriander, nutmeg, saffron, paprika, cumin, vanilla, teas and other fragrant plants were exchanged for precious metals.

In 1697, in a trial trading with India, the English economist, Charles Davenant wrote: *"Silver and gold from America and silver from the European mines put together was equivalent to 800 million pounds. I cannot explain what happened to the 800 million extracted from the ground, except to suggest that the 150 million were swept away and swallowed up in India."*

Due to the development of maritime trade between India, Europe and its American colonies, money supply in India tripled between 1592 and 1639, causing inflation in the prices of many products (sugar, indigo, cloves, mercury, copper).

During that time, **the over abundant production of silver lowered the price of the white metal**, while the cost of production and transportation to Seville increased thus reducing the profits of the mining companies.

Salaries in India expressed in grams of silver per day

In western and northern India, including the Indus plain which forms Pakistan and the Ganges Plain today, much of which is now called Bangladesh, the salary of an unskilled worker rose from 0.67 grams in 1600 to 1.40 in 1700 then to 1.80g in 1850.

The salary of a skilled worker rose from 1.62 in 1600, then 2.37

in 1700 and finally 5.27 grams in 1850.

The price of silver was therefore divided by 3.

The same salary expressed in kilograms of wheat per day over the same period for the unskilled worker decreased from 5.2 kilos to 2.5 due to improved farming techniques and therefore wheat production.

The salary in kilos of rice remained perfectly stable.

Over the same period in China, the salary remained stable, rising from 1.5g of silver/day to 1.7 g/day.

The wages of unskilled workers in India caught up with that of China in 1700, before it exceeded it slightly in 1850.

In England, the price of silver was divided by 4.3. We will see that in 1850 silver had already been replaced by paper money in GB.

Date	Southern England	India	Indian wage
	grams of silver per day		as % of English wage
1550-99	3.4	0.7	21
1600-49	4.1	1.1	27
1650-99	5.6	1.4	25
1700-49	7.0	1.5	21
1750-99	8.3	1.2	14
1800-49	14.6	1.8	12

Since 1645, the silver output from the mines each year was 60 times higher than that of gold.

This proportion did not change until 1720 when the Brazilian Minas Gerais produced 9 tons of gold per year on the average, or 3 times more than the twenty previous years.

This extraordinary improvement in productivity was due to Thomas Newcomen's steam engines that allowed water to be pumped with greater efficiency in the mine tunnels.

ASIA

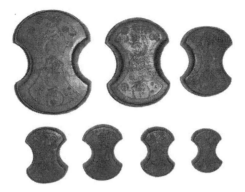

In Japan as in China, silver had currency value. Taxes were levied in silver taels.

The Tael, which weighed 1.2057 troy ounces or 37.5 grams was the unit of weight.

Therefore, these different silver weights had different values.

The Ginzan Iwami Silver Mine in Japan was the first silver mine in Asia. Discovered in 1526, this mine produced between 20 and 30% of the world's silver in the 16th and early 17th Century.

It enabled Japan to develop trade and cultural exchanges with the Far East, including Korea and China.

Japan exported nearly 50 tons of silver to the empires in the Middle Kingdom before 1599 then from 130 to 160 tons from 1600 to 1640, until the Portuguese and Spanish vessels came to compete with them with cargoes full of silver from the Americas.

In 1640, the Dutch Protestants obtained exclusive trading rights with Japan and accused the Portuguese and Spanish for wanting to convert the Japanese population to Catholicism.

Just like in India, the influx of silver from Japan and Mexico into China from the Ming Dynasty in the late 17th Century, caused a reduction in the relative value of silver or a high price inflation of all China-made products, which affected the entire population.

CYRILLE JUBERT

CHINA

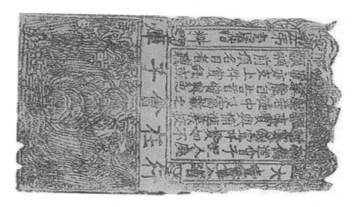

China had a much more advanced civilization than the West. In the 10th Century, the Song Dynasty, by encouraging the clearing of forest and irrigation, allowed the development of agriculture such that China experienced a demographic explosion. This resulted in the unprecedented growth of European cities. Trade and small business sectors thus developed, causing the rich merchants to establish stock companies and valid bills of exchange from one city to the other and from one province to another. The big merchants therefore became de facto bankers.

The copper coins, due to their weight and volume, were not used for big transactions so the merchants exchanged them for paper certificates to avoid carrying the bulk metal around. The government, wanting to regulate this market in which 60 banks were already operating for their own account, created the first Chinese official paper currency in 1024 in Sichuan. The imperial government printed paper notes using about 6 different inks which were valid for only 3 years. Printing therefore started in China and not Europe.

Paper disappeared from the 14th Century as a result of excessive issuance of notes by governments, Mongol invasions and the abundant silver provided by the merchants of Venice.

The plague was endemic in China but localized in some provinces. The wealth of the Chinese civilization stirred up the lust of the Mongol hordes who spread the disease between 1331 and 1393. The plague destroyed one third of the highly urbanized Chinese population before the Mongols and the Venetian merchants trading with the Middle East arrived at the gates of Constantinople and spread the epidemic in the West

The thirst for Chinese silver was due to the fact that from the 11th to the 15th Century, China used fiat money. The latter had been logically devalued several times over the centuries that the paper notes were worth almost nothing.

At the end of the 16th Century, the Chinese population represented ¼ of the world population, and its cities were over five times bigger than the European cities. It had already exceeded one million inhabitants. The transition to a silver monetary standard in a country which did not have it previously explained this thirst for the white metal from China. Issuing silver coins for an economy of this size involved a huge demand which explained the tremendous increase in the price of the silver metal.

Manila in the Philippines was built by the Spanish to be the hub of Asian trade. It was a large cosmopolitan market where European, Indian, Chinese and Japanese merchants could trade their goods.

Europe soon realized that the market was a one-way deal. The Chinese civilization was very advanced and extremely refined and did not want the relatively unsophisticated European goods, whilst Europe was hungry for Chinese products: silk, fine China and tea could not be exchanged for silver. In China gold was considered like a commodity just like silk, but not as a currency as such.

While the Spanish authorities limited the export of silver to Asia to 500,000 pesos (12.8 tons), the flow that passed through Manila, the gateway to Asia, exceeded 5 million pesos (128 tons) annually and even reached 12 million pesos (307 tons) in 1597.

Chinese silver was worth twice in China than anywhere else in the world. At Canton, from 1592 until the middle of the 17th Century, gold was exchanged at a ratio between 1/5 and 1/7 against 1/12 to 1/14 in Spain.

It is estimated that 30 to 40% of silver produced by the mines of the Spanish Empire ended up in China.

CYRILLE JUBERT

A RATIO OF 5 IN 1585'S CHINA

This graph shows the fluctuations of the ratio in France, China and Japan from 400 to 1650, explaining why the international merchants obtained huge profits by trafficking in precious metals between Europe and the Far East.

Silver was much more valued in China and Japan than gold. The merchants carried silver along to use it to buy gold and then sold it in Europe with fabulous profit.

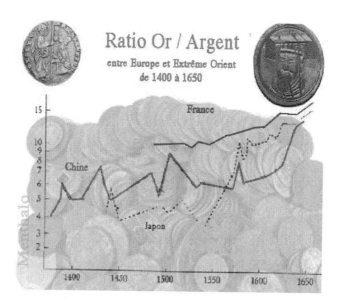

Confirmation in this document.

The precious metal exported to Asia every year was estimated at one and a half million sterling [42]. Other observers at that time attested to the amazing capacity of India and China to absorb the white metal. Henry Bornford, employed by the British East India Company, wrote in London in 1635 after his return from a business trip in the Portuguese town of Macao in China, that the commodity mostly sold there, was the silver-metal and in particular the 8 reales: <The Chinese sought for the latter with such ardor that they did not want to go back to where they came from. They supplied their goods with an extraordinary boldness, preferring to get rid of their own blood than these coins once they took possession of them. > [43]. Duarte Gomez had already understood the technical reasons allowing such large quantities of silver to cross the West to Asia. While the catholic powers tried to fix the gold/ silver standard at 10 (between 1585 and 1600), it was only 5 in China [44], which was a high premium on silver. Most of the sources confirmed this diagnosis. The change in the gold/ silver standard undoubtedly determined the composition of the metal treasures which were sent to Asia. Throughout the 17th Century, the silver that arrived in India was in such large quantities that, for some time, it was cheaper than the gold in Spain. During this short period, gold exports dominated the East Indian companies. A contraction in supply throughout the Middle East coupled with the development of trade between southern Asia and China seemed to have restored the balance and even created a silver shortage in the short term [45]. The reason why silver was preferred to gold in international trade in the Indian Ocean is not difficult to explain. Traditionally, silver and copper were the monetary standard of southern Asia and China [46].

From 1570 to 1580, the Ming Dynasty wanted to modernize the tax system by introducing the "Single Whip" Reform, which allowed the farmers to replace previously mandatory chores and taxes as a percentage of their production with payment in silver.

But over the years, the relative value of silver in China declined while the prices of agricultural products and handicrafts experienced high inflation. Revenues of the Middle Kingdom were fixed but they decreased in value each year, leading to the impoverishment of the state and the fall of the Ming Dynasty.

The influx of silver from the Americas, mismanaged by the Chinese Ministers, caused the collapse of the Empire.

Conversely, silver from the Japanese mines, strictly controlled by Shotgun, allowed the Rising Sun Empire to set up the small feudal lords by unifying the country on one hand, while developing the Japanese international trade throughout the Far East, on the other.

Japan was strengthened after this historic phase.

In 1635, the silver fever fell on China. The price of gold shot up at a ratio of 1/13 compared to silver.

PAPER CURRENCIES IN EUROPE

While paper money disappeared in China in the 15th Century, it reappeared in Amsterdam in 1609 to solve the problems of a growing international trade in Flanders, which had just gained independence from the Spanish Crown.

This independence allowed the rapid expansion of Protestantism. The latter did not prohibit loans with interest contrary to the Catholic religion. The bankers were able to refine their practice officially. Like all other big trading ports which had to manage the influx of foreign currencies, Amsterdam resorted to private banks to manage the change.

In 1600, nearly 800 different metal coins, more or less clipped and doctored, were circulating in Europe. This made it necessary for complex quality controls to be imposed with each exchange. The Bank of Amsterdam proposed to withdraw all coins below their actual price to melt again and turn them into coins with genuine quality.

The new coin cost 8% of the withdrawal fee otherwise the money remained in an account. Bills were settled with simple "bills of exchange." Since there were no charges for bank transfers between accounts, it attracted many customers to this city dedicated to international trade.

The bank kept the silver stocks of its customers and charged them storage fees every six months. When customers exchanged their metal into paper currency, **"banco guilder"**, they received a 5% premium. The Guilder Banco did not circulate in small business sectors.

By banning the traditional changers, the Bank of Amsterdam granted itself a de facto monopoly. It became **the first Central Bank**. At the time of creation, it was defined as the bank with no right to grant loans. Brilliantly managed for a century and a half, this bank made Amsterdam one of the major financial centers in the world in the 17th Century.

CYRILLE JUBERT

"THE GLORIOUS REVOLUTION" ENGLAND UNDER THE DUTCH YOKE

Holland's financial power, born from the combination of a united, high performing, free and well managed banking system, the "Dutch East Indian Companies", allowed the Netherlands Princes of Orange who had become very powerful to land in England to overthrow the English dynasty in **1688**.

This palace coup called the "Glorious Revolution", allowed the Holland Protestant princes to establish a Constitutional and Parliamentary Monarchy to replace the aristocratic government of the Catholic Stuarts. By decree, the Catholic King was henceforth banned from ascending the thrown of England.

This religious antagonism, which seems unimportant today, was extremely sensitive at that time. The United Provinces of Netherlands had long fought against the Spanish suzerains to obtain religious freedom.

At a time when the Spanish Crown and the Catholic Powers still dominated in Europe and the world and when the Vatican banned the Catholics from engaging in financial transactions including loans with interest, this decree had considerable importance. It gave birth to the City of London in the world-class of international finance.

The "Glorious Revolution" was inspired, if not instigated, by the bankers in the United Provinces who were worried about the huge debts issued by Britain, whose currency had drastically depreciated on the markets.

CREATION OF THE BANK OF ENGLAND

In 1694, the new English regime which was partially managed by the Dutch elite created the Bank of England. Like the Bank of Holland which was created earlier, the Bank of England stocked the gold and silver of depositors and created accounts which enabled silver to be circulated through bank bills.

The first major effort to finance the Bank of England was to create the **Royal Navy** by issuing Navy Bills. It was not until nearly ten years after this decision that Great Britain became the mistress of the seas.

The first issuance of bonds of the Bank of England experienced a crisis of confidence in Amsterdam, leading to a fall in the pound sterling (in silver) and a sharp rise in the English Gold Guinea on the Dutch exchange market. Discount in the BOE bonds increased to 12% before it reached 40%.

It must be recalled here that silver from the Americas attracted the greed of adventurers throughout Europe and the piracy blocked the influx of metal to Spain in 1650.

The shortage of silver coins made the Spanish Crown bankrupt on a recurring basis. Major lenders in the United Provinces suffered greatly from this. The Dutch bankers quickly demanded that the Navy Bills and the other bonds issued by the Bank of England be approved by Parliament and covered by the property of the Crown. This new legislation put an end to the monetary crisis by restoring confidence. British debt shot up from 1 to 16 million pounds from 1688 to 1702, then to 48 million pounds in 1714, mainly due to the creation of the Navy. Over a quarter of the exorbitant English taxes at that time were used to fund the creation of the Royal Navy.

There was therefore a true political will and a real strategic vision behind the future British Empire.

While Great Britain lagged behind the other great European powers (Portugal, Spain, Netherlands) in trade and especially colonial matters, the building of this battle fleet marked the starting point for the creation of the British Empire. The construction of military arsenals led to an improvement in techniques and reduction in the construction of commercial shipbuilding in Great Britain. The British ironworks multiplied by 3 in 25 years and England soon absorbed 60% of the iron produced in the mines in Sweden.

Lloyd's and the London Stock Exchange were established at the same time. The former was not yet an insurance company but a stock exchange where ship-owners and merchants exchanged and shared risks on expeditions and cargo.

The Bank of England had to ensure monetary and financial stability in the United Kingdom. It encouraged the creation of commercial banks throughout the country for which it was the lender as a last resort.

The increase in the number of banks coupled with the use of paper money resulted in the acceleration of the British Industrial Revolution.

At the same time, Parliament increased the premiums of investors. The number of patents doubled. This is why the "steam engine" for pumping water in the mines was patented in 1698, prior to the new patent by Thomas Newcomen, which came to improve it in 1705. The improved techniques gave a genuine boost to mining.

You will recall that in 1600, the total annual trade with Asia was 50 tons of silver by all companies.

Silver throughout History

The British East India Company took a substantial part of this trade compared to its Dutch, French, Spanish and Portuguese rivals.

From 1660 to 1675, it was only 7.5 tons of silver per year (240,000 ounces but it multiplied by 6 with 42 tons in the next decade.

The « Nine Years War » ruined trade for 10 years. From 1700, 31 tons of silver were sent to Asia annually for 20 years, then 50 tons for 30 years and finally 60 tons over the next 10 years.

According to some authors and countries, the Nine Years War was also known as "The War of the League of Augsburg", "the War of the Palatine Succession" or the "War of the Grand Alliance". It took place from 1688 to 1697. It was against the King of France, Louis XIV in alliance with the Ottoman Empire and the Irish and Scottish Jacobites (seeking to restore the Catholic sovereign on the thrown of England) to a broad-based European coalition the League of Augsburg led by the Anglo-Dutch William III, Emperor of the Germanic Holy Roman Empire, Leopold I, Charles II, King of Spain, Victor Amadeus of Savoy and many princes of the Germanic Holy Roman Empire. This conflict took place mainly in the neighboring seas of Continental Europe between the English and French colonies and their allied American Indians in North America and lasted through a limited campaign. To this was added a naval war, we must dare to use this term, where privateers from different nations plundered the Spanish colonies and galleons in the Caribbean and Latin America.

Louis XIV finally recognized William III of Orange-Nassau as the King of England and endorsed the "Glorious Revolution" of the Dutch..

As a cold comfort for the loss of Canada, France gained recognition for its occupation of the west of Santo Domingo in the West Indies, making it the world's leading producer of cubed sugar from the 1740s.

Sugar was a very expensive commodity at that time and it helped to enrich the ship-owners and merchants of Bordeaux, Nantes and Lorient, who were very involved in the triangular trade. Sugarcane cultivation required abundant workforce, so the merchants went to buy herds of slaves on the African coasts and resold them to planters before bringing sugar, molasses and rum back to Europe.

Over the years, the intrinsic value of the white metal fell and prices of commodities rose in Asia. At the same time, the economic expansion in Great Britain increased the consumption of imported goods from India, China and Asia in general (Indian tea, spices, silk, porcelain.)

Compagnie Anglaise des Indes Orientales
exportation d'or et d'argent vers l'Asie en kg de fin

Période	Argent	Or
1660-1665	40 145	1 074,47
1666-1670	22 910	1 673,66
1671-1675	49 828	3 669,50
1676-1680	179 252	5 156,62
1681-1685	240 952	6 931,61
1686-1690	30 567	879,18
1691-1695	7 687	221,14
1696-1700	131 511	491,22
1701-1705	166 885	—
1706-1710	173 833	141,11
1711-1715	167 503	145,79
1716-1720	250 851	—
1721-1725	289 349	—
1726-1730	261 401	—
1731-1735	260 102	—
1736-1740	260 378	—
1741-1745	257 882	—
1746-1750	366 289	—
1751-1755	398 041	—
1756-1760	193 458	—

Sources: India Office Records, East India Company Commerce Journals and General Ledgers, L/AG/1/6/ vols. 1-8, L/AG/1/1/ vols. 2-14.

The silver metal was an essential barter commodity in the trade with India and China as these countries were not buyers of finished British products.

Many voices were raised against the drain of precious metal and the cheap but excellent quality goods imported from Asia, that the western manufacturers could not compete with.

This is what Richard Cantillon wrote in 1730 in *"Essay on the Nature of Trade"*:

<It is amazing to see the imbalance between the circulation of silver in England & China. The goods manufactured in India such as silks, painted canvas, muslins etc. Notwithstanding the 18 months shipping expenses remained very low in England which paid them a thirtieth part of its work & manufactured goods if the Indians wanted to purchase them. But they were not so foolish to pay exorbitant prices for our work for much cheaper, while we worked better in their country. Also they only sold their manufactured products against cash ...the Indian goods consumed in Europe only decreased our silver and the work in our own factories >

From 1756 to 1760, trade fell by half due to the war between France and England or the French Company of the East Indies and its British counterpart. The Battle of Plassey in 1758 marked the end of the French presence in India and the beginning of the military conquest of the CAIO.

For the record, the British East India Company gradually colonized some territories with private armies for its own account. It was not until a century later that the management of India was restored to the British Crown.

English economists and financiers believed that the currency did not need to be in gold or silver for commercial and industrial transactions in Great Britain or with their European partners.

"The peak of money circulation has already taken place at home through the bank notes of the Bank of England and private banks", explained the historian Fernand Braudel.

An increasing part of the British money supply was made up of bank notes. Only the average currency and lose money were made of pure metal.

CYRILLE JUBERT

THE REGENCY IN FRANCE

The period called Regency (1715-1723), after the end of the reign of Louis XIV in France was interesting to observe because it was marked by a serious bankruptcy in Public Finance.

At the death of Louis XIV, the Treasury was empty and revenue of the following two years had already been spent. Given the difficulties the Treasury, the Regent, Philippe d'Orléans, listened with interest to the seductive proposals of the Scottish, John Law, who studied the Dutch system. A country, he said, is richer as it engages in more trade. But trade depends on the abundance of money and the **rapidity of its circulation**.

Since money was only a medium of exchange of goods, its nature was immaterial. It was not necessary to use gold, silver or rare metal, which many countries were deprived of. The most convenient currency was paper money which was easily manufactured and transported. The state had to become a banker and issue "bank notes", or paper money that could be easily exchanged for gold or silver.

Commercial banks which were already operating at Amsterdam, Nuremberg, Stockholm and London issued promissory notes in exchange for coin deposits that guaranteed the convertibility of notes at any time, to ensure the security of customers, but the bank was prohibited from granting large loans.

John Law thought that securing notes through incomes from agricultural produce constituted the capital base. The convertibility at any time against hard cash was not guaranteed, but customers had the assurance that the value indicated on each note issued corresponded with the value of an existing property.

This system was a true and proven revolution and a first step towards the abandonment of gold and silver as the only means of payment.

In Law's system, a new currency could circulate independently from gold or silver and it corresponded then to a need for the European economies to have more means of payment and greater flexibility. Europe was on the eve of its industrial revolution. However the arrival of precious metals from the Americas was less abundant, money became scarce and the economies took a downward trend. This state of affairs confirmed the Theory of Mercantilism according to which prosperity depended on the quantity of gold and silver in circulation. Law's system also helped to regulate the issuance of new currency based on the needs of the economy and the state.

In 1716, Law obtained permission to open a private bank, the **General Bank**. The Regent and nobility took part in the purchase of shares of the new bank. It was not a land bank but a bank built on the Dutch model which exchanged coin deposits for bank notes. Profits were made through the exchange and discount transactions. The currency issued was more convenient for the traders and it was soon a success. The bank started increasing the volume of issuance by printing more paper money which had no gold nor silver content.

The success of the General Bank was such that it was recognized as a state bank in 1718.

According to John Law, the state must also be a trader because its profits can be used to settle public debt. Thus Law also established another Joint Stock Trading Company in 1717 under the name of Western Company, and later to **East India Company** in 1719. It had monopoly of all French colonial trade. Finally, the East India Company was mandated to collect indirect taxes. In 1720, John Law merged the General Bank and the East India Company. Everybody wanted to own shares. People paid 20,000 pounds for 500 pound shares. A real stock market bubble.

However, in a few months, the dividends earned by each share reduced and public confidence was eroded.

The situation soon worsened. To break the French tradition of hoarding gold and silver, **Law prohibited the possession of more than 500 pounds of precious* metal by household** under the penalty of confiscation and fines.

A reward was given to whistleblowers and searches took place. On the 11th of March, to discourage the public from using the coin, John Law suspended the discharge value of gold and silver on December 31. Three months later, on March 24, Law's system became bankrupt.

The shareholders presented themselves together to exchange the paper money for coins that the company no longer had. The VIPs, like the prince of Conti or the Duke of Bourbon came in person to withdraw their gold at the headquarters of the Bank Rue Quincampoix which resulted in riots. The share price fell before Law could control the crash.

On July 21, an order established a semi-bankruptcy. Parliament which attempted to resist was sent on exile to Pontoise.

On October 10 an announcement was made for the suspension of bank notes from the 1st of November. The Law system died. Law escaped to Paris on December 14 before he went on exile to Venice.

"In 1720, after the bankruptcy of Law's system, the official denomination of the Livre Tournois became the "Pound" (0.31 grams of gold).

The film "The Hunchback" was based on this storyline. The gigantic crash diverted the French from the stock market for over a century.

(*) 500 pounds = 155 grams = 26 napoleons

THE BANKING CRASH OF 1763

The Bank of Amsterdam was used as a model to create similar institutions all over, especially in Protestant Northern Europe.

Amsterdam bankers went beyond their prerogatives from the start by using "bills of exchange" as loans secured for 3 months by the metal deposits, thus funding the belligerents of the Seven Years War (1756-1763). This conflict was often compared to a world war between the all-powerful European powers, Russia, Prussia, Great Britain, Holland, France. It took place in all the continents. France lost India and Canada as a result.

At the end of the war in 1763, speculations on commodities at the Amsterdam Stock Market were higher and it collapsed suddenly. The stock crash caused customers to rush to the banks to exchange their "bills of exchange" into gold and silver coins.

In Amsterdam alone, 16 banks granted more loans than the metal reserves in their coffers and went bankrupt as a result. The other banks immediately closed the credit tap to their customers.

Dutch companies were the first to suffer and the price of stocks dropped leading to a stock market crash.

As the bank customers were international, the crash spread in Europe. At Hamburg, 48 financial institutions closed their doors in less than one month.

1776 – AMERICAN INDEPENDENCE

In 1776, bankers in the City of London succeeded in getting the British Parliament to pass a law prohibiting the thirteen American colonies from creating a local currency, the **Colonial Script**. The law required these colonies to use the coins minted in London for trade.

The Colonial Script

Since the currency was obtained with interest, it automatically became a perpetual debt for the settlements. The monetarists called it the **currency debt**, which constituted an annuity of the private banks at the expense of the states under this regime.

Upon declaration of Independence of the United States, the founding fathers stipulated in Article 1 of the American Constitution signed in Philadelphia in 1787: *"This Congress shall have the right to mint money and regulate its value"*.

Thomas Jefferson was convinced of the perverse role of international bankers. He wrote: *"I think the banking institutions are more dangerous than the army. If ever the American people authorize the private banks to control money supply, the banks and the corporations developing around them will deprive people of their property until the day when their children will wake up homeless on the continent that their fathers conquered."*

Over two centuries ago, Jefferson had prophesied about the current crisis of the "subprimes" which cast forty four million

American citizens on the street.

After the Americans defeated the British troops, the independence of the American colonies became a reality.

But the London bankers did not concede defeat. They created a private bank under the deceptive name of "Bank of the United States", for people to think that it was a state bank. For 20 years this bank obtained the right to mint money from President George Washington in 1791, in total contradiction of the Constitution.

Twenty years later, President Jackson sought to put an end to the privileges enjoyed by this bank and to enforce Article 1 of the Constitution but to no avail.

English bankers led by Nathan Rothschild lobbied to impose trade barriers on American products and taxes on products to the U.S. so much that the Bank of the United States was able to recover its privileges in 1816.

It was not until Abraham Lincoln's time that an American President sought to oppose the diktats of the bankers. This he did in 1862 by passing the Legal Tender Act. Three years later Lincoln was assassinated.

His successor, Andrew Johnson, who got the message, abolished the "greenback" and restored the privileges of private bankers.

CYRILLE JUBERT

THE ASSIGNATS BANKRUPTCY OF FRANCE IN 1793

History stuttered.

Before the 1789 Revolution, royal finances were in a catastrophic state with a debt estimated between 4 and 5 billion pounds. Half of the royal budget was used to reduce the debt which only increased as the cash was used as annuity for various people. The risk of bankruptcy was close and they had to find new money. The MP, Talleyrand, proposed that the property of the clergy be confiscated (but not to be nationalized because no compensation was paid in exchange.)

This influx of assets, estimated between 2 and 3 billion pounds, was a huge windfall for public finances. The sale was entrusted to the Special Fund created on December 19 1789 and ended on December 6 1790. The sale of all goods had to take at least one year. This deadline was too long because the state coffers were empty and maturities of creditors were such that bankruptcy was announced before everything was sold.

It was for this reason that a decision was made, that very day, to establish a Special Fund whose value was assigned to the property of the clergy. **Then the script was born.**

The operation of the script was simple: as it was impossible to sell all the property of the clergy right away, notes were issued to represent the value of the property. Anyone who desired to purchase domestic goods had to do so with assignats. Therefore, individuals first and foremost had to purchase assignats from the state and that was how money came back into the system. Once the sale was made and money went back into the hands of the state, the assignats had to be destroyed. Thus cash inflow was faster than waiting till property was actually sold.

The first notes issued were valued at 1000 pounds. This significant amount was not meant for use by the population, but for individuals to hoard with the sole aim of getting money back right away into the state coffers. The total value of the first issue was 400 million pounds. The idea was far from a unanimous decision by the constituent Assembly as some cited the bankruptcy of Law's system. This is why MPs like Talleyrand, Condorcet or Du Pont de Nemours were against it. According to them, the major problem with the issuance of assignats was that there should not be more assignats in circulation than the value of national assets. But, at that time, the notes were easily forgeable. There was therefore a high risk of finding a greater quantity of assignats in circulation than the actual number there should be. Besides, the assignats issued by counterfeiters did not bring any revenue to the state. In such cases, the assignats were worth nothing.

By early 1790, the first failures occurred. On the 30th of March, the MP Montesquiou-Fezensac said the assignats were: "the most expensive and disastrous of loans."

Depreciation

On April 17, the assignat was turned into paper money. As the state was always short of money, it used it for all running expenses. The machine got carried away... The state did not destroy the assignats it recovered; worst still, it printed more assignats than the value of the national assets. Necker, the then Minister of Finance, vehemently opposed the conversion of the assignat into paper money and tendered his resignation in September.

The assignat lost 60% of its value from 1790 to 1793.

Although the value of the assignat reduced, the auction of national assets still remained very high and only the wealthy could afford it. This was how some people enriched themselves immensely and bought huge lands and buildings for almost nothing compared to their real value. The legal overvaluation of the assignat allowed the purchase of undervalued property as a result.

To support the assignats, several successive harder laws were passed, as heavy fines and severe prison sentences were imposed on anyone caught selling gold or silver coins or processing paper money or precious metals differently including the refusal of a payment in assignat.

On the 8th of April 1793, the Convention decided that the cost of all purchases and contracts concluded with the state would be stipulated only in assignats. This measure was extended to the private sector on the 11th.

From the early days of the Terror, on September 8 1793, non-acceptance of the assignat was declared punishable by death: the property was confiscated and the informer was rewarded.

On the 13th of November 1793, trading in precious metals was prohibited. In May 1794, any person who asked in which currency a contract would be concluded was sentenced to death.

Despite all this, the political authorities did not know how to handle the economic crisis that ensued and the state continued to issue more and more assignats to finance the war. The number of assignats produced were of 2.7 billion pounds in September 1792 and 5 billion in August 1793. In early 1794, the number of assignats issued increased to 8 billion. However, the authorities finally understood that the continued depreciation of the assignats was due to excess issues. Also, part of it was withdrawn from circulation from 1793 through forced loans. By subtracting the quantities withdrawn and burnt, only 5 and a half billion remained in circulation.

In June 1794, the creation of new one billion assignats , from 1,000 Francs to 15 instituted at the same time as the 100 million forced loans on the rich was launched by the Finance Committee. After new issues, assignats in circulation shot up from 10 billion in August 1795 to nearly 45 billion pounds in January 1796, while the sum total of assignats should never have exceeded 3 billion, value of the property of the clergy. The inflation was due to overproduction of assignats; price controls did not allow their decline but resulted in scarcity.

A large number of fake assignats, made in Belgium, Holland, Germany, Switzerland and Great Britain flooded France, with the complicity of the British government, the greatest enemy of France at that time, interested in accelerating the French economic crisis.

The end of assignats and assessment

By decision of the management board, the assignat was finally abandoned with pomp when the printing presses, punches, dies and plates were burnt at Vendôme Public Square on the 19th of February 1796.

On the 1st of March, the assignat was withdrawn from circulation against a new note, the territorial mandate. The exchange was made on the basis of 30 assignat francs against 1 mandate franc, instead of its actual value of 300 against 1, condemning the new note upon its issue. The territorial mandate experienced more or less the same history as the assignat, depreciating much faster than its predecessor.

On February 4 1797, it was withdrawn from circulation and the hard cash took its place.

The assignat was generally regarded as total failure. However, not only did its creation prevent the near immediate collapse of the French state but contributed to debt alleviation and helped to raise funds needed to finance the war during Year Two.

CYRILLE JUBERT

Silver Throughout History

19th Century Bimetallism

CYRILLE JUBERT

FRANC GERMINAL YEAR XI

After the financial and monetary disruption in the late 18th Century, the Apocalypse of revolutionary currency, the Consulate put in place a bimetallic monetary system, gold and silver which restored economic and financial stability.

The 7th of Germinal Year Eleven or March 27 1803, the First Consul Bonaparte fixed the value of the franc, called "Germinal Franc".

1 Franc was worth 5 grams of silver in 900/1000th or 4.5 grams of pure silver.

By decree, 15.5 ounces of silver was needed to buy an ounce of gold. **The whole of Europe aligned with this monetary system.** That was the era of bimetallic gold.

This system allowed monetary stability for the next 75 years.

All the silver or gold coins minted in Europe, America and the colonies had the same weight and value. This facilitated international trade extremely.

Growth in global money supply was constrained by gold and silver mining production which were naturally limited by the techniques of the time.

Privateers and pirates continued to plunder the seas including the Indian Ocean during the 19th Century.

Surcouf, 1773-1827, the most brilliant of our privateers, was so rich that he covered the floor of his house with Napoleon's gold coins.

During his visit in 1803 to try to convince Surcouf to accept the command of a squadron of his fleet, Emperor Napoleon 1st remarked that he found it so indecent that one thus walked on his face *"Never mind, Sir,* replied Surcouf, *I shall place them on the edge."*

Could Surcouf have avoided Trafalgar?

THE TRAFALGAR OF SPAIN

Napoleon who advocated for monetary stability was one of the causes of the end of bimetallism. The King of Spain, Charles III of Bourbon was related to the King of France, Louis XVI through the "Family Pact" (1761), linking the Bourbons of France, Spain, Naples and Parma. The aim was to counterbalance the British expansionism. At the same time, Charles III was wary of his powerful neighbor and he maintained close relations with Prussia and Holy See. When he died in 1788, his son, Charles IV, inherited the kingdom after finding the place he occupied in Europe in the early 16th Century. Charles IV, very similar in character to his cousin Louis XVI, was more interested in manufacturing shoes, weapons or furniture than public affairs. His promiscuous wife put one of her lovers, Manuel Godoy, in power. Spain was not hostile right away to the 1789 ideas. It was only after the arrest of Louis XVI that the Spanish monarchy closed the Cortes and established a terrible repressive censorship. Charles IV borrowed 2,300,000 pounds from Banque Lecouteult to corrupt his judges in vain. The execution of Louis XVI toggled Spain to the side of the enemies of France and the "Enlightenment". On the 7th of march 1793, Spain declared war on France. The entire population stood up to launch a crusade against the lawless French. The people's contributions to the war was 45 million francs in Spain against 5 in France which was struck with terror. This state of war enabled the revolutionaries to disrupt colonial trade and cut British supplies and finances. Bayonne was threatened, and Montpellier was surrounded by the Spanish. Paris sent troops in late 1793 to chase the Spanish before invading the Netherlands and Cataluña.

The increasing strength of the Spanish revolutionaries and Basque separatists forced Godoy, the queen's lover, to negotiate for peace.

In August 1796, Paris and Madrid put up a common front against London. But the troops and the vessels of Charles IV only experienced setback against the English. Spanish vessels could not leave their ports, trade was blocked and the colonies were in danger. Charles was a weakling, controlled by a woman who had developed strange and decadent tastes as described perfectly in the paintings of Goya. The royal couple was a laughing stock in Europe.

When Bonaparte came to power in France, he managed to have

such ascendancy over Charles IV that Spain was said to be a satellite country of France. As the first Consul, he pushed Spain to war against Portugal in the brief "War of the Oranges" in 1801.

In 1804, when Napoleon was crowned emperor, he wanted to invade England. He designed a large naval maneuver across the Atlantic to keep away the English fleet from the Channel by leading them towards the West Indies. All the Spanish war fleets were involved in this maneuver. But the French and Spanish fleets experienced an overwhelming defeat off Cape Trafalgar.

Trafalgar left the full control of the seas to England. Spain could no longer protect its colonies let alone the convoy of silver from New Spain, as they called the vast kingdom, which run from Florida in Peru to Mexico which was the source of Spain's wealth thanks to its silver mines.

These successive wars weakened the country that was still plagued by famine after several years of poor harvests. The economy was in disarray, and the royal finances were near bankruptcy as the currency continued to depreciate. The "Vales" paper money was worth only a quarter of its nominal value.

The Queen's lover, Godoy, was the Acting Head of Government and played a double game. He swore his allegiance to the emperor but he wrote to his enemies and promised to send his armies to take the French cuffed. His letters fell into the hands of the French in 1807 and Napoleon sent an army through Spain to participate in the war against Portugal as the latter did not want to enforce the continental blockade against the English. Also, he sent Murat and the army to Madrid at the time when there was a conspiracy to overthrow the weak King, Charles IV and put his son Ferdinand VII on the throne. Napoleon took advantage of the disorder in the monarchy to force the two sovereigns to abdicate and he installed his brother Joseph on the throne.

The Emperor mistakenly believed that the French supporters and the "Enlightened" constituted the majority of the Spanish and that Jerome would be acclaimed. However, the opposite happened. Everywhere, people rose against the French, creating a terrible guerilla war, which marked the first defeats of the imperial army on the continent.

In 1812, the Cortes adopted a constitution that was very close to French Constitution of 1791 and the Declaration of Human Rights and Citizenship of 1789.

CYRILLE JUBERT

REVOLUTION IN NEW SPAIN

Placing Joseph Bonaparte on the Spanish throne caused uprisings in New Spain in general and Mexico in particular with a time lag due to the paralysis of commercial traffic between the metropolis and the colonies of New Spain.

The legitimists wanted the return of Ferdinand to the throne while the separatists were dreaming. The Declaration of Human Rights and Citizenship and books of "Enlightenment" were able to cross the Atlantic, raising the hopes of the Creoles who were born in the colonies but did not have the same rights as the Spanish and the mestizos who were even more despised. The revolution begun in the latter part of 1810. The army of the insurgents with more than 80,000 men chalked lots of successes but they committed so many massacres that this barbarism dampened some of the separatists. The leaders were all killed from the very beginning and the rest of the insurgents got back in line. Only a sporadic guerilla persisted in some provinces.

It was not until 1820, after the King of Spain, Ferdinand VII, signed the constitution of 1812, that the war of independence spread in Mexico. The Republic of Mexico was founded in September 1821.

From 1821 to 1850, Mexico had 50 successive governments. Their respective policies had only one constant factor: They prohibited the export of silver, the main wealth of the country by accumulating debts.

Who was so powerful that he corrupted 50 successive governments for such a long time? Who was interested in destabilizing the global monetary system at that time?
Give it a guess: the **Bank of England.**

This was the territory of New Spain in 1819. It included almost one third of the United States of today.

Florida was one of them. King Ferdinand sold it for 5 million dollars (26 million Francs of gold) to repay part of his debts.

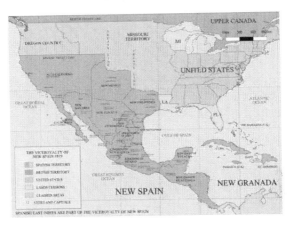

Napoleon sold New Orleans, Louisiana and the entire region irrigated by Mississippi and its tributaries for 15 million dollars or 80 million Francs.

In fact, he realized that he could not develop an empire on the American continent and preferred to sell it to the United States before Great Britain took possession of the territory. This territory was sold for 7 dollars per km².

80 million francs of gold = 4 million napoleons = 1 billion euros in August 2012.

Here are some funny stories that changed the course of history including monetary history.

Uncle Sam

Samuel Brannan was born in 1819 in Maine but his parents moved to Ohio, where he learned the printing trade. Sam, following the example of his parents, listened religiously to Jo Smith's Sunday sermons and soon became one of his inner circle of disciples. At Smith's death, Sam Brannan escaped to New York with a group of Mormons, banned from their county and within a few months he published a newspaper, the "The Prophet". But in New York also, the Mormons were chased out. Sam Brannan therefore decided to go and colonize the virgin lands in the west with his friends. This is how in February 1846, with 40 Mormons, Sam boarded a boat to California, via Cape Horn and Hawaii. He carried an antique printing press in his baggage. This long and perilous journey led them to Yerba Buena on July 31. Their arrival tripled the size of the village at once.

Yerba Buena was then a tent village with several wooden huts along the Pacific. The bay served as a natural shelter for ships that came to exchange goods with a few hundreds of Americans who populated this region that was officially almost completely deserted.

Yerba Buena was part of this new country, Mexico, which gained independence in December 1821. But this very young Republic was nothing but a political disorder. Upper California was mainly populated by some little-known Indian tribes because nobody cared about that distant province.

Well, almost nobody.

CYRILLE JUBERT

FROM YERBA BUENA TO SAN FRANCISCO

During that time in Washington, President James Knox Polk dreamt only of "Conquest of the West" to expand the territories of the United States that had recently celebrated their 70 years of existence. Knox therefore sent a diplomatic mission to Mexico in late 1845, with a mission to buy New Mexico and California for 25 million dollars. Receiving no response, Washington sent troops to the north of Rio Grande in February to press for negotiations to open. As usual, when you put a match close to a powder keg or armed men against other armed men, it causes explosive reactions. In April, after repeated skirmishes between the two opposing armies, tension mounted until a war was declared in May. This was how the Mexican-American war which lasted for 2 years was born. On the 2nd of February 1848, the United States got their hands on 1,300,000 km2, half of Mexico for only 15 million dollars, representing 206 million USD today.

John Sutter was one of the countless pioneers of the Conquest of the West. After moving around pretty much everywhere, he created a fortified village, Sutter Fort, along a small tributary of Sacramento river. Around fire, they told the story of the saga of the Fort Alamo, which took place barely a decade ago and led to the independence of Texas. The songs of the West evoked the great deeds of modern heroes which made them dream of all the adventurers in the New World. Hoping also to go down in history, Sutter joined a small battalion of volunteers in 1846 to free California from Mexican iron rule. On June 15, he was among the 30 settlers who seized the Sonoma garrison to float the Bear Flag of Liberated California. In July, he participated the liberation of Yerba Buena on the Pacific that was immediately renamed San Francisco. By a quirk of history, John Sutter and Sam Brennan, the Mormon, both assisted in the birth of this city.

Demobilized in early 47, Sutter returned home a hero to Sutter Fort, only to discover that all his cattle had been stolen in his absence. Full of energy, he then started again from scratch. All these pioneers who arrived in the West every week in long caravans needed wood to build houses. Sutter then planned to get wealth by creating a sawmill.

Silver throughout History

A carpenter, to be precise, James Marshall, visited Sutter Fort and seemed to know its business. Over a glass of bad bourbon, they developed plans for a modern sawmill whose badsaws would be powered by a mill. Give me five, it's a deal. Marshall, hired by Sutter, went to explore and found an ideal location for their company in Sonoma, 64 kilometers upstream on the American River.

The sawmill started with a few Indians and some freshly demobilized Mormon veterans as staff. Unfortunately, within a very short time, the hydraulic power was insufficient for the bandsaw to work perfectly. Marshall managed to convince John Sutter of the need to dig a forebay, an industrial divide to harness the river to reinforce hydraulic power. A new team of day laborers were hired to work only at night in order not to disturb the operation of the sawmill during the day. The laborers worked at night and went to bed at dawn.

On the 14th of January 1848, at cockcrow, Marshall, like every morning, went to inspect the progress of work of the canal in the rock. His gaze was quickly attracted by flashes of light at the bottom of the forebay. He went down to take a closer look and found extremely glittering rocks as if they were made of pure metal. When he hit them against each other, he realized that those rocks did not break but appeared somewhat malleable. Is that almost pure gold? He picked some of the finds to do some experiments.

James Marshall was amused by this discovery but as an engineer he had nothing in mind except the development of the sawmill. The staff were also excited but they did not have the right to search for gold except during the regulated break periods. Some days later, Marshall went to give account of his work in the sawmill to Sutter. He remained at Sutter Fort and officially became its mayor. He showed him the nuggets and its owner who after some tests acknowledged what was obvious. It was pure gold, worth 23 carats.

Contrary to what you might expect, Sutter did not jump with joy. He rightly feared that the discovery would result in hoarding by the lawless miners in the region, while he dreamt of building an agricultural empire. He then asked Marshall to keep it a secret.

The story could have ended there but some workers in the sawmill went to deliver boards at San Francisco and seized the opportunity to buy some tools to enable them search for gold. One of the shops in this growing township belonged to Samuel Brannan.

This Mormon, who settled down recently, was both a preacher in the church and editor publisher of the local rag , the "California Star" and had a shop where farmers found everything. Sutter's workers went there to buy shovels, pickaxes and gold washing sieves and paid with nuggets. Did this trickster Sam serve them a small rotgut to set their tongues wagging or whether he heard his Mormon brothers confessing it, the story does not say it but whatever it was, Brannan took the right decisions immediately. He started buying all the shovels, and pickaxes available in the region and placed an additional emergency order with his broker. After that, he hired some of his travelling companions to open a secondary shop at Fort Sutter and build a chapel there. According to the local history, due to a single denier of the church, tithes that all believers had to pay, Samuel Brannan became a millionaire.

Once the different businesses were set up, but not before, Brannan published a special issue on the discovery of gold in California in his *"California Star"* of March 1848. All the edition was sold out during the day. Sam walked through the streets of San Francisco shouting "we have found gold in California". Obviously, this special issue highlighted that only Brannan had tools for miners. "charity begins at home!"

Three days later, San Francisco was a ghost town. All the inhabitants went to look for gold.

CYRILLE JUBERT

THE GOLD RUSH

On the 19th of August 1848, the New York Herald was the first major newspaper on the East Coast to report that there was gold rush in California. It is estimated that only 500 pioneers left the East Coast in early 1848 but 6,000 researchers came from Mexico, Peru and even Australia and California in search of gold by the end of the year. At that time news travelled relatively slow and travelling was difficult, slower and more dangerous than today. Nevertheless, in 1849, 90,000 gold-diggers invaded California. Nearly 50,000 were Americans. The rest came from all parts of the world with a surprisingly large proportion of French who fled the 1848 Revolution. Many of these gold-diggers worked for only 6 months and went back home happy for having got the equivalent of 6 years' salary. In 1849, Fort Sutter's single store generated 150,000 dollars sales figures per month. Sam Brannan had stores throughout California and he had considerable wealth. Cleverly, Sam bought all the lands in San Francisco and founded cities in other places that he connected by railway lines. After a costly divorce and his liking for adulterated whisky, this brilliant Uncle Sam died penniless.

May he rest in peace

CALIFORNIA GOLD IN FIGURES

In 1848, the Independent Treasury Act separated the accounts of the Federal government and the banking system and imposed strict standards on the Treasury Department. But the rate of gold-silver conversion overvalued the latter due to the high demand for gold needed to trade with foreign countries, including Great Britain. Under Gresham's Law, there was an influx of silver but gold fled the country. This erosion of the amount of gold in circulation compared to that of silver, made it necessary to prospect gold, which led to the Gold Rush in California in 1849.

Was this gold rush desired by bankers and organized through the media? That was a real possibility.

When the entire world's media started commending the rapid fortunes made by the gold seekers, tens of thousands of people began to search for it. When we seek, we find. That was how it was found almost at the same time in California, Australia, Alaska or South Africa. Small streams make big rivers. This influx of gold allowed the transition to the gold standard that some bankers wanted a few years later.

Production reached its peak in California in 1852 with 121 tons, representing 3.9 million ounces. In 1865, all surface and gold panning was exhausted, leaving only the hard-earned gold in the mines. Production fell to 27 tons.

An estimated 80 million dollars of gold was sent to France by French prospectors.

Historians agree that the world's gold production since man's existence was about 150,000 tons out of which 30,000 got lost or were destroyed by the industry. Before the California "Gold Rush", only 13,000 tons of gold were destroyed, justifying the gold/silver ratio.

It is established that 90% of gold from the mines in the world to date was produced after 1848.

1848 was therefore a pivotal year in the history of silver.

CYRILLE JUBERT

Silver Throughout History

1848-1900

CYRILLE JUBERT

The industrial revolution that was experienced in the second half of the 19th Century permitted the creation of large scale manufactured goods allowing a new form of mass distribution to consumers, with the birth of department stores as well as multiple chain dime stores such as "Felix Potin", the GMMP.

During this century, improved infrastructure and transport equipment (steamers, railways) gradually facilitated national and international trade, by increasing the rate of circulation of money. Industrial expansion in the 19th Century would not have been possible if all transactions were actually paid for with gold or silver coins. After the creation of the Bank of Amsterdam, paper money multiplied and the national banks which were just like the Bank of England structured the financial market by improving international trade. In the 19th Century, the banks played a major role by increasing bank accounts of administrations, businesses and the general public. Scriptural money and commercial paper increased the money supply needed for economic development regardless of the metal mass.

As always, there was more money in circulation than the actual gold or silver stocked in bank vaults. This led to recurrent alarming bankruptcies. Whenever customers were beset with doubts, they requested for their cash in precious metal.

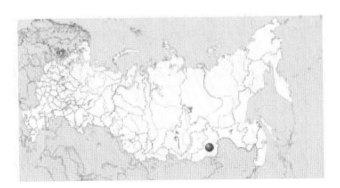

CYRILLE JUBERT

RUSSIAN SILVER MINES

There is very little information available on gold and silver mines in Russia. This is a mixture of observations of a member of the Academy of Sciences, Jean Chappe d'Auteroche (1728-1765) with later information from the late 19th Century.

"If most of the vast Siberian territory is unlikely to be cultivated, the subsoil contains valuable reserves of coal and various metals. At the time of Chappe, the most fascinating metals to man were gold and silver and they were subjected to active exploitation. Gold mines in Siberia, were largely exhausted. The extraction processes used allowed the treatment of only the richest parts. Outside the mines of the Urals mountains, connected to European Russia and those of the Altai, exploited since antiquity, most of the gold ores withdrew from the alluvial lands, in particular those of Lena in the neighborhood of NizhneUdinsk, Kansk or Minusinsk in the Yenisei bassin. Deposits were found at the bottom, covered by swampy lands. Exploitation was very expensive because it required the removal of barren surface layers and transportation of these mine spoils at a distance from the mine. Five groups of mines formed in the middle of Siberia, including about 380 mines, with 260 located in the forest area and 120 in the agricultural area. They employed about 10,000 workers annually and provided about 400 million francs worth of gold (137 tons). The mining district of Altai fell to the second place. The richest deposits were found in the Amur and Lena basins, where large companies were formed for the exploitation of the precious metal.

In 1880, 8.4 tons of gold were extracted by one company, the Olekma Company, for a value of 25 million francs. The extraction value was still maintained in the late 19th Century at 18 million francs or 6.2 tons."

Silver production declined sharply throughout Siberia. In Altai, production was once abundant. 2,000 tons of silver were mined from 1750 to 1863, date for the abolition of slavery.

In late 19th Century, these mines provided only a small amount. At Nertchinsk in Transbaikalie, in South Eastern Siberia, exploitation of silver mines dated back to the early 18th Century. After a slow and modest start, production reached 10 tons per year, around 1763, and it was maintained until 1786. These mines were considered as the worst penal colonies of the Russian Empire.

Two centuries later, out of 90 silver mines in this region, only 10 were still in operation and they provided about 800 kg per year. The whole of Siberia produced 6 to 7 tons of silver at that time. It was necessary to add platinum extraction to the production of precious metal since platinum was abundant especially in the Urals.

CYRILLE JUBERT

JAPAN
THE LAST SHOGUN

Under the regime of Shogunate, Japan was cut off from the outside world.

The silver mines belonging to the Shogun family maintained **a gold / silver ratio of 1/5** whilst that of the rest of the world was 1/15 until 1867 when it changed. Before the Perry Expedition in 1853-1854, foreigners were not allowed in Japan. In 1856, the U.S. Consul General, Townsend Harris, who was sent to negotiate a treaty had to fight tooth and nail for Japanese silver coins to be exchanged for an equal weight against foreign silver coins. Having managed to include this clause, the Consul hastened to change his silver dollars and Mexican Pesos against their Japanese equivalent, before swapping Japanese silver coins against a gold ratio of 5 to 1. He then sent his gold to a correspondent in Shanghai, where he changed it at a ratio of 15 or 16 to 1 against Mexican dollars.

Japan did not have enough gold for this game to last for a long time. In less than two years, Japan aligned the gold/silver ratio to the rules in force in the rest of the world.

In 1867, Emperor Mutsuhito seized power and imposed an "enlightened government" equivalent to the "Enlightenment

Century" that Europe experiences in the 18th Century. This period will go down in history as the Meiji Era. The emperor modernized and opened up the country to foreigners.

After attempts to introduce a silver standard, it was ultimately the gold standard that was put in place in 1871. Nevertheless, the domestic currency was temporarily in silver. Japan tried to impose a silver currency for the foreign trade, "dollar trade" hoping to supplant the Mexican dollar but it was in vain. The gold standard was initially a failure. The Japanese government adopted a bimetallism as a ratio of 16 to 1.

The modernization of Japan enabled it to adopt a parliamentary monarchy and put in place an economic structure for rapid development of its industries including metallurgy. It modernized its army at the same time and very soon its expansionism put it into open conflict with China, particularly for the control of Korea. Japan won the Sino-Japanese conflict from 1894-1895, and received significant war reparations which it demanded in gold. This windfall allowed it to successfully establish a gold standard in 1898.

From 1871 to 1898, 165 million yen silver were minted. The 2/3 were exported because of foreign trade and they were melted into other currencies including Chinese. Only 11 million silver yen came from abroad and were added to the 75 million in circulation in Japan which the Central Bank repurchased.

However, the Spanish-American wars raised the value of silver which fell sharply compared to gold after the demonetization of silver by Bismarck in 1870, then by India in 1885. The Bank of Japan was able to sell the bulk of the silver in China and Korea by losing only 5.5 million yen.

CYRILLE JUBERT

QUEEN VICTORIA & THE OPIUM WARS

The Chinese used opium to relieve pain. Some Chinese used it as a drug from the 17th Century. The Portuguese navigators with their strong trading posts in India were the first to exchange opium against Chinese products

The **British East India Company**, whose international trade increased from 40 tons of silver in 1660 to 280 tons around 1720, was faced with a serious problem. The Europeans adored porcelain, furniture and paintings from China. They loved tea which they consumed in very large quantities.

The Middle Kingdom was self-centered and cultivated the tradition of opposing any innovation and support from outside. Trade was strictly controlled by state officials and there were choke points for any foreigner who sought to buy or sell goods. The emperor refused to buy any product coming from outside and demanded that all goods bought in China should be paid in silver bullion.

Traders of the East India Company seeking to reduce this silver drain which weakened the company's accounts, were interested in the trafficking of opium. In 1729, 200 cases of opium were introduced into China and traded illegally against silver. The emperor reacted immediately by promulgating an edict condemning smuggling.

But the British East India Company was not ready to let go of this extremely lucrative trafficking, especially since it had invested in large plantations in India to supply the parallel trade. In 1795, it was no longer 400 but 4,000 cases which entered the Chinese ports.

Emperor Jiaqing (1796-1821) hardened the law in 1796. Traffickers faced death penalty and consumers faced prison sentences. In 1800, cultivation was prohibited in the Middle Kingdom.

In 1813, a case of opium was worth 240 silver rupees in India and 2400 rupees in China. The company made ten cubits per trip.

In 1765, the rupee was worth 176 grains of pure silver or 11.4 grams.

In terms of daily minimum wage, a case of opium from India was worth 1520 workdays of a Hindu (4 years and one month) against 40 years of work by a Chinese worker.

The B.E.I.C. increased its trafficking from 100 tons of opium in 1800 to 2400 tons in 1838. The opium market then represented nearly 1000 tons of silver per year and two million opium addicts in China.

Trade with China finally became profitable for the British.

A great debate about opium was opened by the emperor. Should we legalize its production in China to reduce trafficking and the margins of traffickers? It became imperative to stop the silver hemorrhage. The emperor appointed Lin Zexu Imperial Commissioner to stop the trafficking. Lin confiscated all the stocks of the dealers in 1839 and seized 200,000 cases of opium of which 1188 tons were destroyed. The traffickers experienced a dead loss worth 500 tons of silver.

In addition, Lin wrote to Queen Victoria stating that opium

smoking was banned in China and that all foreign ships would henceforth be searched and then urged her to stop the trafficking. Queen Victoria was only 20 years then and had just ascended the throne. Inexperienced, she fell under the influence of Lord Melbourne, who was removed from office for his foreign policy. Nevertheless, 300 commercial companies lobbied for the British government to raise this issue with the Chinese authorities and asked for reimbursement of their drug shipments.

The Prime Minister persuaded the British Parliament to send an expeditionary force to Canton in the name of freedom of trade. There was exchange of gunfire between the Chinese junks and British merchant ships so in January 1840, the emperor prohibited British ships from anchoring in the ports of China.

When the news arrived in Great Britain, there was heated debate between supporters for the discontinuation of drug trafficking and those for freedom of trade demanding reparations from China. Those trained to use the saber gained victory. The British squadron made up of 16 chartered battleships, 4 gunboats et 28 transport ships with 540 guns and 4,000 men got the upper hand. On arrival in Chinese waters, the British bombed Canton and occupied the neighboring archipelago. The emperor's weak troops were quickly defeated and Canton and its region were conquered by the British troops.

In August 1842, a British squadron went back through Yangtze River to Nanking, to force the Chinese government to sign a treaty.

The opium trade was tolerated. Chinese ports were opened to foreigners. Hong Kong was given to the British Crown. Foreign traders could settle in the neighborhoods assigned to them, like the "concessions" etc. and China had to pay 6 million dollars.

The forced opening of China soon doubled international trade in tea and silk. Opium trafficking increased from 40,000 cases in 1938 to 80,000 cases in 1863.

The End of the East India Company

In May 1857, during the "Sepoy Mutiny", Indian soldiers of the Indian army, CAIO, fought the first war of Indian independence and weakened the company which lost its administrative functions in 1958. Two years later, all the possessions of the Company were placed under the control of the Crown. On the 1st of January 1874, the East India Company was dissolved by decree.

Silver Wars

The government of Great Britain, soon officially followed by the United States and France, used the power of their armed forces to develop this drug trafficking which brought immense financial resources to a few large companies and banks that managed these funds.

This war was primarily a "Silver War".

The Treasury of the Bank of England was emptied of white metal through the trade between the British East India Company and China.
This first opium war was followed by many others.

In the twentieth century, the CIA refined the concept during the Vietnam War, by importing opium from the Golden Triangle. The "Company" developed the system on a very large scale in Latin America with cocaine. More recently, the Afghanistan War helped to get their hands on poppy production which experienced tremendous growth with American efficiency. Production in 2000 was 185 tons. In 2007, it rose to 8,400 tons. Processing plants were created in Afghanistan by the Alliance, to produce morphine and heroine which were easier to export than opium. The production of finished products was 630 tons.

The CIA, like the British East India Company established earlier, was a real American drug Cartel. Financial flows from this trafficking fuelled a banking network, including the largest western world banks, were essential ingredients of laundering. Napoleon spoke of England with contempt saying "this nation of merchants". Like Holland, England led by its trade, then it later led global financial flows.

CYRILLE JUBERT

NAPOLEON III AND SILVER

The discovery of gold in California in 1849, then the simultaneous discoveries in Australia and Siberia made gold more abundant than silver. The world's gold production in 25 years, from 1850 to 1875, exceeded production of the 350 previous years.

Gold was flowing everywhere. There was such a profusion that its relative price reduced whilst that of silver increased. France and some other nations whose monetary systems were based on silver, experienced a severe shortage of white metal. Since the law was promulgated in 1803, the official gold/silver ratio was 15.5.

Aware of this shortage, people hoarded silver so much that there was very little left to produce coins.

In 1854, Belgium, independent for 22 years, stopped producing coins due to cost and outsourced the minting of its currency in France. It was the year France minted the least coins since the 1789 Revolution. Silver imports by Belgium from France shot up from 6 million francs in 1850 to 78 million in 1859. France was desperately in need of silver metal. At the same time, Switzerland was facing the same problem. Speculation of the people led to the hoarding of silver coins which in turn worsened the shortage.

The withdrawal of silver coins resulted in a crisis of regulation and monetary circulation, due to lack of monetary signs in sufficient quantities. In this respect, the reduction in minting of silver coins in France between 1856 and 1864 was significant:

Minting of gold and silver coins under 900%, in France between 1856 and 1864 (in millions of francs).

Silver throughout History

Year	Silver Mints	Gold Mints
1856	54.4	508.24
1857	3.47	572.56
1858	8.63	488.67
1859	8.38	702.70
1860	8.08	446.04
1861	2.52	84.66
1862	2.51	210.16
1863	0.25	230.20
1864	0.16	273.84

CYRILLE JUBERT

THE MEXICAN ADVENTURE

In 1861, the American Civil War was raging and the northerners put up a naval blockade of the southern ports, prohibiting the export of cotton from the states of the Confederation.

This greatly affected the then thriving French and "Indian" cotton textile industries. This shortage made many small mills bankrupt whilst the largest textile companies faced serious financial difficulties. Quickly, 223,336 people lost their jobs, affecting the purchasing power of nearly 670,000 French people. Importers had to turn to India reluctantly because Indian cotton was of lower quality. Its fiber was short, more fragile and brittle. In addition, producers in the South of the **States preferred payment in gold. India demanded settlement in silver.**

Only Mexico produced silver at that time. It represented ¾ of the world's supply. The largest reserves were around Sonora, in the desert to the North West of Mexico

Since the conquest of the Aztec Empire in 1519, Mexico flooded Europe with silver from its mines and irrigated India and China through trade.

Mexico's War of Independence from 1810 to 1820 put an end to this continuous flow. Between 1821 and 1850, Mexico had fifty successive governments. In 1836, the first war against the United States caused it to lose Texas. The second war (1846 to 1848) cost it 2.4 million km². A new civil war from 1859 to 1861 left the country exhausted, crippled with indebtedness against England, Spain and France.

In the 1850s, the Apaches carried out regular raids in the Sonora region, whose habitants were unaware of the huge silver reserves in the subsoil. Recent defeats against the USA left the Mexicans ruined and demoralized. The gold rush in California brought a wave of adventurers to Sonora because they thought the region was rich in gold. They lost interest in silver.

The Marquis Charles de Pindray who fled France during the 1848 Revolution landed in the United States. In 1849, he joined a caravan of settlers to conquer the West. With nearly 88 French adventurers, he went to Sonora to exploit the mines. There were about 150 people in his colony but due to lack of food supplies by the Mexican authorities in the desert, and harassed by the Indians, the colony collapsed. Pindray himself was killed on 5 June 1852.

A second French expedition was launched in 1852 by Pierre Charles de Saint-Amant, who was then Consul of France in California. He left San Francisco with 80 men but they also failed in their attempt to exploit the mines in Sonora.

The Count of Raousset-Boulbon in 1852, inspired by Pindray, tried to use diplomacy instead of force. In Mexico, Raousset founded a new mining company, la Compañia Restaudora del mineral de Arizona. The main shareholders were the Mexican President, Arista, France's ambassador to Mexico, and Jecker & Torre Bank. The Mexican government allowed him to explore Sonora and establish mines there. In exchange, the state undertook to provide men to protect the mines from Indian attacks.

Back in San Francisco, he recruited 270 men ready to go on an adventure. Raousset had no intention of playing the role of prospector that was assigned to him. Northern Mexico presented itself to anyone who wanted to take it. The American or European adventurers like William Walker or Charles de Pindray dreamt of building an independent states there. Raousset showed himself as a republican but he had monarchical intentions. He thought of establishing a state to provide a throne for the Orleans family. French diplomats in Mexico did not look unfavorably at the prospect of a French colony, rich in silver mines. Napoleon III, who did not officially support the count was expected to reap the benefits.

Arista relinquished the presidency in 1853 and his successor, Santa Anna, cancelled the contract on silver with France. Napoleon III did everything in his power to get Mexican silver but in vain.

Mexican debts caused Spanish, British and French forces to land in Mexico. They served as a pretext for Napoleon III to implement his proposed Mexican empire of which he wanted to entrust the throne to the Archduke, Maximilian of Habsburg. Geographical conditions were optimal, as the lively northern neighbor was engaged in a protracted civil war.

In 1863, Napoleon undertook his war of conquest but the French armies faced a sustained guerrilla. Mexico City was conquered in the early summer of July 1863. The prominent citizens of Mexico gave the imperial crown to the Archduke of Austria, Maximillian of Habsburg.

Short-lived Empire !

The French army sought to pacify the country by eradicating the guerrilla, but it was dealing with riders, while the French were travelling on foot.

In 1865, president Juarez in exile at the American boarder, surrounded by his troops, reinforced by veterans of the American Civil War, obtained help from the United States.

Under pressure from North America, without debate, nor battle, Napoleon III withdrew his troops gradually from Mexico, Puebla and Vera Cruz. In 1867, the last French ship left the shores of Mexico. The Archduke, Emperor of Mexico, was shot by the Mexicans.

During the American Civil War, the Rothschild Bank of London financed the Northern United States, while the Rothschild Bank of Paris financed the South, extorting money from both sides at usurious rates close to 25%.

Behind the Mexican war of independence, the policy of the young republic in relation to silver metal and the revolutions that followed, there was a strategy of a very powerful actor, who manipulated the monetary balance secretly at that time. This power was the Bank of England and its private shareholders, who were the first to move to the gold standard. The pound sterling was the first reference currency for international transactions for the next 50 years.

CYRILLE JUBERT

DIFFICULTIES OF BIMETALLISM & THE LATINA UNION

5 francs, France 1866

The second half of the 19th Century was fatal for the bimetallic system.

The initial difficulties resulted from a depreciation of gold on the market with the start of production of the gold deposits in California, Australia and Siberia, discovered during the famous gold rush.

Meanwhile, remember that from 1821 to 1850, the 50 successive governments in Mexico had only one common element: they prohibited the export of silver, the main wealth of the country. But Mexico was at that time the world's leading producer of silver.

Silver metal was worth more on the world market than the minted silver of the bimetallic countries. Hoarded or melted for export, silver coin became scarce cash in circulation.

In 1865, after several attempts to respond in a disorganized manner, France, Italy, Belgium and Switzerland created the Latina Union, first form of monetary union between the European countries. Following the agreement, the 5 francs gold and silver coins remained unchanged; the other silver coins were converted into currencies with reduced content (835 thousandths instead of 900) and a limited legal tender.

Napoleon III wanted to expand the union and proposed that a conference should be held, on the sidelines of the world Expo of 1867, to "achieve international monetary unification." The conference took place but it was not followed by any concrete results. Only Greece joined the Latin Union in 1868.

From the 1870s, the speculative attacks confronting the bimetallic system were reversed. Silver production boomed and the value of the metal reduced. With a quantity of this metal paid in 16 francs, one could mint four 5 francs coins and exchange them against a 20 franc gold coin. The Latin Union countries were flooded with devalued silver coins as they saw their gold reserves melting.

Even though we continued to officially define currencies in gold and silver, bimetallism became increasingly shaky. The free coinage of silver was abolished in France in 1876 and throughout the Latin Union in 1878.

The Bank of France gradually reduced its silver reserves in favor of gold. Gold monometallism gradually became necessary, although it was not until 1928 that bimetallism was officially repealed. The reference currency of the Belle Époque was no longer that 5 francs silver coin but the Napoleon 20 francs gold coin, also called *Louis*.

Silver Coins of the Latin Union

All these coins have the same weight and value. They are equivalent to the 10 Francs Hercules.

1869
THE CORNER ON GOLD

In 1869, two New York bankers, Jay Gould and his partner James Fisk, tried a corner on the gold. Before the Civil War, (1861-1865), the dollar was exchangeable against gold at a fixed rate of 20.67 dollars per ounce. During the American Civil War, President Lincoln suspended the convertibility to avoid weakening the paper money that he created, the green-back. In 1869, four years after the end of the war, this convertibility had still not been restored. At the New York Gold Exchange, 100 dollar gold, or five 20 dollar gold coins, were traded in green-back (GB).

During the war, though no one knew who would be the winner, 100 dollars gold peaked at 250 GB dollars. The North defeated the South and with the solvency of the government becoming more reassuring, the price of gold dropped to stabilize at 130 GB dollars.

Jay Gould had previously participated in market manipulation on the shares and had mastered the art of throwing euphoria or panic among investors. In mid-September 1869, it resumed an upward trend, which accelerated the week of September 20. Some complacent journalists, were solicited by Gould to write articles on the shortage of gold. On September 24, gold was 140 dollars when the newspapers appeared. Brokers acted on the order of Gould and Fisk and started buying at the opening price of 145 GB. Playing on the warrants, Gould and Fisk controlled 5.5 million ounces, the equivalent of 110 million, equal to the reserves in the American Treasury in 1869.

Each time gold rose by 1 GB, Gould and Fisk gained 5.5 million GB.

That Friday, the 24th of September, remained in our memories as the "Black Friday", when panic took hold of Wall Street, who saw the value of Green-Back drop. All markets collapsed. Those who played the leverage, to meet the margin calls found themselves ruined. Gold rose to 162 GB. At midday, a banker, James Brown sold 250,000 ounces to the brokers of Fisk & Gould at 160 GB, causing other speculators to sell.

The American Treasury announced that it was selling gold against green-backs. When the news spread to the stock market, everyone began to sell. Gold traded at the close of day at 132 GB.

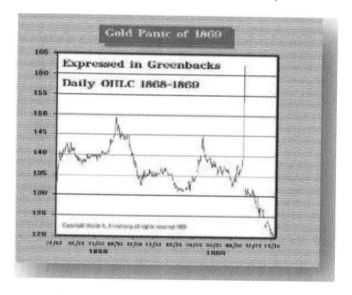

This sharp rise in trading and the sudden drop before the close of day ruined many speculators.

Gould fomented the increase and left his partner Fisk in the center stage, surrounded by his usual brokers to continue to buy on the stock market trading floor. In secret, Gould with his personal broker, had sold his entire position at 150 GB and taken leverage positions on the downward trend in the free trade.

At the close of day, whilst Fisk thought he was ruined, Gould told him the truth that they had gained 12 million GB.

Two million GB was entrusted to the two lawyers to handle the 300 legal proceedings opened against them, and also greased the palm of the financial controllers, stock market brokers and politicians in New York city.

The 1869 manipulation demonstrated quite well the methods adopted by bankers who played on both the physical and derivatives market, seeking to profit from them whatever the collateral damage.

Once again, the bankers used the press to succeed in their maneuver.

Germany was then made up of independent principalities with 31 banks authorized to coin money. They had an exclusive silver standard at that time.

Bismarck, Chancellor of the German Empire, was agitated for some years due to the desire of some people to move to the gold standard, a movement that took place in the United Kingdom at the same time.

The first phase of this monetary change was voted in 1871 **by**

prohibiting the minting of silver coins and imposing on France to pay its war reparations in Gold-Mark.

Then, on July 9 1873, Bismarck passed the German monetary law, establishing the gold standard and created a single Central Bank. This decision actually finalized the unification of Germany.

According to some analysts, the German monetary change worsened the financial crisis already raging in Europe.

1873
DEMONETIZATION OF SILVER IN USA

In 1873, the U.S. Congress passed a monetary law, "the Coinage Act", which did not mention gold and silver and their relative value. In fact, Silver was demonetized, paving the way for the gold standard. This subject created a scandal which lasted for a long time in the United States. The magazine, "The Nations" published an editorial in 1877, accusing Ernest Seyd, who landed in Washington in 1873, for corrupting members of congress and the government on behalf of the London financiers. The newspaper even mentioned an amount of 500,000 USD provided by Seyd to bribe the financial controllers.

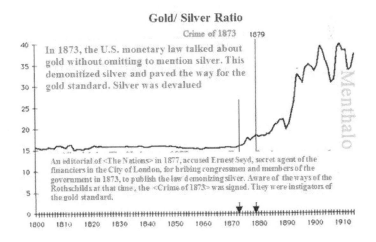

The demonetization of silver was the result of Mexican revolutions and the policy imposed on 50 successive Mexican governments not to sell silver on its markets. This was a secret policy imposed by the financial oligarchy, probably led by the Rothschild's in the 19th Century.

The Rothschild's banks dominated Europe in the second half of the 19th Century. Each of the five brothers ran a bank in one of the dominant European capitals. The London branch was the most enterprising and headed the others. This "1873 crime" seemed to have been signed. The Rothschild's probably wanted to establish the gold standard. For the record, they reigned unquestionably on the London gold market till 2004, date for the launch of ETF GLD. Did they choose this time on purpose to stand out from the large scale fraud which was being established, or as some people argue, were they ousted after a corner on the gold market?

The abandonment of gold-silver bimetallism in 1873 was an economic disaster for tens of thousands of gold seekers from West American States, who in their quest obtained sixteen times more silver than gold. The numerous owners of small silver mines denounced the "1873 crime", the year when congress decided to abolish the minting of silver.

Miners no longer brought their produce to the federal press due to the official price set: (sixteen grams of silver for a gram of gold) which was lower than that on the world market. Their anger led them to politically ally with the farmers within the National Greenback Labor, who won one million votes in the 1878 elections.

In 1878, an initial law, the "Bland-Allison Act", obliged the government to buy and turn them into pieces of silver from two to four million dollars of silver per month.

In 1890, strengthened by the numerous western states who entered the US, the mine owners obtained a new legislation, the **"Sherman Silver Purchase Act"**, stipulating that the government should use redeemable vouchers to buy one of the two metals, and a minimum quantity of 4.5 million ounces of silver per month.

The Great Depression of 1873
An economic winter studied under Kondratiev cycles.

Real Estate Bubble

Napoleon III, followed by a certain number of rulers in Europe, decided a few years earlier to modernize his capital. Under the aegis of Haussmann in Paris, major work was undertaken to ease traffic, sewerage was modernized and vast suburban areas were developed and divided into plots. The French, Austrian or Prussian governments, borrowed money for this work and promoted private investment through mortgage loans. Financiers rushed headlong into the trap, hoping to obtain easy gains. Prices of land soared and the abundance of new buildings springing out of the ground made their sale even more difficult.

The housing bubble, overproduction, drop in prices logically led to the financial crash.

Agricultural Crisis

England, the then leading importer of cereals, chose to import their wheat from the United States, where the beginning of mechanization of agriculture and the introduction of fertilizers resulted in better yield per hectare and a sharp decrease in production costs. Improved transport (railway, steamships) favored this option. Britain's choice brought down the prices of cereal in Europe and Russia, regions where agriculture still remained the mainstay of the economy.

Interbank Confidence Crisis

It is likely that the American decision to demonetize silver threw the finances of European countries still under the bimetallic monetary system out of gear, disrupting inter-bank confidence and causing a cold snap in credit at a time when the industrial revolution was in full swing. During that time, many banks and central banks held significant cash reserves which could have been devalued sharply as was the case of the bank of Florence in the Middle Ages.

Did the banking crisis that hit about one hundred banks in Vienna in May, caused the collapse of the stock market in Austria, Paris and Berlin, before the crash spread to Wall Street?

A series of bankruptcies in the banks and industry brought about a long depression which lasted for twenty years.

THE GOLD STANDARD (1879-1933)

"The Golden Age" (1879-1914)

Until the late 1870s, gold and silver coexisted as monetary means. Bank notes were gradually added during the 19th Century. Since these notes were issued by private banks, they were not always covered by gold and silver reserves, which, iteratively, caused banking crises, exacerbated by competition between banks. The creation of national central banks, which soon became sole operators with monopoly on currency issue, put a stop to this situation.

In theory, central banks were supposed to hold gold and silver reserves capable of ensuring full coverage of bank notes they issued. Upon request, holders of bank notes could apply for their equivalent in gold or silver coins or bullions, at the counters of the issuing banks. The bank notes were only a modality for holding gold of silver due to the full coverage.

The gold standard system, resulting from the failure of the bimetallic system, did not survive the economic and financial crisis created by the first World War.

Principles of Operation

The success of the gold standard was attributed to its automatic adjustment mechanisms. This adjustment capacity was explained by the link established by the gold standard between the national and international economic conditions.

The gold standard therefore assumed a free international, circulation of gold, that is, freedom of movement of capital internationally for it to function properly. The automatic adjustment mechanism of the balance of payment operated under the name of "Hume mechanism". A country that registered a trade deficit and lost its gold benefit to its trade partners, which contracted its money supply and inflated that of the rest of the world, raised the national interest rate and promoted in return, an influx of foreign capital. The excess thus created in the financial account offset the trade deficit. Contraction of money supply in turn reduced domestic prices, thereby improving the competitivity of the country and ultimately tended to restore its trade balance.

Advantages and disadvantages

Under the gold standard system, monetary policy was limited by the world's gold stocks, which were not expandable at will, but depended on mining production. This natural constraint prevented growth in money supply and limited the possibilities of inflation.

Economic activity was limited by the inability to increase money growth. During growth, companies found it difficult to obtain capital to invest in their development. During recession, they were forced to cut down on the number of employees, creating periods of high unemployment.

Limitations of the Automatic Adjustment

In order for it to work perfectly, the automatic adjustments of the various national balance of payments provided by the gold standard, required that each country followed a strict discipline of the gold reserves of its currency and guaranteed the free circulation of capital. In fact, this was not always the case due to at least two reasons:

The first was the economic and financial domination of the United Kingdom, which gave the pound sterling an international currency reserve status, while its management was based on the British Economy.

The second was the cost of discipline in unemployment and the variability of economic growth. Thus, most countries involved in the gold standard system, including the United Kingdom, took certain liberties with regard to monetary management.

The financial power of the United Kingdom greatly facilitated the independence of its monetary management. Before 1914, the United Kingdom was the world's largest exporter of capital, with the strongest net external asset position. Thus, it provided the rest of the world with sterling assets (the "sterling balances") which served as the reserve currency for the other central banks. Under these conditions, it was the Bank of England that tended to fix the interest rate for the rest of the world, but first based on the changing economic circumstances of the British economy, which was not necessarily the same as the other European countries.

Besides, in order to give the British monetary policy sufficient room for maneuver in the event of change in economic conditions, the Bank of England quickly adopted the attitude of not covering its liabilities (notes issued and bank reserves) 100%, **but at best at 30-50%.**

In this way, the United Kingdom partially escaped the automatic adjustment mechanism of balances by disconnecting from the changes in its money supply and consequently, its interest rates and changes in its current account.

Other countries did not hesitate to take measures to break the close link between trade deficits and money supply: limitations on exports and imports of gold; coverage of national bank notes ensured more by international currency reserves (pound, but also the French francs and German mark) instead of gold reserves.

In spite of this, the gold standard system worked relatively well. Despite the differences, the United Kingdom, mainstay of the system, kept interest rates relatively high, by linking the issuance of notes to its gold reserves, whilst it always kept very little gold, much less than France, for instance. Such a policy put some credibility behind the pound but slowed down the rate of investments and growth of the British economy.

Before 1914, the role of the pound sterling as an international currency reserve remained relatively low, compared to that of the dollar after the Second World War. The "sterling balances" remained low, amounting approximately to the surplus of the British balance of services. The two world wars excessively inflated it (multiplication by two and then by six), by financing of the war that they brought about.

At the declaration of war, on the 5th of August 1914, the franc entered a period of price freeze and the obligation on the Bank of France to repay the bank notes that were presented in gold was suspended.

The exorbitant cost of the war led the government not to requisition assets in gold and silver, but appeal to patriotism and ban the export of precious metals. In the summer of 1915 the French patriots brought approximately 725 tons of gold in exchange for paper money.

With the development of the black market for gold, on **12 February 1916, the French government banned the sale or purchase of coins above their legal price.**

This ban had to be renewed at the end of the war and maintained until 1928, end of the fiat currency.

THE INTER-WAR PERIOD (1919-1939)

The First World War marked the end of the gold standard system in its original form with the suspension of the gold convertibility by all belligerents (mandatory price). The inflation that followed the war was so high that the return to the gold standard was long (from 7 to 10 years), partial and temporal (it was permanently abandoned in the 1930s). There were therefore three periods:

1919-1926, free float period;
1927-1931, return to the gold standard;
1931-1939, the managed float.

Free Floating (1919-1926)

The main concern of European economies in the aftermath of the First World War was the struggle against inflation, caused by four years of conflict and reconstruction. European economies experienced higher inflation than that of the United States. There were significant differences in inflation in Europe itself. Thus, under the purchasing power parity rule, the major European currencies began to float.

British policy focused on restoring the value of the pound through a strong deflationary policy, marked by tight monetary and fiscal austerity. By 1921, the pound recovered its pre-war parity with the dollar, but remained overvalued due to the decline of the British economy. UK prices were too high compared to US prices. The free international movement of gold was restored only in 1925.

France also returned to the gold standard in 1926 with Poincaré's stabilization.

The British disinflation policy was criticized as early as 1930 by Keynes. It was intended to maintain the United Kingdom's financial leadership, but it proved disastrous, particularly for its industry and economic growth.

Over the period 1919-1930, the average annual GDP growth of the United Kingdom was practically zero, down from 2.10% in the United States and nearly 4% in France. The low economic activity resulted in a high level of unemployment, around 8-9% during the

1920s, whilst it fell to less than 2-3% in the United States and France.

REPUBLIC OF WEIMAR

Germany, Austria and the Central European countries only joined the gold standard after curbing their respective hyperinflation.

For the record, Germany and Austria were ordered to pay war reparations that were much too high when they lost the war. 132 billion gold marks were imposed on Germany whilst Keynes advocated to limit this indemnity to 20 million gold marks.

France and Belgium who experienced the war in their territory requested for the replacement of their industrial base. While the Germans sought to renegotiate the payment of their indemnity, the French and Belgian armies invaded the Ruhr industrial basin in January 1923. The occupying armies deprived the unoccupied Germany of coal. The Ruhr factories were dismantled and exported, depriving Germany of part of its production machinery and limiting its capacity of repayment.

The German currency quickly lost all its value.

In 1919, an ounce of gold was worth 170 marks.
In January 1924, an ounce was worth 87,000 billion marks.
Silver shot up from 12 marks to 544 billion marks.

Anecdotally, this is from unconfirmed sources and some doubted its veracity: the Gold/Silver ratio deteriorated sharply during the last two months of the hyperinflation, from 1/16 to 1/160.

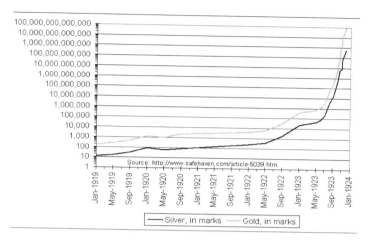

On the 23rd of October 1923, communist riots overran Hamburg. Some Germans remembered the Bolshevik Revolution of 1917, only 6 years earlier, became afraid and sold their silver against gold to enable them to flee abroad, without being overloaded.

With a ratio of 16, the weight of your wealth in silver was 16 times bulkier and heavier to carry than if your wealth was in gold. The panic helped some to foolishly trade away their silver coins. Two months later, the ratio came back to 1/16. Some changers thus gained ten times leap in two months.

In order not to experience this misadventure, quickly move your silver coins into a quiet location where you can retire to, in case of social disturbances.

BACK TO THE GOLD STANDARD (1927-1931)

In 1927, the reconstruction of the gold standard system was completed. It brought together again most of the world except Spain, China and the Soviet Union. However, it was quite different and much fragile than the original system that existed before 1914. The first cause of the fragility was due to the fact that all the countries had abolished the convertibility of banknotes into gold and suspended or limited the circulation of gold coins. Therefore, the automatic adjustment of balances by Hume's mechanism disappeared. Only the external convertibility (currency exchange) and the fixed exchange rates remained. Currencies were convertible into gold but done only through the central bank and there were new rules imposing a 40% coverage rate of gold coins. Normally, the coordination of national monetary policies provided by the 1922 Genoa conference was able to compensate for the loss of automatic adjustment. In fact, this coordination was failing, partly due to the United States refusal of participate.

The second reason for the fragility of the system was its dual nature. Since 1918, it was dominated by two rival centers, London and New York, as well as two international currencies, the pound and the dollar. Now, at that time, the United States was not ready to subject its domestic economic policy to the management of an international currency since the United Kingdom no longer had the capacity.

Persistent overvaluation of the British currency soon revealed the shortcomings of the system. France and Germany, countries whose currencies were undervalued against the pound, adopted a strict monetary policy intended to prevent any resurgence of inflation. From 1926, this policy led them to exchange their reserves in pounds against gold, swelling the French and German gold stocks at the expense of the British stocks.

However, the British current account deficit and the current account surplus of the French persisted due to fixed exchange rates and the absence of price adjustments. The absorption of gold by France and Germany pushed the other European central banks to increase their interest rates and restrict credit to defend the reserves which were becoming increasingly rare. The United States managed to restore the functioning of the system. The country had the largest stockpile of gold since 1918, and a U.S. policy for monetary expansion coupled with low interest rates encouraged capital outflows and promoted the redistribution of gold in the world. However, from 1927, the policy of the Federal Reserve focused, on the contrary, on higher rates to curb the stock market speculation and limited the decline in the coverage rate of the dollar against gold caused by the monetary growth in the 1920s.

From 1929, the onset of the Great Depression and the gold leakages melted the British reserves to the extent that the liabilities of the Bank of England became much higher than its reserves. In September 1931, it decided to suspend the external convertibility of the pound and allowed it to float freely.

The managed floating (1931-1939)

The floating led to a sharp depreciation of the pound against the dollar. All the countries with large stockpile of sterling balances, such as Norway or Denmark, saw their currencies devalue at that time.

From 1933, the situation worsened. The United States, the only country still adhering to the gold standard, placed an embargo on the export of gold (the dollar appreciated sharply against the other currencies), exchange controls and the depreciation of the dollar against gold from 2.67 to 35 dollars per ounce.

The rest of the system broke down in 1935, with the devaluation of the Belgian franc, which caused the collapse of the gold bloc formed in 1931 by France, Belgium, the Netherlands, Italy, Switzerland and Poland to maintain the gold parities and avoid competitive devaluations.

However, the then flexible exchange rates fluctuated less than in the 1920s. The Exchange Stabilization Fund established in 1931 intervened on the markets to control prices. The monetary and fiscal policies also appeared less erratic than they were a decade earlier, although the lack of international coordination, often for fear of certain countries resurgence of inflation, significantly weakened the effectiveness of recovery policies.

Dévaluations compétitives, 1931-1938 (valeur des devises en % de leur parité-or de 1929)						
	États-Unis	Royaume-Uni	France	Allemagne	Italie	Belgique
1931	100,0	93,2	100,1	99,2	98,9	100,1
1932	100,0	72,0	100,3	99,7	97,4	100,2
1933	80,7	68,1	100,0	99,6	99,0	100,1
1934	59,6	61,8	100,0	98,6	97,0	99,9
1935	59,4	59,8	100,0	100,3	93,0	78,6
1936	59,2	60,5	92,4	100,1	82,0	72,0
1937	59,1	60,0	61,0	99,7	59,0	71,7
1938	59,1	59,3	43,4	99,6	59,0	71,8

After the war, France was in a state of exceptional economic and financial ruin. Attempts to return to the gold standard in totally unrealistic conditions, that is, without taking into account the inflationist reality of the war period, and the demands of the winners in terms of reparations, paved the way for a series of economic and financial crises which affected the currencies.

In 1914, before the outbreak of hostilities, the franc was defined as 0.2903 grams of gold (actually the germinal franc was originally defined as 5 grams of fine silver per 90%).

In 1928, after a few years needed for the stabilization of the economy, it was then 0.05895 gram of fine gold to obtain a franc Poincaré in 1928.

A devaluation of nearly 80% of Franc.

Summary

Before opening a new page of more contemporary history, it is necessary to pause and summarize the previous centuries.

The Portugal Empire ended abruptly when the king and the country's elite died in battle.

The Spanish Empire was never managed. The wealth that passed through Cadiz was not used to develop micro-enterprises, industry, merchant navy and warships to protect it.

By losing the United Provinces of Flanders, on a religious question, Catholic Spain allowed the Princes of the Orange to create the Bank of Amsterdam and the Dutch East India Company. These Princes of the Orange took the place of the English dynasty and replicated their success in Great Britain. As early as the fifth century, this island was partly conquered by the Angles and Saxons, Germanic tribes of Western Europe. This is just one more cycle of history.

The Princes of the Orange created the Bank of England and the East India Company and immediately mobilized a large loan to build a naval fleet to rule the seas and international trade. This initial investment allowed England to ruin Spain by plundering its colonies and money fleets before cutting it off finally from its colonies at Trafalgar.

The Dutch and English bankers mastered the paper money and used it in the early 18th Century as a weapon of war to enslave nations. They refined these techniques before removing metal currencies to better lead the world in their own way. The two Indian companies and dominant banks shaped the world and continued to manage it furtively.

Silver Throughout History

1900-2000

CYRILLE JUBERT

John Pierpont Morgan

John Pierpont Morgan, (1837-1913) was an American banker. First focusing on banks, Morgan's empire gradually extended to many other areas like electricity, steel, railway and navigation, including the prestigious White Star Line.

J.P. Morgan was in fact the owner of the Titanic which sank a year before his death.

One day, in a bar, Morgan yelled at a server whilst ordering his beer: "When Morgan drinks, everyone drinks!" All the customers took a beer for the general round. Morgan emptied his glass, stack a 10 cent coin on the table, shouting: "When Morgan pays, everyone pays!"

His father, Junius Spencer Morgan, ran J.S. Morgan & Co in London. His son, John, developed the current New York branch of the company under the name J.P. Morgan & Co. At the time of the Civil War, he bought 5,000 faulty guns at $17,500 and sold them to the Federal army at $110,000. Since the guns exploded in use, Morgan was sued but he was acquitted, and a judge confirmed the validity of the contract.

He quickly gained control of some firms including Drexel, Peabody and Carnegie.

In 1891, Morgan merged Edison and Thomson and formed the General Electric. In 1895, seized the Leyland fleet and many other naval lines by creating the White Star, builders and operators of British vessels, Olympic and the Titanic of disastrous memory.

In 1899, J.P. Morgan controlled four of the five major railway companies in America, bringing together the interests of Rockefeller, Vanderbilt and Harriman.

In 1900, Morgan financed Nikola Tesla's research, scientific genius to whom we owe the radio, alternating current, polyphase distribution, AC motor, as well as strong cybernetics contributions, the radar, ballistics, aeronautics, navigation.

When Tesla showed Morgan a system that allowed free distribution of electricity, without wires nor cables, on the whole planet, J.P.M. asked: "But how can I charge?"

The free energy that General Electric provided, allowed JPM to cut all research budget to Tesla and discredit him.

In 1904, J.P. Morgan merged nine steel mills to create the United States Steel Corporation, the first company in the world to have assets worth one million.

In 1912, the Pujo Committee, charged with the responsibility to investigate the activities of US banks, valued the banking group controlled by JPM worth 22 trillion dollars.

In 1913, J.P. Morgan put forward one of his men, Woodrow Wilson, to stand for the Presidency of the United States.

"Only Gold and Silver are currencies, Everything else is credit."

J.P. Morgan

CREATION OF THE FEDERAL RESERVE

On November 22 1910, Senator Aldrich, father-in-law of the oil magnate, John D. Rockefeller, invited leading bankers to a duck hunting, which changed the face of the world during the century that followed. The hunting party took place in a small island off Georgia.

Three of the men heading the J.P.M. banking group were present at this secret meeting on **Jekyll Island**.

Henry Davison, senior partner of J.P. Morgan Company and regarded as his personal emissary.

Charles Norton, President of the First National Bank of New York, controlled by J.P. Morgan Company.

Benjamin Strong, CEO of J. P. Morgan's Bankers Trust Company, and also known as lieutenant of J.P. Morgan. He also became the CEO of the bank three years later, following the adoption of the Federal Reserve Act. These two bankers also represented the interests of the Rothschild's.

George F. Baker was one of the closest associates. Also present were Frank Vanderlip, President of the National Bank of New York, the largest and most powerful U.S. bank. He represented the financial interests of William Rockefeller and the international investment firm Kuhn, Loeb & Co.

Senator Aldrich, probably, the most important personality among the participants was Paul Warburg. He was one of the richest men in the wolrd. His experience in the operations of European banks coupled with his strong personality enabled him to lead this meeting. He was considered as the initiator for the creation of the Federal Reserve. Of German origin, he naturalized as U.S. citizen. In addition to being a partner of the Kuhn Loeb and Company, in 1893, he married the daughter of the banker, Salomon Loeb, owner of the bank in New York. He represented the banking dynasty of the Rothschild's of England and France. Partner with his brother Felix, he also had close relationship with his other brother, Max Warburg, Chief Director of the "Warburg Banking Consortium in Germany and Netherlands".

Senator Nelson Aldrich was Chairman of the National Monetary Commission, created by President Theodore Roosevelt in 1908 as a result of the monetary panic of 1907. Note that the Democrat Woodrow Wilson was elected due to the fact that Teddy Roosevelt ran against the incumbent Republican President, Taft, thus dividing the voters in his own party. A tactic still used today to get the man chosen by the banking cartel.

These financiers represented the common interests of the world's largest banking groups: Morgan, Rothschild, Warburg and Rockefeller. During the secret meeting which lasted 9 days, these bankers created the regulations governing the operation of the Federal Reserve.

The **Federal Reserve Act** was presented to congress in absolute discretion, on the night of the 22nd to 23rd of December 1913 between 1:30 am and 4:30 am, at a time when most of the members of congress were asleep or on Christmas holidays. The House Democrats present, seconded by President Wilson, claimed they voted for the reduction of the privileges of Wall Street bankers.

The bill was passed in the Senate immediately, so that on the 23rd of December 1913, at 6:02 am, the bill was finally adopted.

The Republican MP, Henry Cabot Lodge Sr, said this vote has created a "non-redeemable paper money flows" which would "*swamp the gold currency*" and cause "*huge inflation of the means of payment.*"

John Pierpont died that year on a trip to Italy. At the time of his death, it was discovered that JP Morgan owned only 19% of the shares of his bank. Therefore, he was only the brilliant President of a bank financed by the Anglo-Saxon oligarchy. The name of the Rothschild's was often mentioned.

In August 1914, his successor, JP Morgan Junior, signed a contract with the Bank of England, giving him a monopoly on the issuance of war bonds by England and France. Extremely well informed, his firms invested massively in the manufacture of weapons, of which he now held exclusive right to supply the allies of the Entente Cordiale (France and England). His banks lent 12 million to Russia and 50 million to France to enable them buy their own weapons. All the American and British ammunition purchased during the First World War were manufactured by J.P. Morgan's companies.

In 1929, J.P. Morgan Junior withdrew from the stock market before the stock market bubble. His position as a shareholder of the Federal Reserve obviously allowed him to play one step ahead.

The surge of the New York exchange was due to easy credit. The Federal Reserve lowered the interest rate from 4.5 to 3% in 1927 and the banks lent without difficulty. Speculators borrowed at low rates and played the stock market with a lever of 10. Soaring shares created a true speculative euphoria. R.C.A, for instance, shot up from $80 in 1928 to $505 in September 1929, multiplying by 6.5.

During the summer of 1929, the Federal Reserve raised the interest rate to 6%, endangering the speculators who had borrowed. The first negative event triggered an unprecedented stock market crash. The financial barons including the secret shareholders of the Federal Reserve were able to buy the most flourishing American companies as well as **two thirds of the agricultural lands to the West of the Mississippi for next to nothing**.

That was the Great Depression. The middle class were wiped out, the working class were thrown into the street and a lot of finances were ruined. JP Morgan saw his companies, General Electric and US Steel losing 90% of their market value. But JPM, short seller, took advantage of the crash like his fellow shareholders of the Federal Reserve. They were able to redeem their competitors to nothing. As a result, the banking sector was heavily concentrated after 1929.

In the USA, in 1900, the 20 largest banks controlled 15% of deposits against 27% in 1939.

MEXICAN REVOLUTIONS
1910-1920

From 1910, Mexico was shaken by political unrest. The famous bandit Pancho Villa and his band of 400 guerilleros, were hired by a politician, Francisco Madero, a wealthy Portuguese- Jewish apostle of the revolution to take part in the revolution. Madero became President and after a while, Pancho Villa was put under house arrest in his El Paso residence. But the assassination of Madero in 1913 revived the revolution. Pancho Villa took control of the mining centers.

Mexico and the United States were the largest producers of silver. The American silver producers had an interest to disrupt production in Mexico, so much that silver was no longer the universal monetary standard, indispensable to all central banks.

The Americans supplied Pancho Villa with horses and modern weapons (guns, machine guns, ammunition) against silver metal. In 1914, Pancho Villa signed an exclusive contract with the American film company, "Mutual Film Corp", to film his battles for $25,000. These films showed the atrocious cruelties committed on behalf of others. Mutual Film paid an additional bonus of $500 to Pancho Villa to film each execution.

On March 9 1916, Pancho Villa and his armed forces entered the United States to attack New Mexico. Kaiser Wilhelm promised Villa some 800,000 marks to create problems for the United States and force them to divert some of their troops so that they did not enter Europe.

Germany negotiated effectively with Mexico, for the latter to open a second front, promising that Mexico would recover the states taken by the United States during the Mexican American wars. Some attacks were effectively organized by the Mexican, or German spies, who destroyed the steel mills and US ammunition depots. The revolution was followed by the civil war until 1920.

From 1910 to 1920, copper and silver production in Mexico fell by 65% and gold production declined by 80%.

It is obvious that the decline in Mexico's silver production benefited its major competitors, the US copper and silver producers.

As a result of the war, the price of copper increased from $13 per pound in 1914 to $37 in 1917. All the copper mines worked at full capacity during the war with teams producing 3/8, to meet the demand for ammunitions by war-torn countries.

To think that the US industrial and financial sectors added fuel to the Mexican fire, there is only one step to take.

SILVER FROM 1914 TO 1920

In 1860, a worker earned 2.50F per day in the province. In 1914, the daily wage of a miner was 5 Francs or 22.5g of fine silver.

The First World War brought an unprecedented rise to the price of silver, followed by a sharp fall taking it to its previous levels with depression at the end of hostilities. Bimetallism in the 19th Century ended in failure, due to the choice of certain members of the financial oligarchy. In 1914, only China and some countries playing a minor role in international trade still observed the gold standard.

Silver was still used almost universally to mint secondary coins for domestic use. Some countries had large stocks of coins, like the silver dollar in the United States or the 5 francs coin in France, with legal tender, but these stocks were not increased and gradually lost their significance. In India, the silver rupee still had legal tender and it was reminted as needed. The silver rupee had a fixed value compared to gold. It was worth more than its weight in silver, as had always been the case in history during Emperor Moghol's time. Theoretically, fluctuations in the price of silver had no political influence. In 1914, all commodities which had no military use experienced a sharp decline. Silver in New York fell from $0.58 to $0.52.

Prior to the war, the world's production was 225 million ounces, of which one third, or 75 million ounces came from Mexico. The Mexican revolution further reduced Mexico's production to 30 million ounces, which was soon fixed quota by quota to the United States, which sought to protect domestic production.

Lobbying of the silver mining companies were then very active in the United States. Silver producers were all in the Western United States and traditionally opposed the representatives from the Northeastern States. The Senator of Utah introduced legislation in congress for the government to purchase 25 million ounces of silver to mint coins whilst the average purchase over the five previous years was only 4 million ounces. This law was readjusted because it was deemed to favor the interests of individuals, at a time when foreign trade had experienced a sharp decline, causing a reduction in government revenues. For this reason, silver fell again to $0.46 in September 1915. Many U.S. mines had to close down for lack of returns.

While men took the front lines, the war sent the female population to work. This active population required further boost in money supply, in particular, the minting of silver coins. In USA, minting of silver coins grew from $3 million in 1913 to $9 million in 1916.

UNITED STATES COINAGE OF SUBSIDIARY SILVER, 1913-1921

Calendar Years	Millions of Dollars
1913	3
1914	6
1915	4
1916	9
1917	29
1918	25
1919	11
1920	25
1921	1

This phenomenon was repeated at the same time all over the world.

India imported 84 million ounces at a time when China and other European countries had increased their demand for silver to mint coins. All the surplus was exhausted in 1915.

In 1916, the price of silver rose to $0.77 in May, then $1.08 in September 1917.

Silver throughout History

Fiscal Year ending March 31	On International Markets	U.S government Pittman Act
	In ounces of fine silver	
1915–16	7.989.000	
1916–17	115.195.000	
1917–18	65.604.000	
1918–19	98.429.000	141.079.000
1919–20	48.285.000	56.240.000
Total	335.502.000	197.319.000

Purchase of Silver Currency by India 1915 - 1920

In 1917, India had considerable difficulties finding silver to mint new rupees needed for currency circulation to provide backing for the paper currency.

The silver rupee remained the reference currency in India and its fine silver content of 0.917 **had not changed since 1835**. The rise in silver prices above the face value of the rupee increased the risk of the currency being melted to meet the demand for jewelry. This put the entire economy at risk and it could even destabilize Britain which was deeply involved in the world war. The British government had to enter into negotiations with the U.S. Treasury to boost the production of silver in America and streamline its distribution at the price previously negotiated between the U.S. and British governments.

After negotiating with the mining companies, the price of an ounce of silver was pegged at $1 per ounce, to allow the reopening of the mines, which claimed they would not be able to make production more profitable below this price.

Nevertheless, the share that was allocated to India in this new American production could not meet its cash needs.

It was decided that 259 million silver dollars from the Treasury reserve then totaling $500 million of silver be melted and delivered to the BOE on behalf of India. Since this huge amount of silver had to be replaced in the Treasury by an equivalent volume in the following years, it became necessary for the silver to come from the American mines. Silver was ordered from the mining companies at a fixed price of $0.99.

This resolution was passed as the **Pittman Act** on the 23rd of April 1918. Once melted, these 259 million silver dollars represented 200 million ounces of silver for India.

After the war, the price of silver dropped on the international market to $0.70 per ounce allowing some American mining companies to make handsome profits from little, as they feigned to import silver from abroad by smuggling it and then selling it back to the Treasury as a national production. All attempts by Congress to create control boards on this issue failed. The legal battle between the silver Cartel, Congress and the Treasury Secretary about the price of silver and its origin lasted until 1926.

Silver which was worth 0.46$ in September 1915 peaked at 1.37$ in November 1919. Its price was multiplied by 3.

In the whole of Asia (India, China, Indonesia), but also in Latin America (Mexico, Chili, Peru) the countries experienced severe depreciation of their paper currency. The rise in the price of silver metal caused the hoarding of silver coins, whose value in weight exceeded the face value. Traders refused to give small change for paper notes in silver coins. They preferred to refuse a sale than to part with hard cash.

Governments were forced to mint coins over and over again with lower and lower silver content.

Great Britain had to increase its coinage from 900/1000th to 500/1000th. The composition of these coins were 500 parts of silver, 400 parts of copper and 100 parts of nickel. The yellowish color made these coins unpopular. The British government in turn banned the export of silver.

France had a very large stock of 5 francs silver coins and numerous coins with lower face value in circulation as well as bank reserves. It experienced the same problems. In 1919, as soon as the price of silver exceeded its face value, the coins disappeared from circulation. The French government banned the melting of coins and export of silver. Bronze coins were minted but the Bank of France refused to print notes worth less than 5 francs.

With the decline in silver price in 1920, the devaluation of the franc kept the silver coins above their face value. It is estimated that 2 billion francs in gold and silver coins were hoarded by the people during this period.

In 1926, the government offered a reward to bring out all hidden reserves. He bought 1 gold franc against 5.70 francs notes, and 2.40 francs notes for 1 silver franc. The offer lasted for only three weeks. It was quickly withdrawn due to the fall in the international rates for silver. To prevent hoarding, the French government minted new 10 franc silver Turin and 20 francs silver Turin coins in 635/1000th in 1929.

At the end of 1920, the revolution and the American Civil War ended, allowing mining production in Mexico to return gradually to levels before 1910.

The world's production, which fell to 160 million ounces in 1920 and 1921 returned to 250 million ounces in 1923 and stabilized at this level until 1930.

This level of production occurred when the demand for war related raw materials (oil, rubber, copper, steel,...) was in sharp decline on all markets, resulting in a general slowdown. Demand for silver from the American Treasury was contractually limited to domestic mine production and did not affect world markets. India had purchased a large quantity of silver directly from the American Treasury and bought very little silver for a few years and China entered a turbulent period.

Additional production in Mexico occurred with very low market demand and caused prices to fall.

The price fell again to $0.52 in June 1921, then in the autumn of 1921 to 1926, it fluctuated between 0.62 and 0.74 before returning to a range between 0.53 and 0.60 until 1929.

The price of silver dropped in 1929 to reach its absolute lowest rate of $0.24 per ounce in December.

1933 Argent monétaire en Millions d'onces

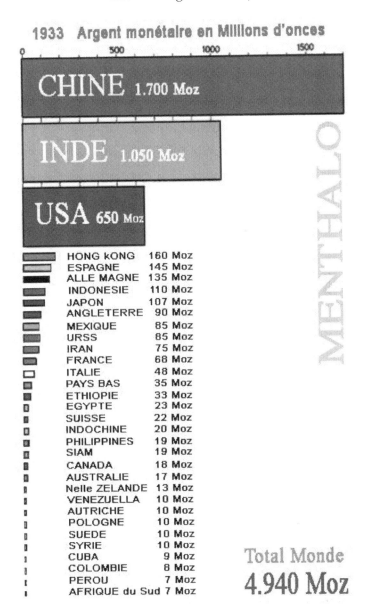

CHINE	1.700 Moz
INDE	1.050 Moz
USA	650 Moz
HONG KONG	160 Moz
ESPAGNE	145 Moz
ALLEMAGNE	135 Moz
INDONESIE	110 Moz
JAPON	107 Moz
ANGLETERRE	90 Moz
MEXIQUE	85 Moz
URSS	85 Moz
IRAN	75 Moz
FRANCE	68 Moz
ITALIE	48 Moz
PAYS BAS	35 Moz
ETHIOPIE	33 Moz
EGYPTE	23 Moz
SUISSE	22 Moz
INDOCHINE	20 Moz
PHILIPPINES	19 Moz
SIAM	19 Moz
CANADA	18 Moz
AUSTRALIE	17 Moz
Nelle ZELANDE	13 Moz
VENEZUELLA	10 Moz
AUTRICHE	10 Moz
POLOGNE	10 Moz
SUEDE	10 Moz
SYRIE	10 Moz
CUBA	9 Moz
COLOMBIE	8 Moz
PEROU	7 Moz
AFRIQUE du Sud	7 Moz

Total Monde **4.940 Moz**

CYRILLE JUBERT

1934
THE SILVER PURCHASE ACT OF ROOSEVELT

From: President of the United States Of America, Franklin D. Roosevelt
To: United States Congress
Dated April 5 1933

I, Franklin D. Roosevelt, President of the United States of America, do declare that the said national emergency still continues to exist and pursuant to the said section do hereby prohibit the hoarding of gold coin, gold bullion and gold certificates within the continental United States by individuals, partnerships, associations and corporations and hereby prescribe the following regulations for carrying out the purpose of this order.

On April 5 1933, President Roosevelt banned the possession of gold by individuals. Gold was taken up by the government at $20.67 an ounce.

On the 31st of January 1934, the dollar was devalued to $35 an ounce.

Simultaneously, the Silver Purchase Act of 1934 obliged the American Treasury to purchase huge quantities of silver; the government wanted the silver reserves to be worth one third of the gold reserves. In the U.S., the future market for silver was then removed.

Roosevelt nationalized the silver of individuals in the United States and purchased all the silver available for sale from abroad.

This high demand in the U.S. increased the international price of an ounce of silver by three, from $0.24 to $0.82.

Silver throughout History

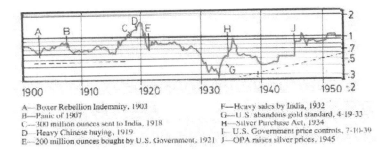

A—Boxer Rebellion Indemnity, 1903
B—Panic of 1907
C—300 million ounces sent to India, 1918
D—Heavy Chinese buying, 1919
E—200 million ounces bought by U.S. Government, 1921
F—Heavy sales by India, 1932
G—U.S. abandons gold standard, 4-19-33
H—Silver Purchase Act, 1934
I—U.S. Government price controls, 7-10-39
J—OPA raises silver prices, 1945

Due to the sharp rise in silver price, China was obliged to abandon its silver monetary standard.

CYRILLE JUBERT

1927-1935
CHINESE BANKS IN THE STORM

Until 1927, China had a relatively liberal banking system. Private banks operated throughout China. The largest Chinese banks and the few foreign banks had their headquarters in Shanghai. They issued bank notes which were exchanged against their face value in silver, the monetary standard in force. The notes of the different banks circulated without any problem nor government regulation. Healthy competition limited abuse.

In 1927, Chinese banks found themselves trapped between nationalists and communists. Violence organized by the communist leaders weakened the industry in Shanghai. Tchang Kai Check made an offer to the banks in Shanghai that they could not refuse. His forces would prohibit strikes and stop violence in exchange for loans for the nationalist government. In 1927, for the first year in the nationalist government, these loans represented 49% of state revenues. The government continued to increase spending and debts.

In the spring of 1928, Soong, brother-in-law of Tchang Kai Check, very well versed in Triads, forced the banks in Shanghai to buy high yielding government bonds. Skeptical or recalcitrant bankers were arrested. In 1932, The banks in Shanghai held between 50 and 80% of government bonds.

In 1928, Soong founded the central bank modeled on the U.S. Federal Reserve, the state bank of the Republic of China. Soong appointed several private bank managers on the board. Government apparatchiks who controlled the issuance of bonds were invited to sit on the boards of private banks. Exactly as in the West, these insiders, aware of the future manipulations of the

Central Bank, became a privileged class of plutocrats.

The spark that exploded the relative freedom of the Chinese financial system came from the New Deal administration of **Franklin Roosevelt**.

In 1933, the U.S. government began to purchase large quantities of silver. In June 1934, "The Silver Purchase Act" passed in Congress, pushed the USA to purchase silver until the monetary value of this stock reached one third of the value of the U.S. gold stock.

As a result of the American manipulation, the price of silver tripled between 1933 and 1935. The debts of the Chinese whose currency was based on silver tripled suddenly, at a time when businesses were collapsing and many workers became unemployed.

The nationalist government banned the export of silver, thus breaking the principles of the silver standard, the very thing the Western central banks did to the gold standard. Taxes on silver were implemented with the aim of prohibiting the profitability of silver trafficking to the West. Soong's Central Bank was the only bank exempted from these taxes, which helped him to make it the most profitable Financial institution in China. Though this bank represented only 11% of the wealth held by all the banks in China, it represented 37% of profits in 1934.

The largest private bank, the bank of China, sought to cut ties with the nationalist government which began to sell its Treasury bonds at a loss. Tchang Kai Check then nationalized the Bank of China, and the second largest private bank, whose management was replaced by finance officers.

In June 1935, Kung, the Minister of Finance used the power of three nationalized banks to purchase all the bank notes on the market issued by the other private banks in Shanghai, before presenting the notes at the counter to demand its equivalent in silver. None of them was able to do this immediately. Kung declared them bankrupt, nationalized all the private banks together in July 1935 and seized all their property.

On the 3rd of November, 1935, the nationalists announced the launching of a fiat currency which was no longer redeemable against silver. Only the bank notes issued by the three largest banks, Central Bank of China, Bank of China and Communications Bank had legal tender at that time.

Roosevelt and Chinese Silver

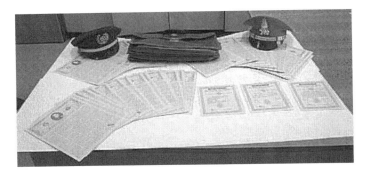

On the 4th of June 2009, in the Chiasso's station close to the Italo-swiss border, the Italian customs seized for 134 billions dollars in authentic US T-Bonds from 1934. One of the bearers was the brother in law of the ancient governor of the Bank of Japan.

2 months later, 180 billion dollars in US T-Bonds from 1934 are seized at the Milan Airport.

In April 2011, a Chinese envoy reveals the existence of trillions of Dollars in US T-Bonds of 1934.

A descendant of a Chinese high official at the time told me that the Americans had brought to China **a dozen machines for printing bonds**, *and that* **the machines have printed from 1928 to 1936**. *According to him, Soong May-ling, widow of Chiang Kai-shek, got her money back for such bonds, mainly owned by descendants of the Kuomintang and of the Chinese Imperial Family.*

"Each box of bonds contains 120 large envelopes, in each of these envelopes there is a nominal value of U.S. $300 million (10 sets of 3

bonds of $ 10 million each), so 3.6 billion dollars per box! And of course, we must take into account not only the face value, but also the interests since 1934!"

This box is declared sealed and registered by the Department of Treasury on April 22, 1934, Washington D.C. U.S.A., containing Lawful instruments for redemption engagement and other commercial purposes.

Witness, the seal of Department of Treasury and signatures of duty authorized Officers this 22nd day of April, 1934, Washington D.C. U.S.A..

All these coffers and suitcases stamped by the different Federal Reserve banks are full of boxes stuffed with enveloppes with US Treasury Bonds in them. Some treasury bonds are later than 1934 and signed by John Kennedy. They are worth trillions of Dollars, backed with gold and silver.

Jean-Marie Le Ray on adscriptum.blogspot.fr wrote pages following this extraordinary story.

I think that after WWI, a deal had been sealed for a new world order, with a unique international currency unit backed by gold and silver, under one central bank, under the responsability of the IMF, UNO and the World Bank. That American military oligarchy violated this deal after the end of WWII and took the power after Kennedy's assassination leading to new wars against Asia. All that Gold and Silver had been stealed by American Banksters and oligarchs, among them a few famous American Presidents. (End of this bracket)

CYRILLE JUBERT

Nationalization of Chinese Silver

All institutions and individuals were obliged to change their silver metal reserves against the new currency within 6 months. The Chinese nationalist government repeated exactly what Roosevelt did to gold in 1933.

Once the fiat money was launched, the government of Tchang Kai Check set the machine to print notes to try and reduce budget deficits.

Between 1935 and 1949, prices multiplied by 1000.

The demonetization of silver in China caused an oversupply of silver on the market and a sharp decline in prices from 1935.

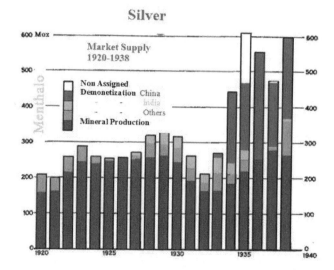

From 1934, the U.S. government purchased the bulk of the silver put on the market by the countries which demonetized white metal. It seemed that there was an agreement of the global financial oligarchy in early 1933, to replace the gold and silver monetary standards with the future dollar king's Gold Exchange Standard, which was launched in Bretton Woods in 1944.

The U.S. Treasury prepared the dollar to take up its role as international reserve by strengthening its monetary reserves. Its huge stock of silver allowed it to control the price of white metal for the next 5 decades.

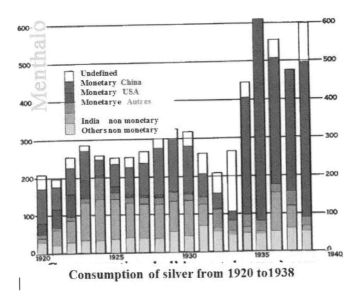

Consumption of silver from 1920 to 1938

The various currency crises (dollar, pound sterling, mark....) pushed investors once again to drop notes and hoard coins.

The increasing demand for gold at the counters of the Bank of France, in exchange for paper money, pushed the government to enact an Act, on the 1st of October 1936, inviting those in possession of gold to declare and return their assets, at the purchase price at the Bank of France.

Thus, 87 tons were recovered by the Bank of France.

In the wave of such enthusiasm, the government decided to take tougher action in a decree adopted on the 7th of February 1937, by equating the possession of gold with smuggling. The unpopularity of these decisions prompted the government to backtrack its decision on the 9th of March, only weeks later. People were free to possess and trade in gold once again. The Treasury repaid those who brought their gold.

The cost of the world wars ruined the treasures of the European banks who were forced to sell their gold to repay their war debts. This led to postwar devaluation of most of the currencies against gold.

In 1944, at Bretton Woods, American power was such that a monetary system was put in place with an international fiat currency, the dollar. The latter could be traded at any time against its equivalent value in gold, whose price was fixed. An ounce of gold was worth $35.

That was the Gold Exchange Standard.

SILVER COINS IN THE UNITED STATES

In 1934, Roosevelt published notes called "silver certificates", of ordinary one, five or ten dollar notes, that the owners could change at any time against the "Silver Dollars", of the hard cash in silver.

The U.S. Treasury, main buyer of the silver from American mines, bought up to 90.5 cents an ounce to sell at 91 cents. The average price ranged from 25 cents in the 30s to 75 cents in 1950. Its weight on the market tended to check the price of silver. However, the market was theoretically free.

Officially, the U. S. Treasury was entitled to purchase silver:
-To the tune of $1.29 an ounce of the monetary value of silver.
-As long as the monetary value of silver stocks did not reach one third of the monetary value of gold stocks.

After the war in 1950, demand for electrical reconstruction, on one hand, and the development of the consumer society, on the other, strongly reinforced the demand for silver. The US Treasury took advantage of this, and sold part of its excessive stocks which reached a peak in 1950 at **2 billion ounces or 56,700 tons**, or 7 times the silver that ETF SLV possessed in January 2012

Until 1960, the government sold its stocks to lower silver prices and kept them under the official price of $1.29 an ounce, to prevent the Americans from melting their coins to sell them in the form of bullions on the market. Without this policy, the international rate for silver would have shot up sharply right from the beginning of the sixties.

On June 4 1963, Kennedy signed the Executive Order n° 11110 by which the government found its power embodied in the Constitution to create its currency without passing through the New York Federal Reserve Bank. He printed 4.3 billion of 1, 2, 5, 10, 20 and 100 dollar bank notes, which were secured by the gold and silver reserves of the Treasury and they could be exchanged for coins or hard cash.

Silver had a fixed price of $1.29 per ounce. These notes were denominated **"United States note"** instead of **"Federal Reserve note."**

Kennedy abolished the Silver Purchase Act of 1934 and all the laws prohibiting Americans to purchase silver. The U.S. Treasury at that time had only 1.7 billion ounces of silver. The demand from individuals and speculators was extremely high, forcing the U.S. Mint to increase production from 1.6 million coins to 4.3 million.

The attempt by Kennedy to regain the power that the private bankers held since 1913, was probably the major motive for his murder five months after his monetary reform on November 26th 1963.

After his assassination, permission to print the new notes was repealed and the implementation of the Presidential Decree was

Silver throughout History

suspended.

Demand was too high and the 1965 Monetary Law brought about the reduction of silver content in coins by half a dollar, from 900/1000th to 400/1000th. Silver was removed from coins with lower denomination and replaced with cupro-nickel.

The new government put in place a policy aimed at cutting the link between the currency in circulation and the silver market.

Between the early 60s and late 60s, the silver used by the U.S. Treasury to mint coins in circulation increased from **180 million ounces to 40 million ounces per year.**

Lyndon Johnson, in 1965 noticed with lucidity that silver was very scarce and that its price would rise accordingly. To remedy this, Johnson decided not to mint silver coins any longer and committed the government reserves to keep the price low.

Here is his speech delivered on the 23rd of July 1965, announcing that the silver coins would be withdrawn from circulation.

"Now, all of you know these changes are necessary for a very simple reason:
Silver is a scarce metal.

Our uses of silver are growing as our population and our economy grows. The hard fact is that silver consumption is now more than double new silver production each year. So, in the face of this worldwide shortage of silver, and our rapidly growing need for coins, the only really prudent course was to reduce our dependence upon silver for making our coins. If we had not done so, we would have risked chronic coin shortages in the very near future.

If anybody has any idea of hoarding our silver coins, let me say this:

Treasury has a lot of silver on hand and it can be, and it will be used to keep the price of silver in line with its value in our present silver coin. There will be no profit in holding them out of circulation for the value of their silver content."

The government sold its reserves to keep the price of silver at the face value of the dollar, $1.2929 an ounce. This policy lasted until July 14 1967, when the Treasury no longer had the means to prevent silver from being revalued.

In 1969, silver was gradually phased out of all coins in circulation in the United States. The other European countries took the same step some months or years later. The coins were melted and converted into bullions for manufacturers, jewelers and a few investors.

GOLD EXCHANGE STANDARD WOBBLES

Loss of confidence in the dollar

Over the years, U.S. monetary policy became increasingly lenient so some countries, including France, sold the dollars from the proceeds of their foreign trade in exchange for gold, thus putting the United States Treasury in danger.

Creation of the London Gold Pool

On November 1st 1961, after a series of virulent attacks on the dollar, eight Central Banks, at the instigation of John Kennedy, formed the "London Gold Pool" to try and contain the value of gold at $35. The United States had to provide 50% of gold offered for sale in this interbank agreement.

United States,	50% 120 tons	($135 MM)
Germany,	11% 27 tons	($30 MM)
United Kingdom,	9% 22 tons	($25 MM)
France,	9%, 22 tons	($25 MM)
Italy,	9%, 22 tons	($25 MM)
Belgium,	4%, 9 tons	($10 MM)
Netherlands,	4%, 9 tons	($10 MM)
Switzerland,	4%, 9 tons	($10 MM)

Whenever the London market investors rushed for gold, the central banks sold large quantities to bring down the prices. When gold prices went down, the central banks bought gold to replenish the common fund.

The "London Gold Pool" worked perfectly well for six years, until France withdrew after a shattering speech by General de Gaulle in February 1965:

"The fact that many nations, in principle, accept dollars as being the same as gold when making up any differences which exist to their credit, in the balance of payments between themselves and America has meant that Americans can incur debts with foreign nations with complete impunity since such debts can be paid, at least in part, with dollars, which they can themselves issue at will.

Given the consequences that could well arise from such a state of affairs, we think that a timely step to avoid them should be taken before they happen. We consider it necessary that international exchanges should be established, as was the case before the great disasters which have befallen the world, on an indisputable monetary basis that bears the mark of no one particular country. On what basis ? The truth is that, it is difficult to envisage that there could be in reality any other criterion or standard than gold."

De Gaulle, the President of France, turned the talk into action and demanded that the U.S. exchanged the dollars from foreign trade with the Bank of France against gold.

The May 1968 riots owed nothing to chance. That was a bit of a tit for tat but this is far from our subject.

In 1967, an attack on the pound sterling and gold forced the Bank of England to devalue the pound on November 18.

Investors fearing the devaluation of the dollar, weaken by the cost of the Vietnam War, triggered a new gold rush.

The End of the London Gold Pool

On the 5th of March 1968, London had to sell 100 tons in the day, representing 20 times more than the usual. The following Sunday, the London Pool reaffirmed its determination to keep the price of gold at $35 per ounce. The President of the Federation, William McCesney-Martin said he would defend this price **"to the last bullion"**.

From the middle of the week, a real air cargo of gold was set between the United States and London to meet demand. On Wednesday, London sold 175 tons, 30 times the usual demand and on Thursday, it exceeded 225 tons.

That evening, an emergency meeting was held at Buckingham Palace and the Queen decided to close the banks the next day, Friday 15th of March. Roy Jenkins, the then Chancellor of the Exchequer, announced the decision to close the gold market "at the request of the United States", to the press.

The gold market was closed for two weeks, during which the Paris and Zurich markets remained open. Gold traded at $44 an ounce, or 25% higher than the official price in London.

The latter re-opened on April 1. A new rule was introduced with a price freeze on trade between central banks at $35.20 and a free price for the Free Market. Gold shot up quickly on the latter to 3 times its official value.

At that time, the American Treasury was actually emptied of its gold, **"to the last bullion"**. The Fort Knox gold has been a myth since then.

A whole book would be necessary to tell the truth about Fort Knox, the Lead bars shown to the Congress and the tungsten bars created later. Gold is not the subject of this book

CYRILLE JUBERT

End of the Gold Exchange Standard

In August 1971, Nixon announced that America had abandoned the "Gold exchange standard" unilaterally. Officially, the dollar no longer had any value other than the confidence placed in it. It became the fiat money (from the Latin fides = faith)

A currency, which is not guaranteed by any tangible asset, like gold, is still valued by the tax authority of the issuing state as well as the balance of its budget.

In a growing economy, confidence in the currency is strong. In an economy in recession, production and consumption weaken, reducing the potential revenue of the state (through VAT and other corporate taxes). Confidence in one's currency weakens it even further.

The Vietnam War, and the outsourcing of industrial production weakened the U.S. economy and eroded the value of the dollar.

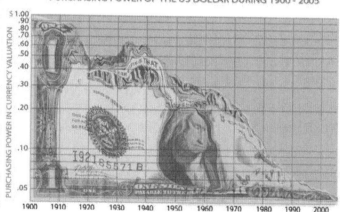

PURCHASING POWER OF THE US DOLLAR DURING 1900 - 2005

In 1945, after the Japanese surrender, USA signed an agreement with the "Zaibatsus", industrial conglomerates in Japan, which built the military power of the Rising Sun. The latter had to transform their industrial base to produce high consumer products for the West. In return, the United States pledged to keep their boarders open, so long as the Japanese re-invested a pre-determined percentage of the dollars thus earned in U.S. Treasury Bonds.

At that time, the U.S. Treasury Bonds were worth the value of gold in the right sense of the word and they accumulated more interests. The Americans then bought equipment or consumer products through the perpetual credit system which resulted in massive debt half a century later.

Right from the beginning, the system was a pyramid scam. It would not have been possible without the massive corruption of the elites of the "producer–lender" countries.

The corruption was made possible thanks to Yamashita's Treasure, see "Operation Golden Lily". The treasure of the Japanese booty in their wars of conquest in Korea, in Manchuria and China were largely recovered by General Mac Arthur at the end of the war. Since 1945, Yamashita's gold financed the American right wing black operations, including active corruption of the elites, to implement, and then maintain an unfair world order, "Pax Americana."

By relocating their production first to Japan, then China, the United States depleted their industrial facilities, thereby reducing American wealth creation.

America concentrated its wealth creation on the tertiary sector (finance, insurance, research, pharmacy agronomy). Its military power enabled it to impose fertilizers, GMO seeds or questionable drugs on the nations of the world, just to mention a few examples, before imposing that all financial transactions should be done in dollars and with approved clearing companies. Thus a real racketeering was systematically implemented.

America in 2012 has nothing to do with that of 1945.

Since the 1950s, the number of government officials has been multiplied by 3. There are 22 million civil servants in the United States today against 11 million workers in the industry. New York city has 1.5 million civil servants against only 0.67 million people working in the financial.

For decades, the U.S. budget was totally unbalanced and the U.S. government was so indebted that it was at the brink of financial cataclysm, which has been delayed due to the increasing falsification of statistics of economic and market data.

THE 70'S

Kennedy sought to restore U.S finances and policies including the reduction of U.S. participation in the wars in Indochina, Lyndon Johnson (63-69), then Nixon (69-74) gave in to the military-industrial lobbying by involving the United States in the Vietnam War, which cost the U.S. Treasury dearly.

General De Gaulle denounced the American monetary hegemony and a monetary system that allowed the U.S. "to incur debts with foreign nations with complete impunity."

Nixon's decision led to a de facto devaluation of the dollar against gold, the universal monetary standard. The price of silver multiplied by 4.

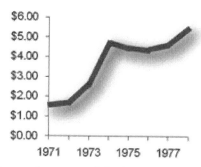

In 1970, the increasing cost of the Vietnam War generated high inflation in USA. The external trade deficit and the balance of payments caused international financiers to prefer to hold gold instead of the dollar. The U.S. Treasury thus saw its "official" gold coverage fall from 55 to 22%.

On the 15th of August 1971, Nixon closed "the gold window" and unilaterally terminated the Gold Exchange Standard established at Bretton Woods at the end of the war.

The U.S. economy was at its worst, galloping inflation, the dollar was under attack, Wall Street and London City shook. Gold prices soared on the open market.

Oil Crises

It was then that a strategy was developed and presented by Kissinger in May 1973, to the Bilderberg group, composed of 84 most influential people in oil, finance and politics during the meeting at Bilderberg Hotel in Sweden. This strategy caused the "Yom Kippur War", the false threat of oil embargo by OPEC and "the oil crises", which resulted in a 400% increase of the price of oil per barrel in early 1974.

London, Washington and Wall Street were saved by an agreement signed with OPEC, forcing the producers to sell their oil in dollars on the London market, through the Bank Cartels. A percentage of these dollars had to be invested in U.S. Treasury Bonds. If the plutocrats found it lucrative, the others experienced an inflationary tsunami.

CYRILLE JUBERT

The Hunt Brothers' Silver Corner

William H. Hunt and Nelson B. Hunt at their trial.

text by **Tristan GASTON-BRETON**

A real disaster! On the 27th March 1980, Nelson Bunker Hunt and his brother William Herbert, powerless, witnessed the collapse of their speculative empire. Though they succeeded in capturing half of the world's silver stocks a few years earlier, sparking a steep rise in prices, they could not prevent the prices from collapsing. In just one day, the price of an ounce of silver was slashed into two, sweeping the International Metal Investment Group under the rug, the company created by the Hunt brothers with the help of some investors in the Middle East. An abrupt end to the ambitions of the two Texans, orchestrated from the beginning to the end by the federal authorities, Federal Reserve at the head. For Nelson Bunker and William Herbert, it was, as a journalist would say, "the party is over".

Humiliated, this failure was demeaning for the two brothers, since from an early age, they lived with a fixed idea that: a rich man is never rich enough! It was their father, Haroldson Lafayette Hunt, who instilled this way of viewing issues in them. This self-taught surprising character became one of the richest men in the United States. Born in 1889 in a prosperous family at Illinois, he left his parents' home at the age of fifteen and did many "odd jobs": lumberjack, farm worker, dish washer in a restaurant, mule-driver, and even basketball player!

The death of his father when he was twenty-two years, helped him to recover some thousands of dollars. With these savings, he went to Arkansas where he created a cotton plantation from scratch. Almost ruined by the collapse in prices caused by the first World War, he resumed his wanderings and moved to El Dorado (Arkansas), where oil had been discovered. Specializing in the sale and purchase of lands, he quickly amassed comfortable fortune which enabled him to launch successfully into oil exploration. Owner, of about a hundred wells in Louisiana, Arkansas and Oklahoma in the late 1920s, he had the foresight to purchase the huge deposit discovered in 1930 at Kilgore, near Dallas, a deposit which the major companies did not believe in.

This stroke of a genius made him one of the leading independent oil magnates in the United States and one of the richest men in the country. In 1940, his revenue exceeded one billion dollars. These sums of money were re-invested in other companies. Hunt was not only a rich oil magnate at the head of several independent companies like the Hunt Oil Company or the Placid Oil Company but also one of the greatest farmers in the United States. In the mid-1950's, his interests span over five continents ranging from oil to drugs and property to cotton, livestock and timber! His activities were grouped in a myriad of companies in about twenty countries of which he personally owned 90% of shares.

More Texan than the Texans themselves, this man, married three times and as a legendary avarice, he utilized all the clichés of his adopted country: Puritan in excess -which did not prevent him from indulging fully in his passion: poker- close to the extreme right-wing groups, he funded some radio and television programs denouncing liberals, communists, federal social programs, taxes and intellectuals confusedly. In early 1960, he confessed the strong hatred he had for President Kennedy so some even suspected him of being one of the sponsors of the assassination in Dallas.

"As rich as Croesus, as clever as riverboat gambler, as tight as a new pair of shoes..., he thinks that communism began in this country when the government took over the distribution of mail. If he had more flair and imagination, If he had not been basically a country bumpkin, he could be one of the most dangerous men in the United States of America", according to a journalist. This was the man who served as a model to Nelson

Bunker Hunt and his brother William Herbert.

Born in 1926, Nelson Bunker never set foot in school or almost unlike his younger brother, who went to the university. Like all the children of Haroldson Lafayette Hunt -15 in all- the two brothers experienced a golden and totally reckless life in Dallas, the city of choice for the family.

"Do what you want" their father said repeatedly, too busy with his business to take care of his children. Taking advantage of the immense fortune of their father, Nelson Bunker and William Herbert created their own oil drilling company, the Penrod Drilling Company, before their father gave them one of the riches of the huge Hunt empire the Placid Oil Company. We were then in the mid-1960s and the demand for oil was in full swing. After a first crushing defeat in Pakistan -which still cost a whopping 11 million dollars- Nelson Bunker and William Herbert launched an onslaught of new deposits on the planet. One country that attracted their attention in particular was Libya.

In the mid-1950s, large oil reserves were discovered there, causing a real rush of large companies. One of the "black sheep" of the Hunt family also gained a major concession there : Armand Hammer, independent just like them but made a mistake, according to Haroldson Lafayette of being a "communist". Was he not nicknamed the "red millionaire" due to the numerous connections he maintained in the URSS? More interested in business than politics, the Hunt brothers also got a foothold in Libya. In the early 1970's, their interests alone in this country was estimated at 7 billion dollars. Like their father, Nelson Bunker and William Herbert were among the richest men in the United States.

That was when everything started going wrong!

There was first of all, in August 1970, the decision by Colonel Gaddafi, who had just overthrown King Idris of Libya, to increase the royalties paid by the oil companies by 20 % per barrel. The two brothers and their ageing father -who died in 1974- ranted in vain, nothing worked! The family was forced to accept the humiliating conditions of the new Libyan leader. Up for grabs: profits reduced significantly. And that was not all ! At the same time, inflationary pressures were felt around the world which contributed to the further trimming of their margins.

These tensions literally exploded after the first oil crisis in 1973. Undoubtedly, due to the sharp rise in oil price per barrel, the Hunt brothers, gained back from one side what they lost on the other. By all standards, the outcome was positive on the whole! But for both Texans and especially for Nelson Bunker who was naturally pessimistic, there was nothing good in all that. Convinced that the economic situation would get worse, and that inflation would reach new heights in the United States, already weakened by the Vietnam War, they saw their influence in the world decline very quickly. The two brothers felt that the time had come to take shelter and cover themselves as much as possible against the economic turmoil. Hence the special project they decided to implement at the end of 1973.

The project? It was just about picking all the silver existing on the planet to protect themselves against inflation!

Nelson Bunker and William Herbert would have preferred gold, but the U.S. Law at that time prohibited individuals from purchasing large quantities of gold. So, they went in for silver, whose world stocks were in the region of 500 million ounces (a little over 15,000 tons). The idea was not so farfetched as it seemed at first. In 1869 the American millionaire, Jay Gould, had already attempted to snap up U.S. gold to make the prices soar but he failed at the last minute due to the intervention of the Federal Treasury. A story that the Hunts should have meditated upon...

Sure of success, the two Texans then began to purchase silver on the world markets. In the early months of 1974, they already had 55 million ounces for a total value of 100 million dollars. For tax purposes, they decided to store the bulk of the silver in Switzerland. For this purpose, three Boeing 707 were hired to commute between New York and Zurich. There, the precious metal was loaded on to armored trucks and transported to six secret banks. Strange convoys travelled at night, guarded by about ten special armed men from the United States of America.

In the mid-1970s, rumors had it that the Hunt brothers had started "cornering" the silver market. The operation included the manipulation of the market with the aim of forcing sellers to liquidate their positions and at any price if necessary. In fact, from the mid-1970's, the Hunt brothers began to accumulate silver contracts to compel sellers to sell their stocks. As expected, the maneuver resulted in a rapid increase in the price of silver: While in 1973 it stood at 1.95 dollars per ounce, it was almost $4 in early 1975. To redeem the stock still available on the market, Nelson Bunker and William Herbert had to be prepared to spend nearly 2 billion dollars. That was a huge amount even if these two Texans could count on their recently deceased father's legacy and their flourishing oil business. It was costing so much to spread their financial risks and to accelerate their acquisition of precious metals, that they decided to appeal to their partners.

In March 1975, Nelson Bunker went to Teheran secretly to propose to the shah of Iran to join the maneuver. But the negotiation failed, largely due to the inability to accurately estimate the gains that the Americans expected to get from that business. Also, at Teheran, people were suspicious of the successful cow-boy ways and there were concerns that this speculation would create problems for the U.S. government. Two other attempts in the Philippines and the Saudi royal family did not succeed. It was not until 1979 that Nelson Bunker and William Herbert finally succeeded in winning the interest of Saudi investors who were seeking lucrative investments for their petrodollars. Thus, in the spring of 1979, the International Metal Investment Group was created.

The company immediately began to gather all the silver available on the market. Between June and December 1979, it acquired more than 150 million ounces of precious metal, for the 200 million total stock of the two brothers and their Saudi partners. At the same time, prices literally soared, increasing from a little over 5 dollars per ounce in early 1979 to 54 dollars a year later. Nelson Bunker and William Herbert won their bet: In January 1980, they accumulated so many silver contracts that their vendors could not meet their commitments, forcing them to buy silver at a higher price on the market. The coming of one hundred speculators on board only worsened the situation. From their ranch in Dallas, the two brothers had every reason to rejoice. Holding half the amount of silver stocks on the planet, immensely rich -their virtual fortune represented several hundred billion dollars- they shared with anyone who would listen that they intended to reintroduce silver as currency to replace paper money. These outbursts, as well as the risk of chain destabilization, pushed the authorities to intervene.

In early 1980, the NYMEX (New York Commodity Exchange), supported by the Federal Reserve, suddenly decided to change the rules of the game. To break the speculation, deposits charged to new buyers were credited to prohibitive levels. In addition, professionals were allowed to replace silver delivery by cash, which immediately relieved the "short" market. In addition, the number of contracts that could be held by one person or an entity was drastically limited. The effect was not long: between January and early March 1980, the price of silver fell sharply from 54 to 21 dollars.

On March 26 1980, the famous "Silver Thursday", the price dropped sharply to 10.8 dollars! Hundreds of speculators were ruined. The Hunt brothers themselves were forced to declare bankruptcy. They were sentenced in 1988 for manipulation of the market. As in 1869, during the Gould case, the federal authorities managed to break clear the speculation.

In the early 1980s, the sharp drop in oil prices ended up ruining the Hunts. Any living relative was ruined and today, the family is still in possession of many assets in oil. But that was the end of the flamboyance of the Hunts. They played too much with money and ended up burning their fingers.

Courtesy: **Tristan GASTON-BRETON**

Silver costing $1.95 an ounce reached $4 in 1975.

Between June and December 1979, the Hunts acquired more than 150 million ounces of precious metal, bringing the total stock held by the two brothers and their Saudi partners to $200 million.

At the same time, prices literally soared, rising from a little over **5 dollars per ounce in early 1979 to 54 dollars a year later.**

CYRILLE JUBERT

In early 1980, COMEX with the support of the Federal Reserve, suddenly decided to change the rules of the game.

To break the speculation, deposits charged to new buyers were carried to prohibitive levels. Professionals were allowed to replace the delivery of their silver by cash, which immediately relieved the "short" market. Finally, the number of contracts that could be held by an individual or entity was drastically limited.

The effect was not long: Between January and early March 1980, the price of silver fell sharply from $54 to $21.

On March 26 1980, the famous **"Silver Thursday"**, prices lost 50% of their value and fell sharply to 10.8 dollars. Hundreds of speculators were ruined. The Hunt brothers themselves were forced to declare bankruptcy. They were sentenced in 1988 for manipulation of the market. The Hunt brothers and their partners bore the cost of administration, in the service of the financial oligarchy, seeking to defend the fiat money.

Today, it is not two individuals but a block of powerful states, rising against the current monetary system based on the enslavement of nations through debt, on one hand, and the endless devaluation of the currency, on the other.

CYRILLE JUBERT

Silver Throughout History

1985-2012

CYRILLE JUBERT

This chapter will tell you events of the recent years, trying to sort out the information we received and putting them in perspective. If you pull a thread, you will discover chain scams, economically and politically motivated killings, whose motives dated more than 10 years back.

It also happened that after a project has been developed by one of the factions of the oligarchy, a project whose implications were global, we witnessed its annihilation in a totally unexpected way by a move of one of the opposing faction on the chess board.

It has been the case in the spring of 2011, with the overthrow of DSK, the IMF boss, followed by the overthrow of the governor of the Bank of Egypt and the different political authorities in North Africa. One of the goals of the "Arab Spring" was to stop the monetary revolution, which was about to replace the unconditional reign of the dollar as an international reference currency with a new gold standard.

We are at a pivotal moment in our economic, political and monetary history. We don't have only one script writer but several. Each one of them is trying to impose his own version of the story by any possible means, with extreme violence. These uncertainties of contemporary history are very chaotic. It is difficult to see the trend and give coherence to the whole, especially as the reality is permanently concealed by government propaganda.

Nothing is ever fixed. The paradigms of yesterday and the day before yesterday are no longer true today. Will the truth of the day be the same tomorrow? We can only show snapshots of the market and try to explain them.

That's why this chapter looks often as a collection of chronicles.

CYRILLE JUBERT

MONETARY GEOSTRATEGY OF THE US EMPIRE

THE DOLLAR FORTRESS

Kissinger in 1972 negotiated an agreement with oil-rich countries of OPEC. He committed to reduce the production of U.S. hydrocarbon, on one hand, and buy oil at a higher price from the oil-producing countries, on the other, provided that :
- OPEC oil was exclusively traded in USD,
- petrodollars were to be channeled through banks in London,
- a fixed percentage of the petrodollar windfall had to be invested in U.S. Treasury Bonds.

This secret agreement, negotiated on behalf of the "seven sisters" of the oil cartel, was the secret origin of the Yom Kippur War and the misleading threat of oil embargo of the Arab countries, which led to the famous "oil crisis" in 1973. The sharp rise in oil price put the industry on its knees, and probably caused its relocation. This agreement provided warranted earnings for the U.S. successive governments, who could get into debt endlessly, sure to find captive customers to fund the U.S. debt.

The first part of this secret agreement allowed the USA to safeguard their own oil resources, while exhausting those of their vassals. The Peak Oil is a hoax created at that time. Lindsey Williams revealed in his book, "the energy non-crisis", that huge oil reserves were found in Alaska in the 70's, reserves that the oil Cartel decided to keep secret and are still unexploited today. They would not do it till the price of oil reaches $200 a barrel. Will that price be reached sometime in 2013?

These gas and oil deposits in the Bay of Gull Island in Alaska represented 150 years of U.S. energy consumption. Bore-holes were drilled and oil and gas pipelines were built in 1975. It is just a matter of opening the valves to flood the U.S. with very cheap oil, but the Cartel (Standard Oil, BP, Shell) wanted to raise the price of oil.

All the iterative tragi-comedy between Iran and Israel, and the potential blockade of the Strait of Hormuz is part of the monetary strategy of the Anglo-American Cartels. The drama in Syria today is about the control of the gigantic layer of gas in the Eastern Mediterranean and the oil and gas pipelines crossing this territory.

11ᵀᴴ CONGRESS OF CPC

In 1972, the indefatigable Henry Kissinger organized a meeting in China between Richard Nixon and the ageing President Mao Tse Tung. The capitalist "paper tiger" laid the foundations of a long collaboration with the communist devil. The West agreed at that time to contribute to the financing and equipping of communist China, which was then mainly an agricultural country, living in total autarky.

At the 11th Congress of the Chinese Communist Party in December 1978, Deng Xiaoping, without changing the communist rhetoric, launched the country into large capitalist economic reforms. It took decades for China to form a skilled workforce and qualified managerial staff, but after PRC worked on the basis of the five-year development programs, it began its modernization process patiently.

Ultra-modern ports, brand new factories with latest technology, worker's housing estates built around industrial centers, cheap and abundant labor, enabled China to become the factory of the world with unbeatable prices.

In 1972, Kissinger offered China an agreement similar to the one signed with the Japanese Zaibatsu after the war. He committed not to put tariffs on Chinese products and urged American manufacturers to outsource their production to China. In exchange, China had to invest its trade surplus in U.S. Treasury bonds. When Nixon stopped the Gold Exchange Standard, the U.S. dollars were no longer redeemable against a fixed value in gold. China therefore worked on credit, paid in funny money, which had been devalued at a fast pace over the years.

The United States located their processing industry to developing countries, reserving the tertiary sector for the West (banking, research & development, Insurance, services,...) which now accounts for 80% of U.S. gross domestic product.

This also explains why China currently has huge currency reserves stored in U.S. Treasury Bonds. But the Chinese are one of the oldest civilizations in the world. They knew that U.S. agreement was worthless without a stable currency, which was not the case with the dollar. An ounce of gold was worth $35 in 1971 against $1,600 in 2012.

The Chinese had been paid with funny money.
Tensions aggravated from 2006 for various reasons, including the acceleration of the pace of the depreciation of the dollar expressed in ounces of gold.

JPM DEVELOPED THE HEDGING OF MINES

In 1988, J.P. Morgan Bank, the Samurai defending the U.S. monetary policy, went to see the mining companies and offered to buy their gold reserves even those deep in the ground of their mines. The mining companies found the idea of selling gold which had not yet been extracted, an excellent financial operation for short term cash. The mining companies repaid this "loan" in kind, after gold was extracted.

It was assumed that the gold hedged was sold below the normal price, but that was not even certain. Indeed, JPM, working for the New York Federal Reserve, was paid by the latter for any operation to maintain confidence in the dollar and control the price of gold against the other fiat currencies.

Initiated with Barrick Gold, whose offices were upstairs above those of JPM in New York and some of the largest gold mines, this agreement covered only 300 tons of gold in 1988. It reached 1000 tons in 2001.

This policy helped to lower the price of an ounce of gold for three years up to $250, then limited the increase till 2005, despite the external pressures.

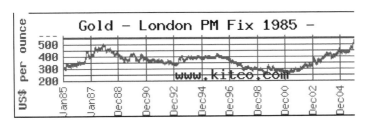

This policy had been applied to silver as well, knowing that all the gold mines also produced silver and that the large copper mines were owned by the banking oligarchy, Rothschild at the head, whose purpose was to **maintain confidence in the fiat money.**

At that time, China refined 80% of Silver, a highly polluting metallurgy that the West outsourced willingly in Asia, where the citizens were not bothered about pollution and the quality of life.

The share of refining of silver from China decreased, when China began to oppose the U.S. monetary policy of continued devaluation of the dollar.

1998
"LONG TERM CAPITAL MANAGEMENT"

The founder of the hedge fund was John Meriwether, famous and brilliant head of arbitration, then interest rate trading at Salomon Brothers, he had to leave after an obvious market manipulation. By establishing LTCM, Meriwether recruited the trading dream team of Salomon Brothers, by adding 2 Nobel Prize winners in Economics and a current Vice Chairman of the Federal Reserve. All the large WS business banks participated in the round table. The team was brilliant and their mathematical models seemed to win every time. In fact, they had insider's information from the Federal Reserve, and their counterparts in the Bank of Italy.

In the same way as Goldman Sachs did for Greece, LTCM fiddled with the Italian accounts in order to enable Italy to join the European Monetary Union. LTCM, in particular, advised the Bank of Italy and the Italian Exchange Office (UIC) to use some cavalry tactics, with the former, selling a few tons of the national gold to the latter, who in turn resold them to the former, generating fictitious profits. So, Italy managed to be integrated into the Monetary Economic Union, and the Bank of Italy thanked LTCM by leasing them 400 tons of gold. The Hedge Fund sold that gold on the market, hoping to be able to buy it back cheaper. But LTCM traders were taken off balance in 1998. LTCM played with huge leverages on bonds, many of which were "junk bonds", and they were washed away in a few hours by the 1998's Russian Bond Crisis.

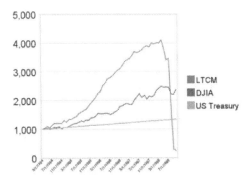

The New York Federal Reserve brought together all the heads of the largest investment banks on Wall Street and Europe and forced them to recapitalize the hedge fund to avoid a systemic crash.

Only one bank, **Bear Stearns**, refused to finance this rescue plan. The Bank was then considered by the New York Federal Reserve as an **"enemy of the state"**, the bank to be pulled down.

After its bankruptcy, LTCM was dismantled and shared among the different banks.

JPM inherited the short position on LTCM's gold.

1999

The Bundesbank, the German central bank, is at the heart of the construction of the European Union and its monetary system. The ECU (European Currency Unit) launched in 1979, which was a unit of account with a basket of the different currencies of the member countries, disappeared in favor of the **EURO**. At this time, Euro was only a unit of account for European financial transactions. The Euro became the common currency in 2002 only. In 1997, long before the European Central Bank launched the Euro, one of the European officials in charge of preliminary studies for its implementation, Bernard Connolly, published a book: *"The Euro, rotten heart of Europe."* He was already saying that it could only be a source of conflict between economies that were too disparate.

On October 24 2012, declassified documents revealed that Germany in 2000 and 2001 has repatriated two thirds of its gold reserves stored at the Bank of England, 960 tons out of 1,440. The rest of the German reserves are in Paris and Frankfurt but mostly stored in the NY Fed. Its last serious and comprehensive audit go back to 1979/80. Since then, the auditors have seen the sealed boxes in NY, but were not allowed to open them. Strange, isn't it?

When Germany repatriated some of its gold from BoE, the price of gold began to rise in what we called the Bull Market of the Century. In 2000, the Bundesbank was already opposed to the Anglo-American policy.

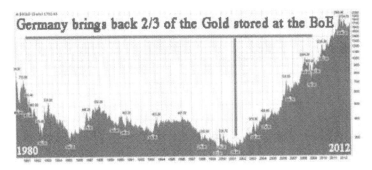

2000

We saw in the historical section that the original "gold standard" could not survive the First World War. The United States was the main financier and supplier of commodities and equipment (weapons and vehicles) for the belligerents of the "Triple Entente". They enriched themselves while Great Britain, France and Germany became poorer and fell into debt. As a result of these commercial and financial transactions, the Americans had the largest stock of gold on the planet. Since most countries had abolished the convertibility of bank notes into gold, the nationalization of gold by Roosevelt in 1934 announced the introduction of a new monetary system, in which gold was strictly reserved for trades between Central Banks.

As early as 1932, an agreement had probably been signed between the international financial oligarchy preparing this monetary reform, which would only be formalized in 1944 at Bretton Woods. The Silver Purchase Act of 1934 led to a sharp increase in the price of silver, exploding (all or part) of the monetary system that remained within the silver standard (China, India, Latin Union), causing the United States to purchase almost all the silver available on the planet in a few years.

The global stock of monetary silver was 4,940 million ounces in 1933. From 1934 to 1938, USA bought nearly 1.8 billion ounces, to add to their pre-existing stock of 650 million ounces. The United States alone had then **2.450 billion ounces of silver.**

From 1939, the US government established an administrative control, "the Office of Price Administration" (OPA) to control the prices of silver. This administration fixed a different price for the silver purchased from U.S. producers at 70 cents and that from the international producers at 35 cents.

The price was not allowed to rise until after Bretton Woods, when the dollar became the single currency used for international trade, and exchangeable with gold. Silver was no longer used to trade between the central banks.

In 1950, the US stock of silver was 2 billion ounces.

To this official stock, we can probably add part of the Yamashita

Treasure, which instead of returning to the U.S. Treasury, remained in the hands of the military industrial lobby. The latter were then headed by the Rockefellers, who had quasi-monopoly of the U. S. oil (Standard Oil = S.O. = Esso = Exxon), and a dominant position in the refineries, bulk chemicals and fine chemicals (pharmaceutical laboratories). The "black operations" to defend the dollar were carried out by the Federal Bank of New York and the Rockefeller Group Bank, Chase Manhattan Bank, which merged with JPM in 2001.

In 1963, the U.S. Treasury then had only 1.7 billion ounces that the government sold to maintain the price of silver at its face value against the dollar or 1.2929 USD an ounce. This policy lasted until July 14 1967, when the Treasury no longer had the means to prevent the silver from being revalued. In June 1968, the price of silver soared to $2.565 an ounce at the very moment when the price of gold in London blasted the "London pool".

When Nixon denounced the Gold Exchange Standard in 1971, speculators invested in gold and silver, seeking a hedge against inflation. This led to soaring prices from 1979-80 due to an attempt by the Hunt bothers to corner silver. The Cartel then changed the trading rules to lower prices and punished speculators severely.

In 2002, the U.S. Treasury had only 200 million ounces of silver. **In 2004, the Treasury was completely exhausted of its reserves.**

Through Geithner of the New York Federal Reserve, or JPM, the United States officially borrowed 300 million ounces of silver from China (maybe more, no one can tell the specific amount involved) using Treasury bonds as collateral. By a contract dully signed by the Federal Reserve, China had the opportunity at any time to recover its 300 million ounces of silver after four years upon request.

The graph below shows that this loan was used to inflate the COMEX stocks in February 2000.

Were there several loans? I didn't find informations about that.

A few years later, when China requested for the refund of its 300 million ounces of silver, its American counterparts at the New York Federal Reserve told the Chinese that their request could not be granted because the silver had been sold on the market.

"But you have treasury bonds as collateral, keep them", said the Federal Reserve to the Chinese representatives. **But the Chinese had an acknowledgement of debt guaranteed by the American government on 300 million ounces of physical silver.**

We will see how they will use this weapon.

China International Trust and Investment Corporation, giant Chinese financial company established in 1979 at the instigation of Deng Xiaoping and its policy of "four modernizations."

The original purpose of CITIC was to attract and use foreign capital, introduce advanced technology, and convert to international financial management practices.

CITIC was the MAINSTAY OF SILVER EXPORT extracted or refined in CHINA, representing 80% of the world's Silver from 1985 to 2000.

In 2005, China exported 3,000 tons of silver per year, or **96 million ounces. BEAR STEARNS Bank**, which was then the 5th largest bank on Wall Street, used to hedge the production of Chinese silver on behalf of CITIC, in a very normal and healthy manner.

In 2006, the WSJ revealed that CITIC was preparing to take a stake of nearly 20% of the capital of the BEAR STEARNS Bank. CITIC renounced this agreement in March 2008, at a time when Bear Stearns was forced into bankruptcy, which was a banking assassination as Wall Street in general and JPM in particular, has the secret.

Bear Stearns was known for taking positions with a strong leverage on the markets. They were easy to disrupt when the time came. Precisely, it turned out that Bear Stearns **had a huge "long" position on gold**.

JPM with the complicity of the WS financial Cartel, grouped around the Federal Reserve of New York, at that time headed by Timothy Geithner, will voluntarily cause the bankruptcy of Bear Stearns in 2008.

Timothy Geithner, first trained at Kissinger Associates, second at the Council of Foreign Relations, was then President of the New York Federal Reserve. He ordered JPM to buy Bear Stearns, which was completely strangled by the market. BS was sold off at $2 a share, a quarter of the value of its building in New York. That was a real murder.

JPM covered its "short" position on gold inherited from LTCM with the Bear Stearns's "long" position. JPM inherited, at the same time, a very long short position on Silver, the usual CITIC's hedges on Chinese silver production.

JPM being politically very committed to the defense of American interests and therefore that of the dollar, these "short" positions on precious metals were included in the monetary policy of the Washington Agreements on Gold between the G8 central banks, defending the stability of the fiat currencies.

JPM is at the forehead of the enforcement of this policy.

Simultaneously, as seen in the embassy cables published by Wikileaks, China was aware of the manipulation of the prices of precious metals and raw materials by the banks on Wall Street and that these manipulations were done to its detriment.

China decided to change the game.

In 2007, an American analyst of Chinese origin, Song Hongbing, published "Currency Wars". In this book, the author explains how some European private bankers took control of the global economy at the dawn of the nineteenth century and are now spearheading a permanent currency war. This book was sold to 200,000 readers and has generated over 400,000 pirated copies. The mandarins of the CPC and of the largest Chinese companies were required to read it. In his book, Song Hongbing recommended China to change its monetary reserves from fiat currencies to precious metals. This wise advice seemed to have been followed, as we will see.

How China Squeezed JPM

China, through CITIC asked JPM to sell 300 million ounces of silver on the future of COMEX. At the same time, China bought 300 million ounces anonymously from the London market through Asian Hedge Funds. This huge sale of silver on the COMEX in New York brought down the prices, allowing China to purchase real physical silver cheaply in London. In the London Metal Exchange (LME), a buyer could ask for delivery 48 hours after his purchase. China, well informed about the inflow of gold and silver into the LME warehouses, organized raids there for delivery to be made as soon as a shipment of silver arrived.

When the COMEX authorities obliged JPM to deliver the quantity of silver sold on the "futures", the bank asked CITIC to supply his warehouses in New York with the 300 million ounces of silver that had been sold on his behalf. CITIC then gave JPM the acknowledgement of debt of the 300 million ounces signed by the Federal Reserve, asking them to honor that delivery and append their signature. This episode, in my humble opinion took place in August 2009. Some more light should be thrown on this story.

We recall that in June 2009, when Geithner was giving a talk in a university in China and repeatedly mentioned the strength of the dollar and the U.S. Treasury bonds, he triggered a general hilarity among the students, probably encouraged by their supervisors. This event was widely spread in China on the internet, with the blessing of Chinese authorities.

Geithner totally lost face that day. In China, "losing face" is worse than death.

Keynes's BANCOR

On March 23 2009, a few days before the G20 summit, Zhou Xiaochuan, governor of the Chinese Central Bank published a text in Chinese and English on the bank's website so that it had the greatest possible impact. "**Reform the international monetary system**".

You can find this document on the BIS's website.

"**The desirable goal of reforming the international monetary system, therefore is to create an international reserve currency that is disconnected from individual nations and is able to remain stable in the long run, this removing the inherent deficiencies caused by using credit-based national currencies.**"

Zhou writes also : "Back in the 1940's, Keynes had already proposed to introduce an international currency unit named "**Bancor**", based on the value of **30 representative commodities**. Unfortunately, the proposal was not accepted"... "the Keynesian approach may have been more farsighted."

The Chinese will could not be more clear. They want a kind of bimetallism with Gold, Silver, Copper, Oil ... etc.

You could stop reading this book here. Everything had been said. Silver is **NOT** just an industrial metal.

Throughout 2009, journalists wrote at regular intervals on the impending sale of IMF gold, and China's desire to strengthen its gold reserves to balance its monetary reserves and stop depending on its U.S. dollar reserves. But IMF sold the gold to India, to some small countries like Sri Lanka and Mauritius without giving the Chinese a chance to bid.

China announced that it had at that time, **1054 tons of gold**, or the equivalent of 1.7% of its monetary reserves, but this percentage was still ridiculous compared to that of some countries like France (2400 tons), Germany (3.400 tons), Italy (2400 tons) or the United States (8.100 tons). The latter were then described in the U.S. accounts book as "deep storage gold", but we must understand that most of the gold that had been extracted from the ground, the Fort Knox reserves, had been sold in 1968. All these observers fantasized about the thousands of tons of gold that China was getting ready to buy to catch up with the Western countries' reserves and balance its accounts.

According to analysts and speculators, the price of gold could only soar with such a buyer to sustain its price.

Six months after the G20 summit, China, the world's leading refiner, banned the export of silver metal. You could not find a single article to make the connection between IMF's 200 tons of gold, that China did not seek to buy and the **4,800 tons of silver banned from export**.

One of the oldest civilizations in the world, who always had **silver as monetary standard**, blocked the export of its metal and encouraged its citizens to hoard it in bullions and silver coins…

This should indeed get us into some serious thinking.

Russia, China, India and Brazil united to fight against the unipolar world that the Anglo-Americans are seeking to perpetuate. South Africa, major producer of precious metals, Iran and the United Arab Emirates, gas and oil producers, have joined this core group to try to establish a new monetary order.

2009

Three months later, in July 2009, a G8 meeting was held in Italy. The various participants received coins samples supposed to become the future world currency "United in diversity". This photo of Medvedev brandishing one of the gold coins saying, "this is the currency for tomorrow" spread around the world.

In the highlights of the official announcements, the press stated that the coin was worth €2,800, but it weighed only 15.55 grams of pure gold, or €180 per gram. A gram of gold was worth €32.8. I concluded that the price of gold could be multiplied by 5.4 with the monetary reform. That means the 20 francs Napoleon gold coin at €1,000 and an ounce of gold could be worth $8,000.

A wall of silence reigned over the silver coins given with the gold coins at Aquila. No photo, anywhere, no mention of weight or price, yet **150 silver coins were given with the 20 gold coins.**

The silver coin shown above, to the right, was never issued. Once again, the total silence of the media and politicians on these silver coins, speaks for itself. It's "Omerta"!

Note the ratio of 7.5.

In 2008, silver production in China stood at 9,587 tons,

representing 308 million ounces. The export quotas were 4,800 tons or 154 million ounces in 2008.

Net Monthly China Silver Imports (kg)						
	2010	2009	2008	2007	2006	2005
Jan	204,653	-65,470	163,339	-46,805	-70,849	-201,134
Feb	260,615	-38,279	46,246	-145,764	-52,372	-232,463
Mar	415,361	-1,197	-35,123	117,395	-200,770	-410,228
Apr	302,090	132,507	127,307	-160,452	-96,107	-226,929
May	353,726	49,753	275,710	23,552	-144,677	-234,016
Jun	325,477	3,438	246,189	-289,271	83,335	-270,668
Jul	419,286	67,657	130,870	232,151	-49,916	-272,292
Aug	205,721	352,004	320,853	406,077	-80,782	-222,724
Sep	282,019	-34,035	437,985	469,040	-97,034	-176,773
Oct	191,770	148,158	412,260	403,714	85,291	-218,745
Nov	211,315	171,813	-2,380	-20,968	-251,954	-229,989
Dec	303,362	90,476	-158,722	129,933	-199,366	-238,694
Ann	3,475,394	876,825	1,964,534	1,118,602	-1,075,201	-2,934,661

This table shows that China started purchasing silver from the markets since 2007, when China was the third world producer. China has therefore been accumulating strategic and/or monetary reserves since 2007.

1,118+1,964+876+3,475=5,557 tons of net import, to which must be added the 4,800 tons/year banned for export by decree in August 2009.

China's currency reserves on the eve of January 2013, should be about 2,000 tons of gold and 15,000 tons of silver which could be valued as follows after the monetary reform:

Low Hypothesis (price from Jim Willie)
2,000 tons of gold = 64 M Oz @ $3,000 /Oz = $192 billion
20,000 tons of silver = 640 M Oz @ $200/Oz = $128 billion
Or 10% of their foreign exchange reserves of $3,000 billion

High Hypothesis (see **Amero valuation**)
2,000 tons of gold = 64 M Oz @ $10,000. / Oz = $640 billion
2,000 tons of silver = 640 M Oz @ $1,000/Oz = $640 billion
or 42% of their foreign exchange reserves.

Xia Bin, one of the officials of the Chinese Central Bank, during an interview with a business magazine, China Daily, in January 2011 said:

"China must increase its gold and silver reserves."

Have you ever heard Greenspan, Bernanke, Trichet or Draghi talking about silver reserves from the Fed or ECB?

NEVER!

AUGUST 2009

Bill Winter was JPM's CEO for risk-management. Regarded as one of the most brilliant men on WS and the City, he had been suddenly fired after 25 years in the company, "thrown out of the window" as reported by Reuters. Bill Winter's violent expulsion in September 2009 took place a few days after **China's announcement authorizing its companies to default on derivatives linked to commodities, on August 31 2009.**

JPM had always been at the forefront of innovation in derivatives. These new financial markets created around 1997, experienced a spectacular growth, allowing JPM to generate new phenomenal sales figures. Blythe Masters was one of the inventors of these sophisticated products. Bill Winters was the head of the department that caused a tremendous growth of the bank. JPM owned about 40% of the shares of this market, which rose from 0 to 600,000 billion USD between 1997 and 2010. The financial bubble of the century!

It is obvious that if there was any personality in the world who knew the exact conditions of JPM derivatives on commodities and especially, those hedging JPM's "short positions" on silver, it was Bill Winter. If there was any person in the world who knew the exact relationships binding JPM and China on white metal, it was him.

He knew the exact quantities available in the London warehouses, those of COMEX, SLV and all other ETF on the planet...and therefore, he knew exactly at what point in time and the extent to which there was cornering on silver.

In June 2010, Bill Winter was appointed to the restricted management board of the UK Banking Commission. Approached several times to assume leadership of the various investment banks, including the Royal Bank of Scotland, he refused all these prestigious offers saying that he would no longer work in a bank.

In August 2010, the financial press saw the establishment of an equivalent of "Black Rock" together with a brilliant financier of the City, **Clive Cowdery**. The latter, after selling his insurance consulting firm, set up a new insurance company for the Rothschild Group.

In late 2010, the press revealed that Bill Winter had reached an agreement with Lord Rothschild, leader of the English branch of the famous banking family in Europe.

Winters created a global company with an alternative management, Renshaw Bay, of which he owned 50% and was both the President and CEO. Its partners, RIT Capital Partners, chaired by Lord Rothschild, and Reinet, controlled by Johan Rupert, shared the rest of the stocks.

Johan Ruppert is a South African billionaire and a major shareholder of the Richemont Group, the world's number three producer of luxury products with brands like Cartier or Van Cleef, beside Reinet Investments. John Ruppert is also a gold tycoon in South Africa.

Is this a battle between finance dynasty's leaders?

Rockefeller against Rothschild? As you see, Bill Winters had the best introductions to the highest levels of global finance. He will not just play on the small silver market, even if the upward potential of white metal is phenomenal.

For the record, the silver market officially represented 889 million ounces in 2009, when an ounce was sold at an average price of $14.67.

So, the silver marked in 2009 was worth about 13 billion dollars, only one thousandth of the volume of the derivatives traded daily on the foreign exchange market. If we consider Bill Winters' two current partners, Richemont's market capitalization is 29 billion dollars plus that of Reinet which is 6.6 billion dollars for the first. Then that of RIT Capital Partners is 3 billion dollars, for the second. It is obvious that the new group, Renshaw Bay, will have no difficulty at all in raising capital to weigh heavily on the small silver market. It is recalled that in October 2009, China, leading producer of silver on the planet (mining production+refining) banned the export of white metal. According to my calculation, it was 154 million ounces that China withdrew from the world market. Figures of net silver imports from China show that it was even heavier on the market.

It was 3,475 tons, equivalent to 111 million ounces which was added to the 154 million ounces, that is, 265 million ounces of silver monopolized by China at the expense of the world market. 30% out of the 889 million ounces available supply in 2009 was melted in 2010, bringing the actual silver supply to 624 million ounces in 2010. At $14.67 an ounce, the physical silver bullion market in the West was then only worth $9 billion.

In 2011, the average price of an ounce of silver was $35.12. The whole silver market weight only **22 billion dollars.**

Jason Hommel, famous analyst of the silver market, pleaded his case time and again with his "dear billionaires of the world" arguing that if only one of them invested a small part of his wealth, he could blow up the small silver market.

He compared the silver market with the $18,000 billion financial products. The annual physical investment was represented by only a small part of paper money, the virtual money. In a market where the supply has not been able to meet the demand for more than 70 years, if the investment in silver was doubled, according to Jason Hommel, it would be enough to send the price of silver to $200 an ounce.

Certainly, Bill Winters had greater power of conviction than Jason Hommel, to persuade a few handpicked billionaires. Playing of China's monetary policy, Winters and his allies quickly doubled the price of silver. These players, like China, exploited by accumulating physical silver bullions, the most formidable and efficient leverage to skyrocket the price of silver.

ESPIONAGE AND CYBER-WAR

Sergey Aleynikov earned a good living. As a Russian analyst-programmer, he emigrated to the United States in 1990, where his talents were quickly recognized. Recruited by Goldman Sachs, for $400,000 a year, he took two years to write a confidential software, which would allow the bank to purchase and sell in nanotrading. An extremely vicious system!

When a client gives a purchase order, the bank buy a few fractions of seconds before reselling the title to the customer, after taking a nano-commission in addition to the official one. The same for sale. Obviously, this system demand powerful computers but also top quality connectivity so that the bank's orders arrives on WS market ahead of other competitors. This is why many trading companies concentrated on the immediate environment of WS computers to earn a few millionths in seconds. Sergey's software was of this kind, which put Goldman Sachs a few months ahead of the bank's competitors.

In June 2009, Sergey left GS for a start-up in Chicago Teza Technologies, which tripled his salary overnight. Sergey left GS but he kept a copy of the nanotrading software's sources which he had created. He even downloaded a copy on a German server, which was recognized but charges of industrial espionage were leveled against him.

Some market commentators even said that Sergey sold this software to Germany and Russia, to enable them to counter Goldman Sachs on their own ground. Goldman Sachs got Sergey arrested and tried. GS won the trial in the first instance and lost on appeal in March 2012. Sergey was then released and he could return to his country with the honors of his motherland, if he so desired.

To complicate this story, Teza Technologies, which was obviously specialized in nanotrading, recruited a new programmer-analyst in May 2010. This newcomer, Yihao Ben Pu, is as Chinese as Sergey is Russian.

Obviously Yihao made a wild type copy of the sources of this nanotrading software and downloaded it on a Chinese server. Arrested in turn, Yihao confessed that he wanted to set up a hedge fund in China. Obviously this story of Hedge Fund in Asia was just a hoax.

Yihao offered China a tool to counter the western bankers on their own ground.

These trading tools allowed China and Russia, in particular, to dominate the gold market in the first half of 2012, by countering in nanotrading the gold swaps between the major Bullion Banks (JPM, GS, UBS, …). It has been a real carnage as we will see it further.

SEPTEMBER 2010

After the sharp rise to $21 in early 2008, the price of silver dropped drastically until November following the crash related to the Lehman bankruptcy. The increase took nearly one year before returning to the price in January 2008. The price then fell in November 2009 due to the resistance, and again in May and June. It was not until September 2010, that silver finally broke the resistance to $19.96, paving the way for new highs.

This figure is a consolidation triangle. The rise from the lowest is performed in successive waves in a very distinct bullish channel.

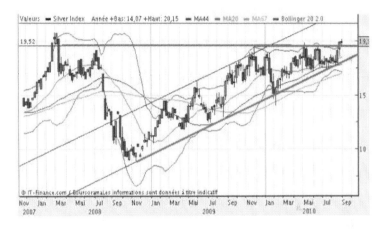

The increase after the break in the resistance of a consolidation triangle was always at least equal to the depth of the consolidation. An increase to a minimum of $30 was therefore expected from September 2010.

A Major Silver Event on September 3 2010.

On September 3 2010, the COMEX dealers were able to deliver only 45,000 ounces instead of 14 million ounces they were supposed to deliver. This was a very rare event.

CYRILLE JUBERT

Beginning of shortage

The lack of delivery note reminded Bill Murphy, founder and chairman of GATA, of a similar event that occurred in May 1987 on the copper market. He then purchased all the possible options to raise the price of the metal.

In April 1987, the copper price was $1,483 per ton, which was at the top of the range at that time.

In May, the price shot up to $1,518, then $1,693 in July... $2,866 in December 1987...

In December 1988, copper cost $3,496 before it took a downward trend.

There was a 230% increase over 20 months.

The 230% increase raised hopes that silver could rise up to $46 an ounce.

Why was this a strong signal ?

Traders in the metal markets paid the storage, security and insurance fees for their silver bullions and bars. These costs burdening upon the potential capital gains, traders better ask for the "delivery note" earlier from the vendors, and gave it to the buyer who then pays the storage fees.

The last day to request for the delivery of the contract in September was August 31st 2010. Vendors had a 30 days grace period to notify buyers through this "delivery notice" that their metal had been delivered. The absence of a "delivery notice" showed that the sellers had sold metal they did not have in stock and that they found it very difficult to get the quantities required by their buyers. The open interest of September 2010 was 3,002 contracts. Each day of the second week of September, deliveries were made in small quantities. There were 1,544 forward contracts before the end of the month so that the market would not be put in "default". The contracts were for 5,000 ounces but the vendors sought for 7.72 million ounces including 230 tons of silver before the end of the month.

On September 7 2010, these short sellers leased 2.3 million ounces of silver to COMEX customers, or the equivalent of 460 contracts, in order to meet their obligations. These rental expenses in addition to security fees (etc.), made the operation very expensive for the seller.

The COMEX dealers published at that time that they had 54.1 million ounces of silver in their warehouses but they were unable to deliver 13million ounces. (end of quote of my letter of September 2010)

Indeed, this first technical signal led to the wave of increase expected in 2010 and 2011.

The price shot up from $20 to $48 in 8 months.

Israel Friedman, mentor of Ted Butler wrote in 2006:

The Three stage of the coming silver shortage

"Price Points and the Coming Silver Squeeze.
To define what I mean by shortage in silver, I say categorically that I'm not interested in the level of world inventories of silver, COMEX inventories and the guru's stories. I am only interested to know if the users are receiving their shipments of silver on time. When a delay of silver shipments occurs, and affects most the users, I will consider this as a shortage.

1) Pre-shortage: users will have to wait between 3 to 6 extra weeks for their shipments. Then the prices can rise to $20-30

2) Shortage: users will wait between 6 weeks and 4 months for silver. Then, the price can rise above the old all-time highs of $50.

3) Super shortage: users have to wait more than 4 months for their silver shipments. The prices will range from $100 to prices you won't believe.

If this last scenario occurs, and gold has plenty of supply, the price of silver, at a minimum, will equal the price of gold. And my crystal ball tells me that silver can exceed the price of gold by a great deal.

You should be asking, how did I calculate the prices for the different stages?

My calculation is very conservative. I only take into consideration the future deficits between the producers and users, which is running currently at around 50 million ounces annually. I also take into consideration that private investors have 400 million ounces in bullion and coins that they will sell in some stages.
1) Pre-shortage I think investors will agree to sell 50 million ounces between $20 and $30.
2) Shortage Investors will sell 200 million ounces at a price ranging between $30 and $100.
3) Super shortage The remaining 150 million ounces at this stage will be sold at really shocking prices.

These prices are very conservative, in my opinion, because they don't take into consideration the naked shorts, new investments, or those banks worldwide that sold silver certificates without real silver backing, only derivatives backing. (by Israel Friedman? *The three stages of silver shortage*) (end of quote)

The various stages of shortage have some relationship with the four bullish price channels in the graph below. One can however wonder whether the re-monetization by some BRIC central banks, will both trigger shortage and thus rise in prices.

This is a graph of a trader dated May 2011, showing the potential silver targets.

You will find $72, $200 and $1,000 of the different analyses, but also **$9**, the base figure, that some prophets of doom are considering for the second half of 2013. Anything can happen before the monetary reform since we are experiencing a banking, monetary and systemic crisis.

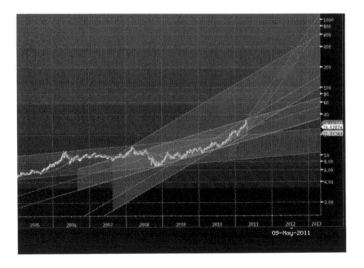

Prices of silver in Shanghai on May 15 2011:
- one ounce silver panda coin = 480 Yuan ($77)
- bullion of 31 grams of silver = 650 Yuan ($100)

On the same day, silver paper was worth $34 on the COMEX.

SEPTEMBER 2010 - APRIL 2011

On the London metal exchange, insiders observed that many traders, who were Asian, German or Emirati, without any apparent link between them, seemed to have taken action together to carry out raids on stocks of precious metals. These raids were even described as "military thoroughness" in their execution.

These raiders seemed informed about the operations inside the warehouses. They knew the exact time precious metals arrived, and as soon as a cargo has been stored, these raiders arrived in their armored vehicles, accompanied by armed guards and an army of sworn lawyers and judges to enforce their rights to remove the gold or silver bars purchased from the market.

Tension rose between the accomplices of Wall Street and the City about the manipulation of prices of precious metals: JPM and HSBC. The former accusing the latter for being traitors and selling themselves to the Chinese. JPM and HSBC shared roles in 2004 at the creation of GLD and SLV ETF. One was the official custodian of the gold reserves, while the other was responsible for the silver reserves. These roles has been sometimes reversed in the secondary storage.

If JPM is a bank with American origin, HSBC, whose full name is Hong-Kong Shanghai Banking Corporation, is a British bank, which had its dominant position in China in the late 19th Century.

The tension in the oligarchy appeared in broad daylight in mid-September 2010 with a violent sweep at the top of HSBC. The President and Chief Executive Officer were dismissed mercilessly.

Mike Geoghegan, Chief executive Officer of HSBC was removed after 37 years in banking and unique in the annals, at the very moment when Stephen Green officially resigned to work with the government. Those who resigned were replaced by former Goldman Sachs. The Wall Street banksters wanted to stay close to their accomplices in the City.

Silver throughout History

A few months after the JPM bank threw Bill Winters out of the window, Blythe Masters, head of JPM derivatives trading and one of the initiators of derivatives, fired the entire team of traders off, including the head of precious metals trading at JPM.

These traders knew the market from the inside like Bill Winters. They knew that JPM had a mountain of silver derivatives, equivalent to **7 years of mining production.** These derivatives were a real danger for the bank. The more the price of silver rose, the more it risked shooting up sharply. Considering the size of JPM, the price of silver had systemic importance. The old JPM traders took advantage of this situation.

These traders bought contracts for 5,000 ounces of silver on the COMEX and requested delivery, knowing that JPM would not be able to deliver. The bank had to negotiate with the traders, asking them not to demand the delivery of their silver, offering a high premium.

These traders were like the Lernaean Hydra. Whenever you cut one head, seven more would grow in its place the following month.

On the expiry date in September 2010, JPM, unable to deliver the silver requested for, had to buy **483 contracts** with 20% premium. The traders with initial investment of $50 million collected the $10 million premium. They increased their investment at each maturity, in the following months.

At the maturity in December, JPM had to buy **3,583 contracts** (7.4 times more), worth **$837 million** because the price of silver had increased from $20 to $30.

Traders with more prominent position demanded a premium of 30%. Their premium rose in December 2010 to $300 million.

At the March 2011 deadline, JPM was forced to purchase **49,725 contracts** which were 13.87 times more than in December. The traders reinvested 100% of their capital again.

JPM supported a Ponzi scheme which fought against itself.

The traders united against JPM released this on the internet:

"There were rumors on WS that Blythe offered a 30 to 50% premium above current forward contracts. One of the group leaders said.
Friday February 25, the group decided to request for their delivery on Monday because they did not want to settle for the 30% premium while the price of silver had been capped at $33.50. Some said Blythe Masters had already offered a 50% premium. In our case, it was very far from the truth. We got 80% premium. That's the truth.
More than $50 on condition that we sold all our contracts. Our partners even planned the threat of systemic bankruptcy like Herstatt bank. (see Wikipedia).
*They even admitted that they would not be able to give us 20 million ounces, and that if we remained in a position awaiting delivery, they would ensure delivery to all others except us, before making default on us, and this could have put us in the uncomfortable position of "unsecured creditors". They told us that they could not allow a request for delivery of 5,000 contracts because they could barely deliver 4,000. As Vito Corleone stated in "The Godfather", "**I will make them an offer that they cannot refuse**"... and in fact, we did not refuse, since we have achieved the goal we set from the start.*
Silver-paper might struggle to exceed $36, if JPM & associates are ready to

pay more than $50 an ounce to dissuade anyone from requesting for delivery. If the price of « silver paper » remained under $36, it means the losses from the derivatives would be fatal for JPM, because they had short sold the equivalent of 7 years of production. This was the main reason behind the suppression of the price of silver.

We don't see any reason why they didn't allow the price of silver to increase since they are happy to pay handsome prices for the contracts, to show the world that few people really care about delivery.

For us, COMEX may not be missing anything except the 4,000 forward contracts pending delivery. We are really anxious to know how far the price of paper silver will rise in this transfer." Posted by Louis Cypher.

In February 2011, JPM bought silver at $33.5 + 80% premium = $60.3.

The operation cost the bank between **13 and 15 billion dollars**.

The Open Interest on silver in late March was 135,654 contracts and the price of silver shot up to **$48 in late April.**

Silver at $36
JPM's exponential losses

The ex-JPM traders indicated that *the derivatives on JPM silver involved exponential losses when the price exceeded $36.*

The JPM « short » positions in April 2011 were 150 million ounces on COMEX against 180 million ounces in August 2010.

For every $10 increase in the price of silver, JPM lost $1.5 billion. But due to the way in which JPM derivatives were made, the bank's losses were multiplied by 5, if the price of silver exceeded $36.

These losses were multiplied by 8 when it was over $45. Indeed, as soon as the price reached $36, provisions were activated to amplify the losses.

Rumor has it that JPM might lose $40 billion, if the price of silver reaches $50.

When the price of silver exceeded $36, JPM took action and began to reflect on the losses. For every dollar gained by silver, the action had to lose 70 cents. When the price of silver reached $60, JPM was worth $10. The increase in the price of silver could ruin the JPM Bank. (Extracts from *Revelations of defectors from JPM*)

We have not heard from the team of traders since then. Were their contracts redeemed in April?

Does this team of traders work with **Bill Winters** and Clive Cowdery or with only Winters in his new company, Renshaw Bay, together with Lord Rothschild, and Johan Rupert?

There has been no news about these traders since February 2011.

THE RED FLAG

We recall that the Rothschild's left the presidency of the London Gold Market in 2004, at the time when the first ETF, the famous GLD was launched. As you know, GLD is an electronic fraud abusing of fractional reserve banking, in the same way as SLV, launched in 2006. One of the main architects of this fraud is the Rockefeller Bank, JPM-Chase.

The famous family of European bankers had always been on excellent terms with the left-wing parties and trade unions, mainly funded secretly by the subsidies of the various factions of International finance.

In August 2010, two of the largest silver mines on the planet, in Bolivia including San Bartolome owned by CDE, were on strike.

In February 2011, all the gold and silver mines in Peru went on strike. In March, the third silver mine in the world, San Cristobal in Bolivia, went on strike for a month and Bolivian silver was totally blocked.

From January to April 2011, Chili's ore export capacity reduced greatly due to the deterioration of the lifting equipment in the main port. Certainly, copper was the most affected but 70% of silver is obtained during refining copper, lead & zinc ore.

These minor incidents taken in isolation have very little significance, but they followed one after the other as go-slow strikes, making supply more difficult for the already hyper tensed silver market. We recall that Sprott Management had to wait for two and a half months for the delivery of its 22 million ounces of silver. To succeed, it bypassed COMEX, and purchased silver directly to the mines and refineries around the world.

The shortage worsened the successive social movements. Fellow union members waved the red flag, emblem of the Rothschild's. Were they manipulated?

The Rothschild's banks control RIO TINTO, one of the biggest mining groups on the planet and a copper producer. They can slow down the flow of silver coming to the market as they wish, thus jeopardizing JPM-Chase already struggling. Have they done it?

FORCED CONSOLIDATIONS OF MAY 2011

COMEX, supported by the Federal Reserves reproduced identically in May and August 2011, the various measures put in place in 1980 to block the Short Squeeze organized by the Hunt brothers.

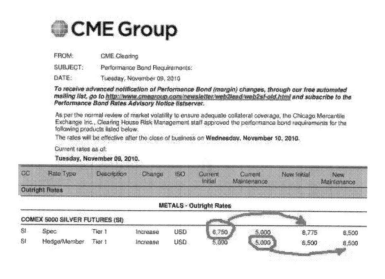

A fraud of the monetary authorities

There were 5 successive margin increases in 8 days in May 2011, to force the consolidation.

On the 4th of August 2011, there was a further increase of 12%.

Maintenance costs, which were $5,000 in November 2010 soared to $12,000. The required margins which were $6,750 was then $ 14,513.

With the standard contract of 5,000 ounces at $40 or $200,000 per contract, the investor was supposed to have a deposit of $14,513+$12,000, or $26,513 or 13% of capital. There was a further increase on Friday, September 23.

The leverage effect on COMEX fell to 6.

This gigantic manipulation of COMEX in May was doubled by monstrous insider trading which should have sent many American market leaders behind the bars but it did not happen.

Even though the CME massively increased security deposits, JPM sold nearly 300 million ounces or all the SLV virtual stocks in bulk on the market, causing a collapse in prices.

For four years, the CFTC carried out an investigation in vain to find out whether or not there were market manipulations on silver prices. In August 2012, the Financial Times disclosed that the CFTC abandoned the survey when they were unable to find sufficient evidence to allow the American law courts to take a decision.

There are none so deaf as those who do not want to hear.

The CFTC came up against the national interest. Silver is a systemic monetary standard. The manipulators that the CFTC was not allowed to bring to justice were the Federal Reserve, the U.S. Treasury and the various Central Banks who were coordinating the monetary system at that time.

End of the story.

CYRILLE JUBERT

THE CHINESE, SAVINGS AND GAMBLING

If westerners think gold is the best metal to guard against inflation, to the Chinese population silver is the only important thing. It is their historic standard.

It was not until August 2009, that China authorized by decree individuals to hoard precious metals. The decree was followed immediately in September by a fully-fledged national communication campaign pushing investors towards the 500g, 1k, 2k or 5 kilos silver coins and bullions.

"The price of silver today is extremely cheap compared to gold.", said JT's announcer.

At that time, about 60 ounces of silver was needed to purchase an ounce of gold. For the record, The gold/silver ratio dropped to 31 in May 2011, proving that the Chinese government was right.

Searching directly on some Chinese websites, in Chinese, I came across many sites talking about the opening of the precious metals market to ordinary citizens of the People's Republic of China calling this change in domestic policy:

"The Second Revolution"

This terminology has all the communist dialectics and it reminds us of Mao Tse Tung's "GREAT LEAP FORWARD".

For the record, in the late 50s and the early 60s, the Chinese authorities wanted to trigger a forced march towards agricultural and industrial revolution. Among others, Mao set a goal to catch up with England's steel production within 15 years. Production was massively increased at that time, but the very rudimentary conditions under which this was done, produced very poor quality steel.

The important thing is that the terminology, "Second Revolution", suggests a genuine political will of China.

Hoarding by the Chinese masses was supposed to limit the amount of silver in circulation, and thus help to fight against uncontrolled inflation, unless I am mistaken.

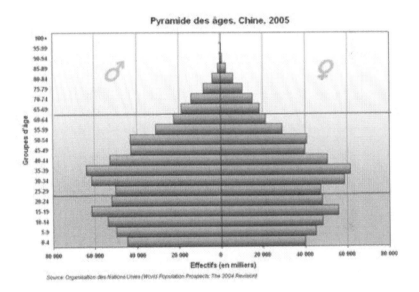

This graph represents the Chinese population. The active population alone, aged between 25 and 64 years, represent approximately 500 million people.

The Chinese savings rate ranges between 30% and 40% of average income. Imagine the potential in terms of demand for gold and silver!

According to a study conducted in 2009, (source Questinnaore.net), "the average income of 10% richest Chinese is 139,000 Yuan", or 20,000 USD today.

Obviously, it is the richest Chinese who have the most means to save. Let's take only the 30% saving capacity.

(10% of the active population = 50 million people) x (30% of 20,000 USD) = 300 billion US.D

If 10% of the savings of 10% of the richest of the active Chinese population invested in the monetary standard in the main Middle Empire, that would be 30 billion US dollars, an amount to be compared with all the silver markets that had not already been monopolized by China, or 10 billion USD.

Success breeds success and chance breeds chance.

The pioneers who followed the government's directive in September 2009 by investing in silver, can only boast of having done a great deal, and therefore, find more followers.

China is becoming increasingly voracious and hungry for silver.

The volume of trade on SGE shot up from 20,206 tons in March to 33,293 tons in April, or a little over 1070 million ounces. A further 65% increase from March to April…

In 2011, the Chinese limited the rise in intraday rate for silver to 8%.

On the 22nd of July 2011, on the occasion of the opening of the Hong Kong Market, the HKMEX, the Chinese authorities clearly expressed their stance.

"On the commodities market, participants in the region have had to rely so far on the western trading markets in terms of price. Our new platform will allow Asia to have a say in the determination of the price of commodities."

The largest shareholder in this market, Hong Kong, is a member of the Russian oligarchy, Deripaska, President of RUSAL, leader in aluminum. This man is Nathaniel Rothschild's nominee, who appears like Rusal's advisor at different levels. HKMEX is now fully integrated in the overall current system.

In December 2011, China strictly prohibited the trading of the futures of precious metal elsewhere other than the Shanghai market (SGE). There was an upsurge in small private markets, like the backrooms of the numerous illegal gambling dens and it was time to put them in good order.

China produced 360 tons of gold in 2011. An increase of 6% year by year.

Hong Kong exported **427,87 tons** of gold in mainland China in 2011 against 118.9 tons in the previous year. **The volume multiplied by 3.6.**

Chinese domestic demand for physical gold (bullion, coins and jewelry) rose to 639.2 tons in 2011.

For the record, the RPC banned the export of gold, therefore China hoarded to guard against inflation as well as increase its cash reserves in precious metals.

CYRILLE JUBERT

CHINA'S BANKING REVOLUTION
31/12/2011

In 2008, China authorized the population to acquire gold. From August 2009, the authorities encouraged the Chinese to invest in silver, which after the message delivered by the TV news was extremely cheap compared to gold.

Since ETF gold and silver were introduced by the Chinese banks in mid-2011, the latter advised their customers to the cash on their account in Yuan, gold, or silver.

Thus, in 2011, in about just 6 months, the ICBC Bank sold 300 tons, or 10 million ounces to its customers. The figure expected for the full year 2011 was 20 million ounces, or more than 2.5% of the world's total mining production. But so far, only 5% of the customers have used this possibility. Analysts believe that the demand could be multiplied by 3 or 4 next year and rise up to 10% of the silver produced in the world in 2012. They also believe that in the following years, this demand will continue to grow to 30/40% of the demand. Is this a large scale trap?

ICBC has 240 million customers, 5% of them or 12 million customers are already using the possibility of keeping their cash in gold or silver and this number is expected to double in the coming months. The gold and silver is mostly virtual. It is gold and silver paper. If the customers were worried about the banking or monetary situation and requested for physical delivery, and if indeed they had the opportunity, it would probably cause a short squeeze of anthology across China.

China has tested its Monetary Reform

In 2009, after that China asked the G20 to reform the monetary system, the BPoC created the Chinese Copper Financing Deals. Banks and companies could get loans from the biggest Chinese banks with commodities with high value to density ratio such as gold, silver, copper, nickel, steel and even soybean.

Las! This has led to a gigantic financial bubble because of re-hypothecation loop and treachery. This bubble is about to burst at the end of 2013 in China. The government of China changed the rules of this CCFD in May. It brought a real crash in Soybeans markets and it could lead to a crash in copper and perhaps silver markets.

At the bank, the Chinese are already changing their Yuan against gold and silver. Just as was the case in the United States from 1776 to 1934 or in Europe since the creation of the germinal franc. The main difference is that the gold and silver rates fluctuate and the gold/silver ratio is not fixed.

So, by encouraging the Chinese request, China is increasing its national reserves whether they are monetary or industrial, putting itself at an advantage at the international level for future production and cash exchanges. Chinese savings are capable of transmuting dollars into precious metals, **while still remaining under government control.**

At the same time, it cleverly took advantage of the banksters' game on Wall Street and the City of London to defend the fiat money in general and the dollar in particular, by beating down the prices of precious metals. The Chinese and their allies took advantage of the reduced prices and bought precious metals to get rid of their billions of dollars in reserve.

By doing so, **China is weakening the dollar.**

Even more effective were the bilateral agreements with Russia, Brazil, Pakistan, Kazakhstan, India and Japan, not to bill them in dollars after trade deals, thus further weakening the dollar on a very large scale. The latest agreements to date with Iran and the United Arab Emirates in which the latter agreed to charge their oil and gas purchases in Yuan just broke the 1973 petro-dollars agreements.

China and the Tungsten Market

In the 70s and 80s, China flooded the planet with tungsten, leading to the collapse of its world price, thus eradicating all competing mines and creating a quasi-monopoly of China on the global production of tungsten.

Once the tungsten concentrate market was under control, China shattered the chain of tungsten transformers to its own advantage. Chinese production of tungsten was on a very small scale due to the large number of small producers. The objective was to bring producers together and reorganize production completely, through internal mergers and acquisitions from abroad.

Then the PRC reduced the overall production of tungsten by limiting the mining licenses in 2001 and implementing export quotas, allowing the authorities to control the world price of tungsten!

The export quotas were designed to adjust supply and demand fairly. China can now create a global shortage on this market at any time and impose its prices.

The strategy adopted by the Chinese indicates that they are very formidable chess players, planning their movements well in advance.

PAN ASIA GOLD EXCHANGE

China was supposed to open a precious metals market in the summer of 2012, known as the PAGE, acronym of Pan Asia Gold Exchange. PAGE should be accessible on the international stage with the price of gold quoted in RMB. On this market, the commodity was supposed to be in 10 ounce gold bullions, numbered and cataloged and then stored in warehouses under the responsibility of the Chinese Central Bank. This was not the market for the "futures", because transactions were completed every day and each bullion actually changed hands. There were no virtual bullions unlike the London or New York markets. Gold is rare and the interplay of supply and demand for real physical gold was completely disassociated from the prices at COMEX and LBMA where the prices were manipulated downwards.

The private shareholders of PAGE appeared to be Anglo-American financiers. In fact, the structure is now quite obscure. PAGE is perhaps only an illusion, a dream.

China had to delay for one year this somewhat unclear negotiation whose motives and counterparties are not yet known. It is possible that we had a silver market instead of a gold market based on the model of PAGE which should primarily open. When this Asian financial center will start booming, metal prices should took an upward trend.

Considering that China is the third producer of silver and the fact that it now holds the largest stock of precious metals as the currency reserves in its central bank, it is likely that it will leave the price of silver to appreciate. The issue is for us to know the proportion, not with respect to a particular "funny fiat money", but **with regards to gold**, on one hand, and wages on the other.

For the record, in the 16th and early 17th Century, **the gold/silver ratio was 5 in China against 10 in Europe**. The ratio was 5 in Japan in 1850, against 17 elsewhere, and during the Meiji era before the opening of the Japanese archipelago.

Considering the current ratio, the Chinese authorities are right for telling the people that silver is very cheap compared to gold. This reminder of the past gives some weight to this prospective study of the gold / silver ratio.

The PAGE has not been launched, but the Shanghai Gold Exchange seems to be the world most dynamic metal market today. **They deliver more gold each day than the COMEX in a month.**

Gold-Silver Ratio

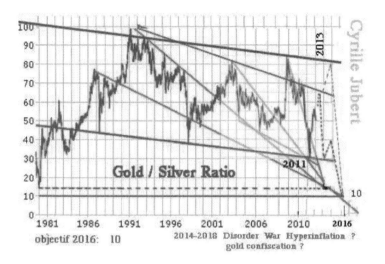

My January 2011 study well anticipated the decline in the ratio to 30 then the blocking witnessed in May, when the ratio came to bounce on the resistance (red diagonal) that had already blocked silver in 1987 and 1999.

This ratio consolidated then between 1/50 and 1/63 for 18 months.

In concrete terms, gold enabled you to maintain your purchasing power while silver enriched you throughout the phase of decline in the gold/silver ratio.

Gold-Silver Ratio II

In early May 2012, a French analyst presented a study on the gold/silver ratio on YouTube, making a connection between the 1968 to 1980 ratio and that of the current period.

Silver throughout History

According to this analyst, the current figure reproduces the 70s/80s scheme. It only lacked a leg drop to 17 of the ratio in the short term.

In my opinion, at that time, we were not at the same point in the figure. We were climbing to point "S".

Monetary disturbances both in Europe and the United States led to a massive rise in the price of gold, while that of silver was pushed down artificially and classified as speculative commodity. The ratio is increasing to a new excess. In August 2013, it seems to me that we are close to the point "T"

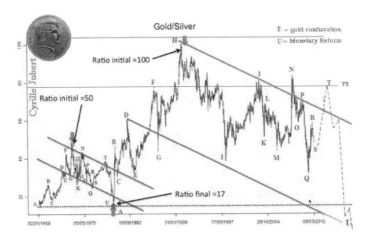

The reason why I recommend to keep some yellow metal is that the price of silver can fall much more easily than gold when manipulated. If necessary, gold can be used to purchase cheap silver by taking advantage of a high ratio.

When gold reaches its target of $3,450 in late 2012 or early 2013, the peak will be followed by a consolidation, a time that governments may choose to nationalize the gold ETF, and gold in metal bullion accounts of banks before limiting individuals' gold possession to a few gold coins per family. This is one of the multiple possible scenarios. The influx of cash from investors for the payment of their ETF or BB nationalized shares will divert the interest of these investors towards silver metal. Investors in ETF SILVER will want to get rid of them and take delivery in physical metal. At the same time, industrial manufacturers will want to secure the stockpiles needed for their respective productions, in order to preserve their production lines of technical unemployment.

The silver market is very narrow. An increase in physical demand by investors and manufacturers will lead to soaring prices, without any limit to the increase.

Moreover, after the deadline imposed by government for individuals to return their gold, the price of gold could be multiplied by 10 probably in the night by a decision of BIS and/or the world government.

The masses will became aware of the hyperinflation and will try to guard against it but it will be too late. Buying gold, at that time, will be forbidden. It is likely that silver will then exceed the highest peak that gold has ever reached on the free markets.

This madness for silver could be the bubble of the century.

Remember the formula of the Rothschild's: "the secret of success is to buy when everyone is selling and sell when everyone is buying."

If you take advantage of this purchasing madness, by stages, and exchange your Hercules and Seeders against other real consumable or non-consumable property, thinking that all bubbles are meant to bust suddenly one day. Note that silver cannot be eaten.

Whatever the depth and the duration of this consolidation during the factual deflation, silver should reach a minimum of $155 in this leg of increase leading to the first monetary reform. The latter had already been postponed twice. Will it take place on October 8 2013, in 2017 or in 2020? As of today, no one really knows.

The value of silver is negotiated at the geopolitical level.

The timings of the different factions controlling the world economy are very unstable and any attempt to set a specific timetable under these conditions seemed doomed to failure. This is why, the only way to play the winner is to hoard silver in a long term perspective.

What you have to remember is the fact that the price of silver will surely rise to extraordinary heights, but we cannot tell when. Safety involves diversifying, on one hand, and on the other, not speculating with financial products whose time value is against you.

You probably already understood that hoarding physical silver totally excludes any shares in ETF, Bullion Banks or any other electronic system. Beware of private safe rented in bank's vault. In case of bankruptcy, you will not be granted access, as it was the case in Argentina.

COMEX SILVER STOCKPILES MELTED

Between August 2008 and August 2011, registered silver stockpiles in the dealers' warehouses decreased from 86 million to 27 million ounces.

Just for information purposes, the open interest on COMEX in the middle of June was 121,325 contracts of 5,000 ounces, or 606 million ounces but there was only 35 million ounces in the warehouses in middle of June.

It was enough for an investor to request for the delivery of 7,000 contracts to cause the downfall of this financial market and free the price of silver. Each month, dealers had to find new strategies to avoid default in delivery. These are some of the dubious systems which operated over some months.

In August 2012, the COMEX silver warehouse stockpile was 35 million ounces. The shortage was always obvious.

The Cornering of Silver

Cornering of silver on COMEX seems to be a permanent reality.

93% of transactions on the COMEX silver market are strictly a financial game. Professionals deserted this "court of miracles", often referred to as the **CRIMEX**, and got their supplies from other markets, directly from the mines or from refiners.

The COMEX Market is Dead. It was already true in 2011 when I started to write this book, it is obvious today. If you look at the Shanghai Gold Market, the small COMEX is just ridiculous. More gold and silver are delivered in a day in Shanghai than in a month in New York. American Banksters won't rule the prices very long now. The decline in current prices is completely virtual. JPM and HSBC sold tons of silver paper from SLV ETF which had no physical reality.

George Soros participated in these raids by massively selling his SLV shares, while he also had a very large position of physical silver that he strengthened at the bottom.

The actual price of physical silver is dissociated from the fixed price by the banksters on COMEX. Like gold, silver is sold for premiums in China, India, Japan…

The Banksters will use all the tricks to delay the moment for the explosion of higher prices. The year 2011 was full of the banksters dirty tricks. Here is a few day by day anecdotes of the last few months.

March 2011

JPM managed to be coopted as one of the leaders of the COMEX warehouses on March 17 2011.

A fund manager complained that HSBC took several weeks to officially "deliver" his silver on COMEX. Even though the silver was administratively delivered on paper, and the fund sent its usual driver with armored truck to transport the metal, HSBC refused to fill the truck, demanding that a number of documents be filled in advance and sent by mail.

Among these administrative documents was the photocopy of the driver's driving license. After sending the folder, the fund's manager called HSBC after 5 days, saying that the driver's license had expired and that another ID was required.

Out of the three contracts, the first one was eventually delivered but the rest were still in the warehouse three months later due to Kafkaesque requirements invented by HSBC.

The warehouses are empty and the banksters do not know what else to invent to delay the time for the real corner.

BANKSTERS, BANDIDOS Y PISTOLLEROS

BANKSTERS

Those banksters who are defending fiat money in Washington or in London, as well as in the ECB and in the BIS are not held by any moral values when it comes to reaching their end.

One can never clearly overemphasize the fact that bankers are lawless people. I am not talking about bank employees behind their counter, doing their job from one week to the other for the sake of their wage. I am talking about those at the headquarters, wherever they are in London, New York, Basel, Paris, Frankfurt, Washington, Rome or Tokyo.

It is necessary to examine the Corleone Family Saga, which began on the docks of Liberty Island and Bronx, continued to indulge in drugs and the glitz of the Vegas casinos, and finally subdued in the universe of High Finance. This saga was inspired by reality, and the model of the Bank of Corleone, was the Banco Ambrosiano, the Vatican Bank, who made the headlines in his time with a cocktail of drug money laundering, CIA, murders, suicides and masonic lodges.

That mafia is certainly made of the new rich. The oldest "families" in the mafia of the banks have more ways and they are "received" everywhere and some for centuries, but they are swindlers and extortionist of money, nothing else.

In 2007, Morgan Stanley was convicted for charging the purchase, guards and insurance of gold bullions that the bank had not even purchased on behalf of its customers.

In March 2011, THE UNION OF THE SWISS BANKS (UBS) was caught for the same fraud.

In 2012, identical lawsuits multiplied for the same offense. The banks gambled and lost gold in the metal accounts of their customers.

This system is practiced on a massive scale by the ETF. Investors who seek to profit from metal rising value buy a share to the bank that manage the ETF. In actual fact, the bank does not buy the metal ordered by its client, but is rather using this cash to the best of his interest in the manipulation of the precious metal prices.

In 2013, ABN Amro, Rabobank and even ZKB proved that they gambled with their clients 's gold and lost it on the market.

BANDIDOS

Rob Kirby reported that the beleaguered HSBC asked the PENOLES company, a Mexican mining consortium to spit out all the mining companies in Mexico of their stock funds immediately available. These raw metal bars were bought below their price. Would you sell below the price? Yes, probably, if blunt arguments are used to convince you off!

The Penoles Company, had just sold the most beautiful of its mines to one of the richest men in the world, the multi-billionaire, Carlos Slim. This man who became rich so fast could be called Slim Fast. There is no need to do extensive research to find his link with drugs. His planes full of cocaine, had been seized a few times. Rob Kirby believed that the manipulations to lower the price of silver was an "arrangement" between HSBC and the banksters' cartel to allow Carlos Slim to purchase Fresnillo, the largest silver mine in Mexico and one of the largest gold mines, at a "reasonable" price. Favor returned after the extortion mentioned above.

...Y PISTOLLEROS

Jesse of Café Américain published another story implicating Carlos Slim, JPM and another mine where this notorious trafficker was a major shareholder. JPM forced the mine, Minera Frisco, to extract very large quantities of silver to immediately close a short sale position, taken when silver was not worth $20. The mine had to accept $1.5 billion losses. At the same time, Minera Frisco was preparing a stock transaction to the tune of $1.2 billion to purchase the reserves of a junior mine. The operation was planned and timed according to JPM's massive attack on COMEX, to purchase these reserves at the lowest possible price.

To complement and reinforce the role of the banksters of HSBC and the latter's close ties with the laundering of the drug money, here is an article of S&P dated May 19 2012.

According to a near record source consulted by Executive

Intelligence Review (EIR), several American senior justice and intelligence services officials agreed to recognize the merits of **John Cruz's** accusations against HSBC. Cruz, who was the Vice President of this British bank in New York, accused his ex-employer for engaging in large scale laundering of dirty money from drugs.

According to this source, a "significant" number of accusations by Cruz proved accurate after several documents provided by the latter to the federal authorities had been verified.

HSBC, in particular, set up ghost bank accounts through which not less than 1,000 billion dollars profits from the Mexican drug cartel were allegedly laundered. Details of the 1000 page document provided by Cruz only confirmed what the investigators of the intelligence agencies knew a long time ago. According to the investigators, it was clear that to launder huge sums of drug money, the Mexican cartels had solid relays on Wall Street and in the highest echelons of the political world in Washington, desperately depending on the money to finance election campaigns.

In the American politics corrupted by money, the correspondent of Figaro in the United States, **Laure Mandeville**, pointed out the disturbing trend in financing of politics in the United States. The article quoted in particular the former mafia lobbyist, **Jack Abramoff**, convicted by court: *"I came to understand it only once I was in prison: the campaign contributions paid by customers in exchange for favorable laws are nothing other than legal bribes".*

In any case, the HSBC affair gave substance to the claims of the former head of UN office against drugs and crime, **Antonio Maria Costa**, for whom contributions from the drug money helped to unfreeze the system of interbank lending in the wake of the 2008 crisis, thus avoiding a total collapse.

According to the source, the Attorney General of Barack Obama, **Eric Holder**, used all his weight to stop the investigations on HSBC. The U.S. justice department just appealed to the Attorney for West Virginia, in charge of the case, to refer all inquiries related to the case to the "major authorities", where the answer was always the same: "no comment."

Historically, the **Hong Kong and Shanghai Banking Corporation**, was one of the key institutions in the laundering of funds from the trafficking of opium by the British in the early 20th century. The bank was under multiple investigations since 2003, but has always managed to escape justice.

In 2013, the Attorney General Eric Holder recognized that HSBC was "Too Big To Jail", You cannot close a systemic bank.

"THE TREASURE OF THE SIERRA MADRE"

An article published in Forbes, reported about the terrible living conditions of engineers in the silver mines in Mexico, including CDE in Sierra Madre:

A rocky desert, peeled mountains, cooked by the sun, miserable people, armed gangs of drug cartels, who held the region to ransom and beheaded police men at regular intervals in remote towns, where Mexican authority had long been theoretical. Shootings and stray bullets in the surrounding villages... constant fear.

The mine is in the heart of a fortified enclosure, surrounded by several rows of barbed wires, guarded by a private militia who were all armed to the teeth. There are increasing numbers of dangerous armored convoys bringing gold or silver bullion to the foundry, who are regularly attacked by desperados.

That is the world of the precious metal mines. At one end of the chain, the bandits, who held to ransom to allow the convoy to pass... ransom, which are part of the normal operating costs in mining business.

At the other end, are the banksters of UBS, JPM, HSBC and those in Washington, London, Brussels or Basle...

Between the two, on one side some Carlos Slim, his lieutenants and the militia, whose men are better paid and armed than those of the Mexican army and the other all the white collar workers totally corrupted of a system that has become a sort of mafia, the SEC, or the NASDAQ authorities with a Madoff at their head, not forgetting the CFTC judges.

The document below is damning to the CFTC.

CFTC Confessions of Judge Parker

On September 17 2010, George H. Parker, administrative judge with the Commodity Futures Trading Commission issued this internal "Order":

"The undersigned administrative judge intends to retire from active service on

January 18 2011. As I will be away most of the time until that date, Seven pending cases currently under my jurisdiction should be reassigned. This is a recommendation on how the cases should be reassigned.

There are only two administrative judges at CFTC, the honorable Bruce Levineand and myself. During the first week of Judge Levine's work, almost twenty years ago, he came to my office and told me that he had promised Wendy Gramm, the then Chairman of the Commission, that he would never decide a case in favor of a complainant. The analysis of his judgments over twenty years will confirm that he has fulfilled this commitment scrupulously. Juge Levine, in his own way of applying the rules, systematically broke all hopes of the complainants, causing them to withdraw their complaints or to accept settlement, regardless of the validity or cause. (see attached survey published by the WSJ on December 13 2000).

In the light of these facts, if I had just announced my intention to resign, the seven pending cases would have been assigned to the only judge remaining with the Commission, Juge Levine. I could not allow this to happen in all consciousness. Therefore, I recommend that the Commission shall, in accordance with Article 5CFR # 930.208(a) of the office of the personnel management, the services of an administrative judge shall be detached from an agency such as the SEC or the Federal Energy Regulatory Commission."

CFTC & THE DODD-FRANK ACT

The U.S Senate passed a bill, the DODD-FRANK ACT, to regulate derivatives, among other products. The CFTC, the regulatory body of the commodities market, confessed to have hesitated for a long time to put this law in practice and in particular the Article concerning the limitation of the positions of the various players. Officially, they felt they were implementing this limitation of the positions for all.

The CFTC could trigger a **systemic crisis**. Why?

The banks, JPM-Chase and HSBC, in particular, short sold gold and silver including derivatives in huge quantities. According to the reports, 3.3 billion ounces of silver (4.7 years of production) and derivate to the tune of 65,000 billion USD were short sold.

If the law obliged the banks to deliver this metal, they would have to supply only the investors whose silver prices were far above the current fictitious prices. Silver was briefly rated at several thousands of dollars. It is likely that the method for calculating premium under the table of JPM would prefer to pay off the buyers, rather than allowing the price of silver to soar.

The judges managing the CFTC were partially changed by Obama in May 2011, thus theoretically giving most of the supporters a major cleaning of the Augean stables.

It appears that during the CFTC's two years recruitment campaign for positions of responsibility within the government agency, many leaders fell in a department that was well known for corruption. The new leaders sought to form new team of incorruptible individuals worthy of the reputation of Elliott Ness.

If this Act was finally implemented, even gradually, the price of silver could soar without limit until all the short positions were redeemed. The sudden and sharp rise in prices could destroy the value of the dollar and lead to an emergency monetary change. This change was prepared long ago but has already been postponed several times. The only thing to watch would be the gold/silver ratio.

The DODD-FRANCK Act which was passed in the summer of 2010 and was supposed to enter into force in December 2011. It was first shifted from July to September 2011, then to December, to January 2012, and March 2012.

On Tuesday July 12 2012, the CFTC finally gave the legal definition of the word, "SWAP". If nothing has changed in the terms of the law, from July 10, players of the derivatives market will have **60 days to get out of all their dominant positions.** It was very Exciting !

Apparently, it is 60 calendar days which would end on September 10 2012. However, it may be that this Act is referring to 60 trading days, that is 3 months, which would end on October 10 2012.

The Bull version
Some analysts concluded that the dominant banks would seek to redeem their vendor positions by outbidding on the prices of precious metals and thus lead to upward target values.

The Bear version
An intelligent programming of the German Constitutional Court's refusal to validate the MES or the new difficulties in Greece, Spain or Italy, led to a sharp decline of the Euro and the markets which were generally correlated to precious metals.

We were expecting a devaluation of the Euro by 25% to 30%, which corresponds to the decrease in the price of silver towards the LT support around $19.8.

At the end of the 60 days, the markets should have experienced violent movements. Beyond this period, the rise in the price of metals should move towards higher levels than expected in the range of: 3250-3450 for gold...

The betting on silver is still open...
It is still true a year later.

JPM BANK SUED

43 lawsuits were filed against JPM and HSBC, for the manipulation of the price of silver.

At the end of September 2011, the Manhattan Federal Court reported of a financial agreement between the 43 plaintiffs and the HSBC Bank and therefore, the bank was no longer prosecuted.

These 43 plaintiffs signed an agreement with HSBC, a system most commonly used in the United States, that HSBC had committed to provide tangible evidence and testimonies, that would let them win the lawsuit against the JPM Bank.

48 hours later, the KingWorldNews website made the "headlines" with the overwhelming evidence of JPM: dates times, Fax, names of stakeholders, exact amounts, etc.

Did the court eventually settle the issue of the manipulators? This is what Bart Chilton of CFTC asked in November 2011… but Bart Chilton played the good cop. He just looked like a game player.

JPM is at the service of the Federal Reserve and the bankers who desired to preserve fiat money. The United States are run by a banking cartel that place its men in all the key ministries and every administration. The whole system is run on "orders". The theoretical plethoric losses of JPM in the defense of the dollar against precious metals are covered by the Federal Reserve. The game is completely distorted.

This powerful banking cartel could only be stopped by a war, revolution or a major event of an exogenous origin…

To delay the corner
JPM put MF Global in Bankruptcy

On October 30 2011, the largest U.S. commodity broker was put in bankruptcy, generating a real storm on the markets.

Gerard Celente, renowned WS analyst, claimed that some

customers of MF Global requested for the delivery of gold and silver from COMEX. The latter did not have that amount of precious metals so they called JPM saying, if you don't do anything, we all jump together.

JPM, knowing that Corzine played short dangerously on the highly volatile markets, deprived Corzine access to their accounts for 48 hours. This was enough to put them in bankruptcy.

Corzine, President of MFG played his customers's money on CDS, betting on the collapse of Greece. The Credit Default Swaps (CDS) are issued by 5 U.S. banks that possess 97% of this market. The most important of these banks is JPM. Two institutions were created to regulate the market and define the rules. The I.S.D.A. (International Swap & Derivatives Association) and the GFMA (Global Financial Market Association), but these 2 associations were created by the dominant banks in the market. They have kept a grip on these regulatory bodies since then.

The ISDA therefore decided that since Greece refused to pay 70% of the capital due to its creditors, it could not be considered as in bankruptcy. This decision was obviously intended to prevent the dominant banks from paying the creditors who were insured with the CDS. If these banks had repaid, they would have risked putting themselves in bankruptcy.

Nevertheless, this refusal to recognize the bankruptcy of Greece, put Corzine in bankruptcy.

The Chairman of MF Global, Corzine, had been Chairman and CEO of Goldman Sachs. He was even approached to become Treasury Secretary of President Obama in 2008. He is therefore a prominent member of the Wall Street Gang.

The fraudulent bankruptcy of MF Global was followed by one of the most outrageous Hold-Up which allowed JPM to steal all the cash outright from MFG customers who requested COMEX delivery of the silver bars and the gold bullions and who to do so, had to bring the full value of their contracts in cash to CME.

JPM simply snapped up all the cash...

The gold and silver bullions of MFG customers, guarded by

JPM on behalf of COMEX, were also stolen by JPM by a simple game of scripture. Openly and known to the authorities, these stocks moved from customers' accounts to JPM accounts. This Hold-up openly prevented the corner of COMEX on last October 31.

HSBC also filed a complaint against MF Global and JPM, claiming to have rights to the gold and silver bullions of the customers of MFG. The latter had mortgaged the customer's' assets to cover its own speculations with HSBC.

Scandal, corruption and fraud are ubiquitous in Wall Street and Washington. No market can survive if the law and order do not prevail.

Dealers in commodities and precious metals preferred to close their case, telling their customers to opt out of COMEX and CBOT of Chicago and invest in physical metals, so long as justice had not put order on the U.S. markets.

COMEX should gradually being marginalized and most of the transactions on precious metals will move to Shanghai, Hong Kong, Singapore and Dubai.

PS: Addenda: in July 2013, The CFTC is pursuing Corzine in Justice.

In the latest report published by the B.I.S. in December 2012:
http://www.bis.org/statistics/dt21c22a.pdf

The gold/silver ratio is around 3.

Table 22A: Amounts outstanding of OTC equity-linked and					
By instrument and counterparty					
In billions of US dollars					
		Notional amounts outstanding			
Instrument / counterparty	Dec 2010	Jun 2011	Dec 2011	Jun 2012	Dec 2012
Total equity contracts	5,635	6,841	5,982	6,313	6,251
Reporting dealers	2,020	2,483	2,257	2,401	2,149
Other financial institutions	2,881	3,558	2,992	3,187	3,347
Non-financial institutions	733	800	--	725	755
Forwards and swaps	1,828			980	2,045
Reporting dealers	524				597
Other financial institutions	995				1,121
Non-financial institutions	309				327
Options	3,807				4,207
Reporting dealers	1,49				1,552
Other financial institutions	1,88(				2,226
Non-financial institutions	424				429
Total commodity contracts	2,922				2,587
Gold	397			523	**486**
Forwards and swaps	230	283		319	295
Options	167	185	215	204	191
Other precious metals	123	144	132	134	**157**
Forwards and swaps	90	86	65	63	63
Options	32	58	67	71	94

Gold : Silver

486 : 157 = 3,09

Expressed as "gross market value", to the right of the table, these derivatives are valued 53 for gold and 10 for Silver.
The ratio is 5.3

The figures of December 2012 in the BIS statistics indicate an increase in silver derivatives ($157 billion against $134 in June 2011). Nevertheless, they represent around 10 years of mining production.
750 Moz x $20/oz= $15 Billions of US dollars

How can banks cover 10 years of mining production in a market which has been in deficit for 70 years?

110 BILLION DOLLARS DISAPPEARED

Without any formal introduction, 110 billion dollars of OTC silver derivatives flew and disappeared as if by magic.

THE FACTS:

OTC silver derivatives for the period of June 2009 shrank from $203 billion to only $93 billion.

By instrument and counterparty
In billions of US dollars

Instrument / counterparty	Notional amounts outstanding				
	Jun 2007	Dec 2007	Jun 2008	Dec 2008	Jun 2009
Total equity contracts	8,590	8,469	10,177	6,159	6,619
Reporting dealers	3,118	3,011	3,479	2,097	2,656
Other financial institutions	4,473	4,596	5,496	3,295	3,277
Non-financial institutions	999	861	1,203	767	686
Forwards and swaps	2,470	2,233	2,657	1,553	1,709
Reporting dealers	658	637	599	361	447
Other financial institutions	1,321	1,262	1,489	927	979
Non-financial institutions	492	334	569	265	283
Options	6,119	6,236	7,521	4,607	4,910
Reporting dealers	2,460	2,373	2,879	1,736	2,209
Other financial institutions	3,152	3,336	4,007	2,368	2,298
Non-financial institutions	508	527	634	502	403
Total commodity Contracts	7,567	8,455	13,229	3,820	3,729
Gold	426	595	649	332	425
Forwards and swaps	141	200	222	116	179
Options	285	395	426	216	246
Other precious metals	88	103	190	96	203
Forwards and swaps	42	51	86	48	101
Options	46	52	104	48	102
Other commodities	7,053	7,758	12,389	3,392	3,101

Change in information between the June 2010 and December 2010 reports: Table 22A: Amounts outstanding of OTC equity-linked and commodity derivatives by instrument and counterparty. Column 2: for June 2009.
Line: other precious metals

By instrument and counterparty
in billions of US dollars

Instrument / counterparty	Notional amounts outstanding				
	Dec 2008	Jun 2009	Dec 2009	Jun 2010	Dec 2010
Total equity contracts	6,471	6,584	5,937	6,260	5,635
Reporting dealers	2,245	2,654	2,101	2,183	2,020
Other financial institutions	3,445	3,248	3,144	3,291	2,880
Non-financial institutions	781	682	692	785	734
Forwards and swaps	1,627	1,678	1,652	1,754	1,828
Reporting dealers	389	445	413	479	524
Other financial institutions	965	950	953	932	995
Non-financial institutions	273	283	287	343	310
Options	4,844	4,906	4,285	4,506	3,807
Reporting dealers	1,856	2,209	1,688	1,704	1,497
Other financial institutions	2,480	2,298	2,191	2,359	1,886
Non-financial institutions	509	399	406	442	424
Total commodity Contracts	4,427	3,619	2,944	2,852	2,922
Gold	395	425	423	417	396
Forwards and swaps	152	179	201	224	230
Options	243	246	222	193	166
Other precious metals	111	93	107	127	123
Forwards and swaps	62	44	76	81	90
Options	49	49	31	46	32
Other commodities	3,921	3,101	2,414	2,307	2,403

The silver price at that time was $15 an ounce. $110 billion divided by $15 is equal to 7.333 million ounces. Has ten years of mining production changed hands?

No! It's not possible. We know that there are no stocks of silver! The mines worked on just-in-time basis and cannot meet the demand, thus creating a permanent shortage. It is more likely that an accounting operation was made to clear a line in the OTC silver derivatives which, on paper, represented 10 years of production.

This is not exactly the same thing.

Rightly or wrongly, we can reconcile with the announcement made by China in August 2009, authorizing its state companies and banks to default on commodity derivatives that the Chinese government considered as a scam.

JPM snapped 110 billion USD on silver derivatives in the summer of 2009. This explains why the then head of risk management of JPM, Jim Winters, was brutally "thrown out of the window" in the words of Reuters.

OTC silver derivatives remaining after the manipulation of entries to the tune of **123 billion USD** was recorded in December 2010.

The average price of an ounce of silver in 2010 was about $25, representing 4,920 million ounces, or **6.5 years of production**.

This confirms the figures provided by JPM Traders.

We will not be able to find merchandize at COMEX to settle, the 4.9 billion ounces. Since precious metals at LME move out faster than they enter and there is a queue at the counter, the situation seems very tensed.

This is really Orwellian. In *"1984"*, the hero serves in the Ministry of Truth. His job is to rewrite historical records to match the past with the official version of the party.

CYRILLE JUBERT

ERIC SPROTT'S APPEAL TO SILVER MINERS

In the current currency and banking, Eric Sprott, chairman of Sprott Management and founder of an ETF considered as the safest in the silver market, launched an appeal to all mining companies saying that :
- If they want to guard against depreciation of currencies, they should keep a large portion of their cash in the form of silver bars that they produced themselves.
Silver has a monetary value.
- If they want to guard against bank failures, they should stop putting their money in the bank and leave them in their warehouses in the form of silver bars.
- If they want to avoid the downward trend in the manipulation of precious metals at LBMA or COMEX, they need to keep their treasure until the price of precious metals appreciates, reflecting the scarcity and imbalance between supply and demand.
- If they want to value their stock on the market, they must take advantage of their production and increase their stocks.

This appeal was well received by the major silver mines. If they apply these principles, the price of silver will appreciate greatly.

In an interview on 20 February 2012 on Silverdoctors, Eric Sprott claimed that the **Endeavor Silver** Mine followed his advice.

In the last quarter of 2011, Endeavor produced 1.2 million ounces but sold only 400,000. Its managers refused to sell at $27.

Thus, with increase that followed, they could not have made a better investment since the price shot up to $33 then $35, allowing them to make good gains.

Eric Sprott weighed heavily on the market in 2010 by purchasing 22 million ounces of silver which he had to seek in London, Zurich or Hong Kong.

He returned in early 2012 after obtaining permission from SEC to increase the number of shares of his ETF, PSLV.

We can rejoice and worry at the same time.

Sprott stepped forward with a single fund and lent themselves to the manipulations of the Federal Reserve or any other American juridical-administrative entity which would play back the incident that affected the Hunt brothers. When necessary, these millions of ounces of silver could suddenly be introduced onto the market and sold quickly, thus causing prices to fall.

The opening of the Pan Asian Gold Exchange or its equivalent silver, though it may occur, should revolutionize the market. If this market opens, it will not be about "futures". This fictitious silver sold in quantities 350 times greater than the actual stocks, as it is the case in London today. This should allow a real review of the price of silver.

The value of the RMB may substantially be re-evaluated to re-balance the industry on the world market. The value of a Chinese worker's wage should be closer to that of its western alter ego. Unfortunately, our manufacturers dismantled their factories to locate them in low-income countries in Eastern Europe, Latin America or Asia. This situation reminds us of Weimar Germany after the 14-18 War. Unable to pay the war reparations demanded by France and England, the latter dismantled their factories in Germany to set up again in France or Great Britain. Germany was covered with debts and without production tools to generate wealth to repay. This is the exact situation in which the United States and Europe find themselves today.

The same causes producing the same effects, we should experience a monetary phase as destructive as that experienced by the Deutsch Mark during the Weimar Republic in the 4 years to come, with acceleration between 2015 and 2017.

The only safe solution is to change your cash into precious metals if it is a lot, or easily exchangeable goods if it is more modest.

PRE-CONCLUSIONS

In June 2012, the silver market was still quite tight.

JPM, cornered in strings, used any trick to find all the silver available, either by raiding the mines or by emptying the ETF warehouses of which it is the official guardian. It caused the downfall of MF Global to plunder the stocks of their customers. It paid the investors so that they do not ask for their delivery or increased trading margins. In June 2012, they brought down a broker in Japan who is two times bigger than MFG, AIJ, probably to empty the precious metals stock of the customers of the Japanese market, the TOCOM.

JPM manipulated the prices at COMEX, but the BRICAD, with China and Russia at their head, took advantage of the low prices of precious metals and bought massive stocks of gold and silver in London, to get rid of their reserves in dollars.

The Cartel was caught in its own game. They could no longer lower the price of gold without emptying the reserves of the central banks, at a time when the latter should have purchased for future monetary reserves.

Gold had a lowest possible margin of decline and I doubt if it can remain permanently under $1,650.

If the Federal Reserves raised the rates to strengthen the dollar, and attract the LT investors, it would probably cause a market crash. This may perhaps lead to the fall in the price of silver briefly to complete its consolidation at $19.9 before a rapid upsurge.

The buyers facing JPM are very powerful. The small hands have let go. The huge appetite of China remains, which consists of strategic or monetary reserves, and the powerful Russia, rich in oil and gas.

And we have the banking and mining houses, notably Rio Tinto, BHP Billiton or Glencore, whose game is never very clear as they have multiple interests. They would be the first beneficiaries of a system like the Bancor.

I think they are playing for a rise and would be happy to pull down a master bank on WS, without absolute certainty.

The banking crisis coupled with the debt crisis should shake the currencies one after the other. The Euro is expected to fall first, and could be followed a few weeks later by the collapse of the dollar.

This little game between currencies is of course relative, the one value to watch carefully is that of precious metals.

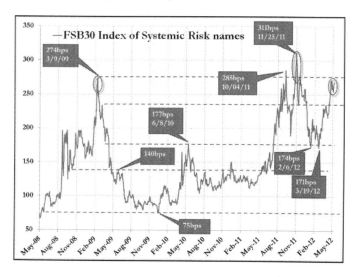

This graph, provided by the Financial Stability Board, the institution responsible for overseeing 30 financial groups likely to cause a systemic crash in case of failure. It gave the instantaneous temperature of the system. Unfortunately, it ended in May 2012, though the fever continues to rise. The whole system could collapse at any moment, but they are likely to find new tricks to keep it for a few more months.

If you look at the graph of financial values, we must exercise extreme caution and get out of the market before banks collapse like a game of dominoes.

The rushes to the counter in Spain and Greece, as well as the arrival at maturity of derivative products have bled the Hellenes and Iberian banks. Nothing has been solved. Spain refuses to cede its sovereignty to the ECB to save its banks and monetary authorities block on Greek debt. Europe is increasingly divided.

2013 should be a difficult year everywhere.

Already at the end of September, on the CME and LME, the thrust on gold and silver almost triggered "commercial failure" of the Majors. The system has almost collapsed. The United States had to export massively silver metal to the UK in May, June and July to save the LBMA, which could not meet the demands of delivering of Asian funds. Exports in July for LBMA have represented 169 tons, five times more than the previous month. This episode is reminiscent of the fall of a "London Gold Pool" in the 60s.

In February, the COT showed that "commercials", that is to say the big banks too big to fail, which had hitherto the master role over the precious metals had greatly reduced their Short positions on gold, but not on silver.

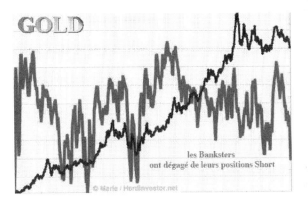

All short positions had been endorsed by the hedge funds, as seen in the graph below.

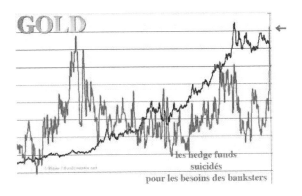

A raid is therefore expected but it is obvious that the 4 systemic banks had been safely set aside from a potential short-squeeze. Hedge funds can go bankrupt without jeopardizing the whole banking system.

Cyprus bankruptcy

The bankruptcy of Cyprus and the "bail-in" process adopted by the monetary authorities of the troika, allowing to repay creditors at the expense of depositors has undermined confidence. Nevertheless we are in a system that relies entirely on trust about the currency and banks. It was followed by a real bank run on the gold deposits of the COMEX and LBMA.

On the following graph of April 2013, we see that JPM's customers withdrawn 95% of the gold they had on deposit.

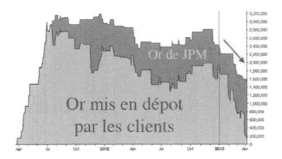

Globally on the COMEX, 30% of gold reserves said "eligible", that means belonging to customers but not for sale, have moved in protection against a "bail in" in case of a default from the bank or COMEX. Trust simply vanished.

In August 2013, JPM is in default. The bank is 2 months late in its gold deliveries.

For Pascal Roussel, analyst at the E.I.B., hyperinflation comes in when trust is destroyed. We are not far from it. When at the beginning of 2014, a global bail-in will be implemented by Europe, trust in the system will disappear and social unrest will follow.

Andrew Maguire revealed on March 15 2013, that on the London market the week before, one of the bullion bank defaulted. It was unable to deliver the gold claimed by its customers and forced them to accept cash instead. That's a fact, the LBMA has defaulted.

Authorities and "commercials" too big to fail had anticipated this and prepared a massive raid on precious metals, which was triggered on Friday the 12th of March 2013 and which got carried on Monday with the same intensity. Gold price fell from $1571 to $1318 in two days.

It was followed by a gold rush in the World. Especially in India, which has imbalance the foreign exchange and the currency, and in China, where demand was such that the HKMEX defaulted and has to give up his clearing license on gold. It turns out that in 2013 the market for gold in Shanghai, the EMS, has become one of the most important places of the World in the gold trade. In recent months, the Chinese have officially consumed the entire world mining production. There are daily deliveries on SGE and on a daily basis we are talking about tens of tons of gold. PAGE finally emerged in another form. Look how the COMEX is nonexistent. SGE delivers probably 20 times more gold than the COMEX.

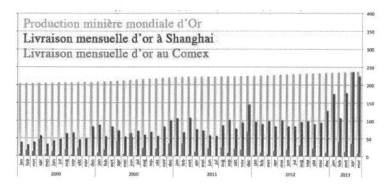

Incredible pictures were shown of 10,000 Chinese queuing in front of a jewelry of an eastern town of China, who made a promotion in June on jewels in gold.

Silver was also violently attacked moving down from $28 to $21,90.

What was the objective of all this? Forcing the maximum of speculators and investors to lay off, in a way that they have no interest to request delivery. Open Interest on Silver on the COMEX was on his highest historical trend with 166,000 contracts before the raid. 159,000 are remaining after. On that point, the raid has failed. For Harvey Organ, only a sovereign fund can remain stoical et keep his position after such a financial loss. He suspect that could be China.

On the next day after the raid of March, to make more investors lay off, the Shanghai Futures Exchange and the COMEX raised margins on the trading of all precious metals. A second raised of 25% has intervened, in May some more should follow in order that the skyrocketing cannot be played with leverage.

Precious metals must be purchased in the form of coins as protection in these times of monetary uncertainty. The coins must actually be held and not left in an account or locked in a bank. Indeed, if a bank default, all private safes are seized. It is the law in France. Be very careful!

A big banking wash is on the way. The bail in act has been implemented in all constitutions of the world. In France, it was voted on June 5, 2013. Banks will go bankrupt in the next coming 9 months. Your private safe and his contents is in great danger to be confiscated. Empty it before being despoiled by bankers or the authorities.

That very day, trust will have been totally destroyed and the fiat money system will be dead.

CYRILLE JUBERT

Silver throughout History

Where will silver go tomorrow?

Is Silver

Just an Industrial Commodity

nowadays?

CYRILLE JUBERT

Speculations on the Forthcoming **MONETARY REFORM**

PREAMBLE

I started writing about the economy and precious metals in 2008. The analyses and futuristic forecasts of Cassandra were largely confirmed by facts.

Splitting the euro is now on the menu of all the tabloids, in the "psychological preparation of the working masses". Some of these pages have therefore lost their freshness. I could cut them but I have chosen to keep the intellectual lines of thought of these past few years, rightly or wrongly.

The history of tomorrow and after tomorrow is not yet written. Drafts are discarded and torn everyday by bankers and politicians caught in the traps they helped to create. Henchmen and minions of the oligarchy follow a plan without even knowing that the former exist, nor the one who designed it. They believe that they have power, but they are just puppets that will be discarded when they outlive their usefulness.

This chapter is intended to try and help you through the next phase during which a systemic crash seems inevitable.

Do not think that taking refuge in gold or silver is "THE" answer. That would be too simple. With the fall of the banking system, a whole Chaos will change your everyday life. Civil unrest everywhere, civil wars will be seen everywhere. You have better to think and prepare to survive to that, wherever you live United States, United Kingdom, Spain or Italy, even Switzerland.

CYRILLE JUBERT

WORLD DEBT

The United States national debt has exceeded $15 trillion.
The total U.S public and private debt is nearly $60.000.000.000.000.

At the end of the G20 summit in 2008, Larry Edelson wrote at moneyandmarket.com that if we were to monetize the public debt of the United States to 100%, an ounce of gold would be $53,000.

Officially, the latest figures attributed to the U. S. Treasury is 8,133 tons of gold or 261,475,950 ounces.

$14 trillion debt of 2008 divided by 261 million ounces of U.S. "official reserves" gold, gives us $53,639 an ounce.

In the records of the Federal Reserve, the gold reserves are described in recent years as "deep storage gold". This gold has not yet been mined. Fort Knox is a fable.

But debt is not the prerogative of the United States. The global national debt is estimated at $40,000 trillion while official reserves of the central banks in the world amounts to only 31,000 tons of gold, about 1000 million ounces, so a trillion of ounces.
Gold should therefore be worth nearly $40,000 an ounce.

Everyone knows that most of the central banks had leased their gold on the market, probably 50% of their reserves. That's why they will have to confiscate your gold.

Information reaching us from the tough negotiations, still underway, there was no question of **short term** and to monetize a small portion of the US national debt for the first phase, with the price of gold ranging between $3,500 and $5,000. But Greece has already defaulted on 70% of its debt and that is only the beginning. Therefore gold should be valued much higher.

A personal confidence in the entourage of bankers set a possible final price close to $32,000.

"11"

An analysis by Tuur Meester, reiterating and developing Vladimir Bukowsky's analysis in 2006, compared the current state of the U.S with that of the Soviet Union just before it exploded in 1991.

I cannot help but make the connection with this magic number which has remained a constant factor:

Franc of Year 11	- Renaissance of bimetallism
1971	- End Gold Exchange Standard
1978 China	- 11th Congress of CCP - Political change
1991	- Bankruptcy of the Soviet Union
2011	- Bankruptcy of the West Block

11 in numerology, these two ones place side by side are added we get 2: Sign of discord and opposition.

But today, we have opposing groups in the oligarchy who do not want to have monetary reform in the same way.

Some want a unipolar world, others multipolar. Some want a basket of purely fiduciary currencies, others want currencies guaranteed by commodities and/or precious metals.

The 11th column of the table of Mendeleev's predicted elements has only 4 elements of which 3 are essential:

Gold, Silver and Copper

This takes us back to the starting point of these analyses done in late 2008.

1 Oz of gold = 1000 ameros / 1 Oz of silver = 100 ameros
These prototype coins show a ratio of 1/10

CYRILLE JUBERT

THE AMERO

Information about the 3 coins above leaked on the net in late 2007. They were engraved Union of North America. The UNA is the North American Free Trade Area, formalized by the ALENA Treaties including the USA, Canada and Mexico. The UNA was built on the model of the European Union.

The EU led to the creation of a single currency, the euro. The UNA likewise ended in the creation of a single currency, the amero. This series of coins was designed by David Carr, designer specialist in numismatics, who worked on numerous occasions for the U.S. currency. These coins were stamped "D" of the Denver Mint, the equivalent of the Paris Mint or the Bank of France. Using this stamp as well as manufacturing counterfeit currency is a crime. Carr was not prosecuted. Therefore, he made these prototypes by order, on behalf of the U.S. government or the Federal Reserve. One of the scenarios studied at the time was:

"The price of gold raise sharply to $10,000; then there is a change of currency and the price of gold came to 1,000 new units."

Silver throughout History

The article above, published in the Financial Post on the 9th of August 2002 by Herbert Grubel explained the need to quickly create a common currency for the North American Economic Community.

A series of bank notes were even printed. This picture was published, among others, in the Russian magazine, *Russia Today*. The other cuts in the background were published by various websites.

Hal Turner, the American journalist who disclosed the amero during one of his radio broadcasts, revealed that containers of bank notes had been shipped to China. He was arrested shortly after under false pretenses and then he disappeared completely from the airwaves.

The Amero was actually in the box at some point in time. Was this project actually abandoned completely?

The only interesting thing about this story was the gold/silver ratio given.
Ten ounces of silver could buy one ounce of gold.

When expressed in the current dollar value, silver shot up to $1000, a figure that has been found on several occasions.

The Federal Reserve created the currency by billions of dollars. Since it did not get any buyers for the treasury bonds the Federal Reserve bought them by printing more dollars. That was the operation "Twist".

It did the same for the worthless real estate mortgages bought from the banks, accounted for in the assets of the Federal Reserve. America entered a sharp recession and since the cost of estates continued to decline since 2007, these mortgages on the Federal reserve's balance sheet no longer have value. And especially at a time where a very large proportion of these mortgages was deemed illegal and considered as a "public forgery" by the American court of Justice. Bankers wanting to speed up the time for the mortgage formalities, fabricated a virtual notarial system, with no legal basis, the MERS, and besides allowed them to evade the payment of property taxes and local registration taxes. The mortgages on the Federal Reserve's balance sheet should be valued to "zero". **The Federal Reserve is therefore bankrupt.** That is a reality. It is under the protection of the U.S. Treasury but the latter cannot pay its debts without resorting to the Federal Reserve's printing press. In all fairness, the system is completely dead.

Since the dollar is a reference currency for international trade, the entire monetary system today is in bankruptcy. This never happened in history.

China is threatening to put 2/3 of its trillions of dollars from US Treasury Bonds on the market, at the very time when the Japanese need to sell theirs to offset the huge industrial debts incurred due to the Fukushima nuclear accident. Meanwhile, Russia had already gotten rid of its US Treasury Bonds.

The Federal Reserve has launched a massive QE3 to redeem all the US Bonds flooding the markets. In one way or the other, the value of the dollar will be destroyed and the people will be terribly impoverished. This news was still scorching in 2013.

Bernanke, Geithner and other officials posed here before a 100 dollars note on which so much has been written about in the blogs. The left part of the note resembles that of the previous notes, but on the right, the pen, handwriting, the "liberty Bell" and the number 100 were printed in gold. According to the GATA analysts, this note announced the return of the "Gold Standard".

Thursday, October 11 2012, a robbery took place at the Philadelphia airport, in which thieves made off with a "large amount" of the new notes, which were intended to reach the Federal Reserve of New Jersey. The FBI declared to the press that the perpetrators could not do anything of their loot, "these notes are only meant to be put into circulation in 2013."

In the spring of 2013, Bernanke announced that this bank note would be released on the 8th of October 2013. This is obviously very exciting if you think it has something to do with the monetary reform.

A year ago my credo was: "These notes may be put into circulation when gold is at 100 times its 1971 value: $3,500. Will silver be worth 100 times its value of 1971, or $155?"

Today, early 2013, I think it is still possible. Gold is at $1300 and a crash seems to be emerging as a result of rising interest rates on markets and a "Credit Crunch" in China. Silver is at $19,50 and might drop even lower. Hedge funds that henceforth hold all short positions aiming a fall of gold towards $800.

In 1979-1980, there was a strong consolidation of 38% of the overall increase, then a very short bear-trap, of up to 44% retracement. Sellers targeted the 50% of Fibonacci, but they got into the trap of a new raise and had to redeem their positions in the disaster, thus accelerating the velocity of the rising value.

Between the lowest point of the consolidation and the high point of gold, there was less than 90 calendar days and only 56 trading days. Therefore, it is possible to see a dramatic increase starting around July 10 and ending on October 8, with in the meantime a massive devaluation of the dollar and possibly other fiat currencies, leading to a sharp rise in precious metals.

We will be fixed very quickly about this.

Will silver be worth 100 times its value in 1971, or $155?

To be persuaded, there is only to seen the rush on the Silver Eagles and Silver Maple Leaf in recent years to understand that silver will find a value closer to the current reality.

The few high-level insiders we know have their fortune in gold, but also hold significant amounts of silver.

Today, in both the United States and France, the old coins in 900/1000th have become much more difficult to find. Many were melted and those who hold what remains are not sellers at current prices, except with consequent bonus.

The monetary disorder, the banking crisis and doubts about the sustainability of the system do not encourage to let go coins with real intrinsic value, for bank notes that have no other value than that you want to grant them.

The Fed announced in early spring 2013, that this 100 dollars note will be put into service on coming October 8. Since then I observe the events on the markets with renewed interest, in respect of this deadline.

Voltaire said that all paper money tend to return to its intrinsic value, that is to say zero.

Whatever the name of the future monetary unit, amero or dollar, after all the Canadians already have the dollar, this monetary unit could be guaranteed by gold in international trade.

But what will be the price of gold, expressed in today's dollars?

Whatever will be, silver should play a brilliant supporting role.

CYRILLE JUBERT

STRANGE PHILHARMONIKER

The Philharmoniker is an Austrian official silver coin. This new one ounce pure silver coin had a face value of €1.5 but it traded at €15 in December 2009.

In 2008, an ounce of silver was worth €12 from February 18 to March 18 but it was not until November 2009 that it reached this level.

€12 + 19.6% VAT on new coins = €15. But why did the face value indicate a value that was 10 times lower than the price of silver at that time?

The phenomenon was the same during the minting of coins in the Paris Mint in early 2009. The face value of a gold coin was €200 per ounce when the rate was €800. In March 2010, I asked myself the following question: Is it possible that the monetary unit of this coin is not the same as the one currently in circulation?

Is it a "New Euro"?

The old franc was in existence until 1959 when the new franc took over from January 1 1960, date on which 100 old francs was exchanged for one New Franc.

Silver throughout History

You will notice that the 1958 coin did not bear the mark, old franc, neither was that of 1960 marked new franc.

We shall probably have a $100 for a new dollar and **€100 for a new euro** in the coming years.

For such a change in the currency unit to be deemed necessary, we should have a very strong devaluation, that is, a strong revaluation of precious metals. We expected the price of gold to rise to $3,500 in late 2011.

This increase and timing were actually programmed by the oligarchy, but the American clan changed the situation on October 31 by causing the bankruptcy of the largest American broker, MF Global, putting off JPM's default for several months.

Doesn't the **$3,500 suggest anything to you?**
Gold had a fixed price of $35 until 1971!
If the price ended on this value, $100 old could be worth $1 new.

Some announced that they would sell their gold around $3,450. They would sell them to invest in agricultural land, forestry, agro-food commodities, oil, but obviously not in fiat money.

Note that the final value of gold stated was 10 times higher, but ownership of gold may be banned and the transactions are likely to be heavily taxed.

Officially, the Chamalières bank note printing unit is expected to produce new series of bank notes, the Euro2, with different colors. These new notes will be put in circulation in early 2013. It is not a secret; the information has been very official for years.

Will the current Eurozone still exist?

Will these €2 have a different purchasing power from the current euros?

During this first Monetary Reform, if it will take place at all, if the metals are officially remonetized, what will be the gold/silver ratio?

Gold preserved your purchasing power, but is silver, this vulgar industrial metal which was forgotten by politicians and ignored by the media, going to improve it?

In the monetary plans of one part of the oligarchy, the European Union and the euro were models intended to be cloned. The idea is funny when we see the obvious failure of the system today and the likely collapse of the Eurozone in the short term.

I mentioned the **North American Union** and the amero earlier, but other similar structures were designed and implemented 'Sugar' or the 'Latino' in South America, the 'afro' in Africa and the 'dinar' in the Maghreb and Arabian countries, (MENA for Middle East and North Africa).

The **ASEAN** is supposed to become the economic, political and monetary community of Asia, bringing the whole region together under the aegis of China. A meeting was held in Hanoi with 13 Asian countries. Florent Detroy of the Edito Matière Première Journal wrote in an article published on May 11 2011 wrote in the subtitle:
   "Is Asia preparing for a monetary putsch?"

The answer is in no doubt "YES".

The successive failures of the G8 and G20 since November 2008 culminating with the G20 snub in Korea in the summer of 2011, where the IMF was declared persona non grata, show that the gap between the geopolitical blocs and factions of the financial oligarchy is widening.

Benjamin Fulford also mentioned the new monetary system that China wants to establish with or without the agreement of the Americans in his confidential letter for two years. The latter should already be operational; they just have to press a button to switch from one year to the other. This could happen at any moment.

During the meeting of Finance Ministers of the European Union in Poland in late 2011, which Timothy Geithner attended without being invited, the German representative was very clear and sharp with the U.S. Treasury Secretary:

"Our new monetary system is fully operational, it is waiting to be implemented at the time when yours will collapse."

In the spring of 2012, when the United States threatened to exclude all the financial institutions working with Iranian banks from the SWIFT interbank system, the parallel and concurrent system developed by the BRIC was implemented, to allow Iran to continue to trade with India, Russia and China in particular. This American threat proved to be a huge diplomatic and geostrategic blunder.

Confidence of one of the Rothschild's in February 2012:
"Monetary reform cannot take place until China gets 3,000 tons of gold."

My calculations assessed the future monetary reserves in China in January 2013, date on which the "first" international monetary reform of about 2,000 tons of gold and 15,000 tons of silver should have taken place.

Low Hypothesis (Jim Willie's price)
2,000 t gold = 64 Moz at $3,000 / Oz = $192 billion
20,000 t silver = 640 Moz at $200 / Oz = $128 billion
or 10% of their foreign exchange reserves of $3,000 billion

We know that the Chinese are still making massive purchases of all the gold available for sale on the London market. This is thwarting the game of the Wall Street banksters who are stuck with their virtual gold. In the first quarter of 2012, China bought 5,000 tons of gold on the LME.

China reduced its domestic production of gold and banned its export as well. It also purchased gold directly and secretly from the South African and Australian mines. This could explain the official decline in the production capacity of these two countries.

The information above implies that the current dollar system will be replaced with a new system where the Yuan will at least play a major role in the basket of international currencies, although it is not playing any role today.

In recent months, China has widened the Yuan's fluctuation range, one of the required stages towards the internationalization of the Chinese currency.

On August 10 2012, the Voice of Russia, reiterated an article published in the Chinese official newspaper, "*Renmin Ribao*":

China Plans To Increase Its Gold Reserves Six fold.

"A gold rush has begun in China. Beijing is preparing to increase the proportion of gold in its reserves, not by only a few tens of percentage, but six times straightaway. This is what emerged from the recommendation of Chinese economists, published on the front page of the state newspaper, *Renmin Ribao*."

The article mentioned 1,000 tons of gold in China that should be increased to 6,000 tons. For me, these data are misleading. China, with its purchases in the spring of 2012, already has the 6,000 tons. The only question that we have the right to ask is this: Has China managed to get 5,000 tons of gold taken to the Bullion Banks in spring?

MONETARY CHANGE

Is it possible for us to experience a change in the dominant currencies in the world: pound sterling, dollar, euro, yen..., with a new dollar, new euro, new yen...etc. in 2013 or/and in 2015?
It would be a vast concerted devaluation.

In an article of September 2007, Roland Hureaux was estimating that the Chinese Yuan was undervalued by 50%, and that the strong euro was crippling Europe, when the salaries of the competing countries were 10 or 20 times weaker. For example, a few months ago, Mercedes decided to manufactured in the USA to take advantage of the weak dollar and low salaries. Renault also announced the relocation of their production of the Clio in Turkey.

These new currencies emerging from monetary change should be balanced to allow a fairer economic competition. The ultimate goal should be the parity between the base salaries of the dominant countries of the West and those of the emerging economies, with a decline in purchasing power in the West, against the revaluation elsewhere. This result will only be achieved after the Second Monetary Reform. Today, negotiations between factions of the oligarchy are in a deadlock. Everyone is only talking about war to impose their point of view.

If BRICAAD* manage to impose their monetary change, silver could be an important part of monetary reserves, with a very satisfactory ratio in favor of those who invested in the white metal.

*BRICAAD = Brazil, Russia, India, China, South-Africa, United Arab Emirates, Deutschland & their allies.

On July 4 2012, China and Australia signed a bilateral agreement, equivalent to the one signed between China and Chili in the previous weeks to bypass the U.S. dollar in their trade and financial transactions.

The decline of the dollar as a reference currency is increasingly becoming a tangible reality. If the current negotiations do not end in an agreement, the monetary reform can only take place in 2016, in a heap of ruins.

By then, Hyperinflation will have completely destroyed

current currencies.

The acceleration that we can witness at the end of the spring of 2013, in preparation of the dismantling of systemic banks, the implementation of the laws of "bail-in" and movements in the price of precious metals, suggest that a large monetary change is prepared for the coming months.

One of our sources announced us mid-June 2013, that in 2014, the oil would be $180. If you look at the current share price, barrel is at $90-95. It's not the oil that will double its price, it's the dollar that will devalue by 50%. Gold is going to rise to nearly $3,000.

double-page of Figaro-magazine of May 2010

In 2009, Jim Willie, who is publishing a very well informed financial letter, suggested an upcoming split of the Euro, between "the" PIIGS currencies, (including France) and the currency of the countries in the North, including the Netherlands, centered around the German economy. Since this scoop is no longer one, all the blogs of financial information talked about it.

We are talking about Northern Euro which would be guaranteed by gold in international trade. Jim Willie's sources are high ranking European financiers, including one, in particular, who acted as intermediary between China and Greece in 2010. The others were German and Swiss bankers.

No currency can provide a gold guarantee all alone otherwise there would be an immediate global monetary disorder and the German export industry would be ruined. These new currencies should be launched at the same time or else none of them will. Jim Willie issued a parallel analysis that can be found in the February 2011 archives.

"China cannot launch a currency guaranteed by gold or by gold and a basket of commodities , all alone, because that would ruin its exports. On the other hand, China can launch such a currency simultaneously with Russia and Germany..."
(addendum: see the United Arab Emirates, India, Brazil and South-Africa)
"Instantly, currencies which would not be guaranteed would be worth nothing. Everyone would try to sell. If the USA do not complied with the Chinese-Russian-German logic, the dollar will be brought straight to hyperinflation. The same thing will happen to the PIIGS currency and the pound sterling."

One of my contacts working at the World Bank and IMF in Washington presented my analyses during a work meeting at the highest level of IMF, in the presence of Nicolas Sarkozy's financial advisor and Strauss Khan brothers. Then an angel passed... A long awkward silence... gazes met... before the then great mandarin in an attempt to avoid the issue said:
"It is impossible to make talk a Chinese who has decided to remain silent."

A second contact of mine said when he explained my theories to a diplomat in Brussels in May 2011, he got a little smile like "you are well informed but I will not utter a word."

A third contact of mine said that during a discussion with a private banker, who was informed enough to have played it brilliantly during the 2007 and 2008 crises, he was asked about the assumption of a split of the euro. He was waiting for an answer like: "crazy hypothesis, etc...". His response was: *"We actually talk about it, there is nothing concrete nor sure, but anything can happen..."* He said with a loud laugh.

During a private conversation with a mutual friend, Marine Le Pen in December 2010, described the split of the euro by giving dates. We are a few months behind the schedule that was announced but the subject is on everyone's lips today.

Were there negotiations to delay this split according to German,

Russian or American electoral timetables?

In the summer of 2012, it would appear that the schedule was thrown into a panic. Some financiers told me in turns that Greece, Spain or Germany had opted to back out. The latter seems to have taken all its time so that its eventual exit from the Eurozone would be on irrefutable legal and constitutional basis. Conversely, it is fighting tooth and nail on a legal ground the European monetary initiatives that put its economic stability in danger.

We talk of a possible split after the German elections in September 2013. A close date from the famous October 8th mentioned earlier.

The Netherlands and Finland have joined forces with Germany to oppose the policy of the ECB.

In mid April 2012, Jim Willie had further confirmation from a German banker that the European currency would be divided between the Euro-mark of the North and Euro-South.

Germany had virtually nationalized the main German Mint (Bundesdruckerei) in 2009, to ensure the confidentiality of his monetary policy. In 2009, the FRG ordered 14 new machines to print bank notes with RFID chips from the Ruhlamat company, based im Marksuhl. The information was quickly censored on the internet.

In 2010, Germany asked its supplier for a huge quantity of watermarked paper it had set aside.

In 2011, Germany limited its production of euro bank notes by 16%, although Germans are Europeans who use bank cards the least and rather use cash the most for their transactions.

Whatever the outcome of the elections, France will not be included in the Euro North. Our currency will be linked to that of Italy and Spain who refused Germany's policy of budgetary rigor. Is there a relationship with the "Growth Pact" announced by Draghi of the BCE? No one knows the exact timing of the outbreak but we are getting close to it very quickly.

France is supposed to lead this split and be the first to plunge itself into it. Don't wait any longer for the lowest gold price before you invest. By the time the split takes place, **the premium would have doubled price of the napoleons.**

It appears that some maneuvers are being prepared behind the scenes between the Russians, Germans and Swiss. Basel B.I.S. would be positioning itself to be an indispensable arbiter between the new currency of the North and the new ruble. The latter would be guaranteed by precious metals, oil and gas.

CYRILLE JUBERT

RESISTANCE AGAINST THE MONETARY PUTSCH

In May 1973, while the dollar was declining, a group of bankers and oilmen, the **Bilderberg**, met in Sweden to develop a scenario. A few months later, Egypt and Syria triggered what became known as the "Yom Kippur War". It followed a threat of oil embargo by the OPEC countries and the first 70% increase in oil prices. The reality of the successive oil shocks was that an agreement was reached between the oil cartel and the OPEP countries for a sharp increase in the price of a barrel of oil, on condition that all transactions on oil had to pass through the banks in the City of London, be charged in dollars and a predetermined share of this windfall had to be systematically invested in U.S. Treasury Bonds. The dollar was saved.

In 2006, **GEAB** announced the impending crisis. According to them, one of the two triggers of the upcoming systemic crash is Iran's decision to open the first oil stock market in Euro, creating a loophole in the system put in place by the Americans to maintain the supremacy of the dollar. This loophole could become a chasm in the coming months. The oil countries, even Saudi Arabia, will be committed to charge their oil in the currency of their buyers, signing the **death of the dollar.**

China, Russia and Northern Europe, most likely Brazil and India all want to establish a new variant of the **Gold Standard** in a short term. This system was supposed to be put in place in late 2011. The currency was intended to be (or will be) guaranteed by a basket of commodities derived from gold, silver, oil, copper, but wheat as well, etc.

America blocked this process by arresting DSK under false pretenses and killing Khadafy who was one of the spearheads of this reform in the Middle East and North Africa (MENA).

Khadafy was establishing a pan African gold and silver currency which was about to be formalized. By overthrowing the heads of state and their clans from power in North Africa and arresting the head of the Egyptian Bank, Mahmoud Omar, also under false pretenses, in the same hotel in New York during that very week, the United States torpedoed the 2011 monetary reform.

Silver throughout History

The war in Libya is part of a strategy to reshape the MENA region by breaking the current countries into smaller poorer states to make it easier to manipulate. This is a balkanization of the region. Libya was split into 3 regions. Mali is being divided. Egypt is supposed to be divided into as least 2 states as in the olden times with High Egypt and Low Egypt. Secular Syria should be broken up. Algeria is also on the list. Mauritania is already in turmoil.

NATO, a mercenary serving monetary policy more than the defense of a common territory, has perpetrated a hold-up on all stock of gold in Libya. This gold crossed France in a convoy of armored vehicles to end up in the Bank of International Settlements in Basel.

It seemed that part of this gold was found to have been filled with tungsten.

This bullion in bearing the stamp of the Bullion Refining Industry Examination, BRIE, but when it is cut into two, you will see that it is filled with tungsten.

For the record, this worthless metal has almost the same density as gold. Several scandals on this huge fraud leaked on the web…

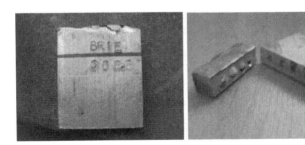

The remaining of the Libyan gold was stored in the vault of the Bank of England. His confiscation was performed with a mere changing attribute on a computer screen.

TWIST

The purpose of the TWIST operation launched by Bernanke in late September 2011 was to make it more attractive for American and foreign investors to invest in Treasury Bonds.

The USA are finding it difficult to get capital and creditors today. The Federal Reserve and the Treasury will therefore raise the prices of all other investment products and reduce the effects of the leverage to force financiers to buy Treasury Bonds. So far, it has been in vain.

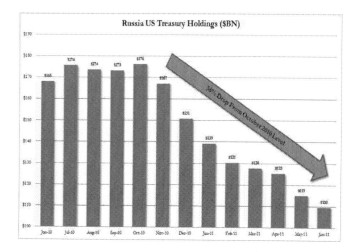

Russia sold half of the U.S. Bonds it held in 8 months and China is also cutting investment as quickly as possible.

Gold and silver are now extremely cheap and China continues to purchase in bulk and request for delivery. Meanwhile, the largest sovereign funds in the world have cut investment in the U.S. securities mortgages (MBS) and the U.S. Treasury Bonds.

The European crisis is in the center stage but the Americans are at least worse off than us, with their biggest states and largest cities in bankruptcy.

China is gradually reducing its stock of US Treasury Bonds by massively importing gold.

Silver throughout History

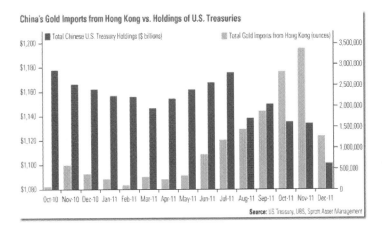

For a few months now, the Federal Reserve has been issuing treasury bonds to two years to redeem all those to 30 years available on the market. The wall of debt in 2013 and 2014 is more than double that of 2012 while the United States is entering recession. The decline in GDP will lead to a decrease in tax revenues and the inability to repay the debt without massive devaluation. That is the "fiscal cliff".

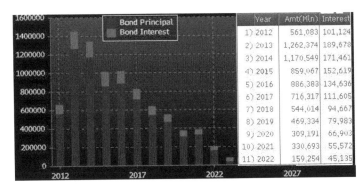

CYRILLE JUBERT

DEBT DEFAULT – QE3 HYPERINFLATION AND DEVALUATIONS

What is going to be the agenda of the US government? All the solutions seem to lead to drastic devaluation of the currency against precious metals and commodities. This will result in a terrible impoverishment of the working masses. Hyperinflation seems inevitable by the end of 2014-2015. The latter could be due to a combination of several factors:

- The different real estate bubble explosions.

- Denunciation of the parallel mortgage system, MERS, created by the bankers who wiped out a large part of the banks' assets, both in the United States and around the world.

- Explosion of the "debt system" reaching saturation, causing borrowers to default and triggering a tsunami of CDS, which will befell the entire world of finance, beginning with the four U.S. banks which issued 94% of this "insurances" called CDS. The four banks are JPM, Bank of America, Citi and Goldman Sachs. They enriched themselves by using these financial products but will be bankrupt if only one country default on its debt. But each of these banks is classified as "systemic", that is, if one collapse, the whole system collapse. The fall of CDS dominoes has already begun.

- Succession of disasters on the main cereal plains in the world: Pakistan, Russia, Ukraine, Australia, Mississippi, Thailand,… in 2010, 2011 and 2012. This terrible *serie noire* which reduces strategic reserves, if it continued, would lead to a surge in food prices.

Monetary devaluation of 50% is expected to double the price of grain. Life will be increasingly expensive.

The QE3, both in the United States and Europe, was a simple timing by the monetary authorities to a further massive devaluation and change of currency.

The price of gold is not rising, it is your purchasing power that is diminishing.

THE POSSIBLE ROLE OF AGRICULTURAL DISASTERS

Due to the heat wave in Eastern Europe in 2010, Russia banned the export of grains. The cereal plains of the alluvial plains of the Indus in Pakistan were permanently flooded in July 2010, destroying fields and plantations. In 2011, Pakistan finally produced 23.5 million tons of wheat, leaving only 1.5 million tons for export. NASA admitted in late 2011 that the plains of the Indus caved in by 3 meters. They are still flooded today.

In January 2011, part of the Australian cereal plains were flooded, drowning part of the harvest of one of the wheat granaries in the world. 40% of the wheat was declared unfit for human consumption. In January 2012, Australia experienced another flood.

In the spring of 2011, the American cereal plains of the Mississippi and Missouri flooded before suffering a record heat wave. This led to a surge in the price of cereals and by extension poultry and meat. The 2012 drought in the United states worsened the phenomenon.

After the winter in 2010, due to the need for treasury and the desire to take advantage of the high prices, many American farmers sold their 2011 harvest on the Chicago Futures market. The 2011 harvest was partly destroyed by the weather and those who sold futures were unable to deliver the expected quantities on the international markets.

Information reaching us indicate that wheat production in France including that of 2012, 2013 and 2014 have already been sold.

The bankruptcy of MF Global ruined large American farmers and brokers, depriving them of cash at the time when they should have invested in the 2012 agricultural season. We recall that in the 30's, the banks played their mortgages on farmers and took possession of most of the American farmland. Reread *"The Grapes of Wrath"* by Steinbeck.

In early 2012, a drought threatened the future maize production in Argentina and Brazil, when officially, USA has only 20 days reserves for consumption. Although Obama removed subsidies for ethanol production from maize, green fuel producers continued to consume maize.

In April 2012, 45,000 hectares of soybean and wheat were drowned in Argentina, due to subsidence of the South American Plate. Part of the harvest was gathered but no one knows the percentage yet.

www.agrositio.com/vertext/vertext.asp?id=133186&se=1000

Just like silver, the brokers plays with the "futures", and always postponing delivery to a later date. But it is a Ponzi, Pyramid Scheme which cannot last forever.

The financial system today, regardless of the sector under study, is a race forward above the void. There will come a time when the whole system will collapse entirely, and leave only economic, social and political chaos.

This graph on maize prices formed a typical figure of cup with handle in July 2012. The resistance greater than $780 was broken in late July, having reached over $823. Logically, they were expected to increase to $1,200. For the record, the price of maize fluctuated from 1980 to 2006 between $190 and $300.

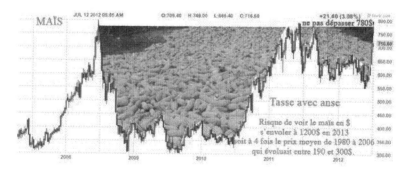

The chart on daily wheat prices shows that an inevitable increase in the price of wheat is in the pipeline. This will bring the price to the same level as in 2008 or $1,100.

Silver throughout History

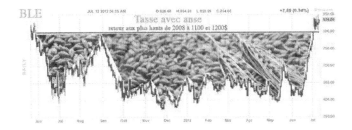

With the exception of rice, all the cereals show a similar pattern. If the trend continues, the price of wheat, soybean, oats could mark further high prices in 2013. Are the price increases already indicating a devaluation of the currency?

CYRILLE JUBERT

DODD-FRANK ACT

This Act is extremely ambitious since it seeks to regulate the huge swap market in particular by introducing transparency on the U.S. markets. In September 2012, only companies linked to cereals (seed, grain, flour, poultry, livestock...) may be able to take positions to hedge fluctuations of grains. Did Goldman Sachs and other pure speculators exit?

Bancor: Will cereals be monetary?

Like gold or silver, cereals are tangible assets which were currencies in their time in the different countries in the world. The Chinese, Russian, Brazilians and Indians have expressed their wishes to replace the current system with a BANCOR. This monetary system that was proposed in Bretton Woods in competition with the Gold Exchange Standard, would be based on a basket of commodities, gold, silver, copper... but also wheat, soybeans, etc. Each of these commodities would be weighted. This was one of the possible scenarios.

Is that why there were so many short positions on cereals, whose prices did not reflect the actual shortages due to adverse weather conditions?
By lowering or controlling the price of cereals, you control the price of a hectare of agricultural area which could be the equivalent of a gold mine if BANCOR is established.
Should we therefore invest in agricultural land? Yet, in the world of tomorrow, landowners could be targets for governments.

In 1929, Stalin put the kulaks (large landowners) to the gulag and collectivized land in a bloodbath. The experiences of the Soviet Union showed the ineffectiveness of these collectivist systems in agriculture. Ultra liberalism has shown the danger to the planet and the ecosystem of an agricultural system based on the sole benefit of the industry (depletion and pollution of soil, deforestation, depletion of water reserves...) Will we find a happy medium tomorrow?

Julius Caesar was murdered because he wanted to limit the latifundia, the large agricultural properties. We also found such laws in ancient Mesopotamia. There was a lot of wisdom in the ancient civilizations.

GOLDMAN SACHS

In the agricultural sector, the US authorities are once again dominant. Actual economic data are manipulated according to the banks' needs for positions on the commodities markets, and in particular, the Goldman Sachs Bank.

Goldman Sachs was criticized by the magazine, "Rolling Stones", in a very complete dossier in 2009, for having initiated and instigated successive bubbles on different commodities of other securities, with the sole aim of making successive financial "coups".

Goldman Sachs is the dominant bank in the United States which put liegemen at all levels of the US departments and administrations.

A statement from the Department of Agriculture announcing a drought caused prices to soar, thus allowing the bank that was pre-positioned upward to make profits... then the bank positioned itself with the leverage downward before the department's, announcement for excellent crops which were much better than expected and collapsed the bubble.

If you examine a sector closely enough, the maneuvers are obvious and they show everywhere.

If you forget these short term manipulations orchestrated by Goldman Sachs, the reality of the prices shows a sharp increase over several years. The price of maize in November 2011 was 3 times higher than during the period 2003-2006 and more than twice the securities of 2009. The increase in the price of maize led to a rise in the prices of chicken and the entire chain of bird meat. An article in the Telegraph in 2010 predicted that the price of meat would be like that in the near future and that the lower class in Great Britain would have to become vegetarians. Joke?

In March 2012, a former vice chairman of **Goldman Sachs** who resigned after working with the bank for 25 years, published an open letter in the Financial Times criticizing the bank. At the end of his studies, he was proud to have been selected among nearly 10,000 applicants to be part of this prestigious bank. The watchword at that time was to serve the customer in the best possible way, even at the expense of the bank's profits. He was proud to have trained several generations of trainees in this spirit of irreproachable ethical standards himself. In his letter, he denounced the new spirit that has dominated for the past ten years, where morning meetings start with "elephant hunting". Elephants are the products or securities which are no longer profitable to the bank so they have to try to sell them to the customers by promising the moon. Customers are no longer respected by the Goldman Sachs brokers. They are just lemons that must be squeezed for the benefit of the bank.

The author of this open letter resigned because he could no longer work without ethics. According to him, a bank cannot survive when it despises its customers.

As we know, Goldman Sachs falsified accounts some time ago to allow Greece to enter the European Monetary Union, causing the problems we know today.

The former vice chairman of Goldman Sachs Europe, Mario Draghi, after being trained in the United States, had important responsibilities at the Ministry of Finance in Italy. He privatized all the jewels of the Republic selling them to the oligarchy: the oil company, refineries, ports, highways, steel mills, etc.

Today, this GS man is the head of the European Central Bank. The ECB balance sheet is totally unbalanced showing a leverage of 36 compared to its stockholders' equity.

After his resignation, the former head of ECB for Germany denounced the mountain of junk bonds stuffing the central bank's balance sheet, making it insolvent in its eyes today.

If the Federal Reserve is bankrupt, the ECB is not any better.

To prolong the survival of the system, the Central Banks can only continue to print bank notes endlessly in trillions. This is what the Bank of Japan, Bank of England, the ECB and the Federal Reserve are doing.

ECB with its LTRO just worsened the imbalance of its balance sheet. The ration with its own funds is now 36.6.

The short term debt seemed to have been partly solved, but to do so, the European countries increased their debt heavily to 3 years.

2012 + 3 years = **2015**

The settlement date comes iteratively, indicating a **hyperinflation** which seems inevitable, both in Europe and the United States.

Are we moving towards a total destruction of confidence in the currency or will a monetary reform be put in place beforehand?

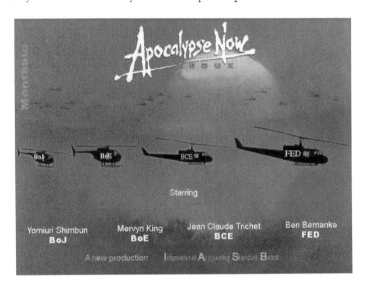

CYRILLE JUBERT

I.A.S.B'S OFFICIAL NOTICE ON SEVERE HYPERINFLATION

Since the second injection of $200 billion in 2008, everyone predicted an upcoming hyperinflation. By crying "wolf", the words lost their power.

If the international body is responsible for setting accounting standards which enacts new rules for the companies to enable them establish an accounting system despite the severe hyperinflation, the words have a completely different emphasis.

The draft amendment was aimed at providing guidance on how the entities should resume submitting their financial statements in accordance with IFRS standards after a period when they were unable to do so due to **serious hyperinflation** *that affected their functional currency.*
The proposed amendment was concerned with the inclusion of an exemption in IFRS. This exemption was to enable the entities that were affected by **serious hyperinflation** *to value their assets and liabilities at a fair value and use it as the deemed cost of these assets and liabilities in the statement of the opening financial statement in IFRS.*
These amendments were effective for fiscal years **beginning on or after July 1st 2011**; *earlier application was permitted.*

Since 2000, the price of silver has been fluctuating in the channel drawn below. The subprime crisis and the fall of Lehman Brothers caused a financial tsunami in 2008 forcing the Hedge Funds to make distress sales with the securities that best resisted: gold, silver, mines.

When the prices tried to exceed the upper limit of the channel, COMEX changed the trading rules 5 times within 8 days which triggered a massive sale in early May 2011. This brings to mind the measures taken to block the corner of the Hunt brothers in 1980.

The authorities reduced the effects of leverage of speculators on COMEX to 1/6.

According to some sources, the first monetary reform which was initially scheduled for late 2011 then expected in 2013, if it does take place, the price of gold and silver should be set at $5,000 and $200 respectively.

Some equally reliable sources predicted higher gold price close to $3,500 and silver at $145 in this phase.

In the 1979 to 1980 increase, the price of silver shot up from $6 to $52 in the space of 12 months. Prices multiplied by 8.5. If the rise started from the base of the current triangle at $26.6, the price could reach $224. If a major attack took place before the rise, and silver started from $19, the price could exceed $160.

If you take the monetary devaluation officially calculated by the Consumer Price Index into account, the $6 at the start of the rise in 1979 corresponds to $19 now, and the $52 in 1980 is equivalent to $145.

The figure for gold that our source predicted at $3,500 matched the analysis I did in September 2011. Indeed, the price of gold for 2010-2011 reproduced only one month apart, corresponded with that of 1978-1979. I therefore anticipated a sharp decline in the price of gold in close to 24 hours and the successive waves of consolidation now, except that the tempo has changed since September 2011. The candles which represented a day on the graphs in 1979, became candles representing 3.5 or 4 trading days in 2012. This was against all odds.

The agenda of the Cartel was changed and it surprised some of our most reliable sources who also followed this model and timing.

This is the graph for 1979-1980 with today's values. When gold hits its highest at $1,919, the increase could be staggering.

This is obviously one of the possible scenarios.

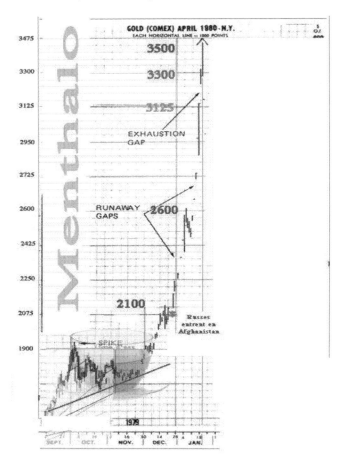

We were then in contact with the medium LT, just before the start of the rise. Will that also be vertical?

The ERSTE Bank's "Gold Report" which can be found online, disclosed in 2010 that the Bank of England sought to delay the re-monetization of gold by pushing it to 2020. According to Erste Bank, the re-monetization will not be total but gradual. The central banks will have the obligation to keep a percentage of their money in gold and the percentage will increase over the years.

Is this the first step towards re-monetization of gold?

A bank that wished to get a loan from another bank or the central bank had to provide collateral. The loan amount depended on the quality of the collateral and it was fixed at 100%, 50%, and 33%... of the collateral, the actual security that secured the loan. With regards to gold, the system took account of only half of the value of gold. It was considered as a risk because it could fluctuate significantly. That will soon not be the case anymore.

Indeed, in early July 2012, the Bank for International Settlements (BIS), which became the supreme authority of the central banks, proposed that physical gold be classified as first-class asset just like money. The FDIC (Federal Deposit Insurance Corporation) simultaneously proposed that gold be classified as Zero Risk Asset.

The proposal, would enabled the banks that held gold in their shareholders equity to record it following the price of gold and not the current rate which is half of the price of gold.

In October 2012, the Office of the Controller of the Currency (OCC), the FDIC and the Board (of Governors of the Fed) were studying a similar project to classify Silver, Platinum and Palladium in Tier One.

This information did not filter in the press, but the NPR (Notice of Proposed Rulemaking) can be found on the website of each of these monetary "agencies" in their official correspondence.

The financial oligarchy is constantly changing its agenda due to negotiations between the various factions. It is possible and even likely that China, Russia and their allies did not allow the West to impose their conditions and agenda. It seems that they are now actually a step ahead of the Exchequer, forcing the Western bankers to act.

At the same time, we can worry because these rough negotiations are dangerously causing the tension in international relations to mount.

You should not try to gamble these movements of gold or silver on the markets because the manipulation of the prices is no longer done by one faction as before but several opposing factions.

Wisdom is telling you to invest in physical gold and silver whilst you wait for the upcoming increase. Those of you who have to think in euro, the next increase in the price of precious metals could be due to a the great weakness of the European currency as a result of the splitting of the Eurozone.

The devaluation of the euro to the tune of 25 to 30% is expected in CT, consequence of a possible exit of a member of the Eurozone and the monetization of debts.

Since November 2008, during the G20 summit, China on its own behalf and on behalf of BRIC, demanded the end of an international monetary system based on the dollar and requested for the return to a system close to BANCOR. This is a kind of expanded bimetallism, where oil and other commodities (copper, corn, soybean...) could play a role. The negotiations that followed bore fruits since the central banks became net gold buyers in 2009 and the following years.

However, one might assume that the Westerners did not give full attention to BRIC, by accepting to return to the gold standard (in the strict sense of the term) but by excluding bimetallism or a larger system. China then protested by banning the export of silver in August 2009, while the production of refined silver from China represented nearly 40% of the market supply.

The effect of China's decision on the price of silver was very sensitive from August 2010, creating a semi shortage which has only worsened since then.

The sharp drop in oil prices in 2008 was a price manipulation imposed by the banking and oil cartels to discipline the oil producers and first and foremost Russia in its monetary and geostrategic negotiations. As a leading oil and gas producer, The Russian economy was heavily dependent on hydrocarbon prices. This did not deter Russia from concluding oil and gas agreements with China for the next 25 years in the form of barter, without taking the international prices manipulated by the cartel into account.

We also know that JPM distorted prices by buying the contracts of players on COMEX since August 2010, by offering them a very high premium. **93% of the financiers playing on silver at COMEX** were just speculators who invested on this market in order to receive the bonus.

The authorities tempered the speculative frenzy on several occasions by increasing security deposits, thus limiting the effect of leverage on financiers. This caused the sharp fall in silver prices in early May and August 2011. The players were forced to play fewer contracts on COMEX.

The current situation is as bad as it was for the financial companies in 2008 and the worst crisis is probably still ahead of us. When the Credit Default Swap, these famous CDS are triggered, the tsunami will be terrible. Many financiers will then have to drop their positions and sell the most resilient assets. On COMEX 93% of financiers and speculators can cause a massive fall in the price of silver paper. The banksters are playing this card and expecting a violent fall in prices which can bring the price to $19.

The maneuvers of LBMA and COMEX, like MF Global's fraudulent bankruptcy and recently that of PGBest for refusing to recognize their failure to deliver can still lead to violent fluctuations in the price of silver paper.

Never lose sight of the fact that physical silver **is a metal** five times more rare than gold bullions or coins and it's an essential metal for various industries.

Do not lose sight of the fact that silver could be remonetized during the next monetary reform with an extremely interesting ratio for those who invested in silver.

Don't play the short term any more. **Invest in the physical.**

NANOTRADING

I mentioned in a previous chapter how Goldman Sachs recruited a Russian programmer analyst, Sergey Aleynikov, to create their trading software which allowed orders to be placed in billionths of a second. Nanotrading was obviously an automatic trading between robots, because nobody can take a decision and enter an order on a keyboard at that speed. The objective of GS was to dominate its competitors through the speed of its orders. But Sergey was recruited by a start-up and he left GS carrying the sources of its software with him. He was arrested for downloading the software on a German server and some claimed when the story came out in 2009 that he offered (or sold) his software to Russia.

The Start-up, Teza Technologies, also recruited a Chinese IT specialist in 2009 who was also arrested for uploading the sources of the trading software on a server in China. His trial took place in the early summer of 2012, accused for industrial espionage and theft of professional equipment.

The methods used by the central banks to contain the upward trend in gold prices and conserve the value of their fiat currencies were officially known. They were the Washington Agreement on Gold. These W.A.G. set the volumes of gold that each central bank had to sell on the market to limit the rising prices. In theory, Berlin sold 100 tons but Paris got wind of it and bought it and quickly resold it to Washington which also sold it to Berlin. Berlin therefore still had 100tons but managed to lower the gold price.

The Majors, big banks who hunted in packs on behalf of the U.S. Treasury and/or the financial oligarchy adopted a very similar technique long since.

They rented gold to the Bullion Banks and ETF and resold very heavily on the market. UBS sold to Morgan Stanley who resold to JPM who also resold to CS who then sold to UBS.

In theory, UBS, at the end of the day, still had the same quantity of gold that it was supposed to give back to the Bullion Banks or the ETF from where it was borrowed.

When these sell-offs took place, the Majors managed to make their sale near an important support. They knew that if a sell-off exceeded the prices on the support, the traders robots of the lambda investors or banks which were not in the know, had automatic sales orders to buy at the lowest price from the next support. The Majors took advantage of this. The traders robots extended and amplified the downward movement. It was enough for the Majors to press the button at the next support again to trigger a second wave of automatic sales.

But since February 2012, this system does not work anymore. When A sells 100 tons of gold on the market after informing B of its action so that B buys at a lower price, the gold does not have enough time to get to where B is standing. A faster hand buys the gold before B.

This hand is not only very fast but also extremely powerful, financially speaking.

From February to May 2012, the pack of the Majors blew 20,000 tons of gold. Do the calculation. That was 705 million ounces of gold at $1,550.

Over 1 Trillion Dollars

Now, make the connection between the stories. You'd probably understood that the Sergey software perhaps has even been improved since then to enable China, Russia and Germany to pinch the Western banksters by picking up the last bet.

The problem with these banksters is that the gold that they played and lost was not theirs. It was invested in the "metal account", the ETF and Bullion Banks accounts. So, there also, gold was entrusted to them by the customers.

Where will they be able to find 20,000 tons of gold?

At what price limit will they be obliged to rise for the investors to agree to sell their own treasures? We can also ask if the delivery of these 20,000 tons was a reality. Or was it just paper?

A the end of 2012, the game was no longer as it used to be. The Majors are bloodless whereas China and its allies have billions of dollars to sell. The exhausted Western system seems to be dominated.

Silver throughout History

Make the connection between this story and the fact that one of ZKB's customers could never take delivery of his precious metals and that he ended up accepting a simple check. In 2013, it's official, ZKB's gold is just paper. They don't deliver Gold anymore. In fact, they lost it.

The same applies to the stories of the trial in Switzerland which was kept a secret from the media and all the customers who were swindled in the same way with their gold account "metal" at UBS or CS. Note that these two banks are only Swiss by their name. Incumbent leaders are American or cowboys trained on Wall Street.

ABN AMRO has warned its clients invested in the markets of London and COMEX, that as from April 1 2013, they could not ask for physical delivery. Then on April 15, Andrew Maguire reported a default in London on the LBMA where a customer could not take delivery of its gold and had to accept a check instead.

This short squeeze implies a very strong surge to follow.

The extremely violent attack of mid-April and June on the precious metals, was a giant bear-trap designed to frighten the weak hands and make them sell their precious metals before the increase. I do not doubt for a second of the great increase that should inevitably follow. All this is monetary and solely monetary.

CYRILLE JUBERT

NEW MONETARY SYSTEM

If we should rely on the official figures, the gold in the central banks and IMF is supposed to represent 30,623 tons.

It was disclosed that in May-June 2012, an unidentified actor raided 20,000 tons of gold, equivalent of 2/3 of the gold in the central banks. It is difficult to see this without being tempted to conclude that it was not for nothing that China, the New World Bank and the BRICS created the Mumbai summit.

If we recall the German Minister's invective to Geithner who imposed his coming to the European Finance Ministers meeting on 16 September 2011 in Poland:

"We are waiting for your monetary system to collapse. Ours is ever ready to replace it."

One may wonder if the powerful actor who swiped the stake on all the markets is not deliberately going to cause the bankruptcy of the Majors, ETF, Bullion Banks, LME and CME, to accelerate the process.

We are living in a great time!

GERMANY RAISES ITS VOICE

Under pressure from the Bundestag and the German press, Bundesbank revealed that 1,536 tons of gold, or 45% of German reserves were kept in the vaults of the New York's Fed, 31% in Germany, 13% in the custody of the Bank of England and 11% in the Bank of France. Conservative MP Philipp Missfelder had been refused an inspection of German gold reserves in the Bank of France.

For several years Germany wants to audit the National gold stored in armored cellars of the Federal Reserve in New York. Since 1980, Germany is facing an end of inadmissibility. By exerting pressures, German controllers were finally able to "see" a gold pallet, but without control. The Bundesbank is committed to repatriate 300 tons of the 1,536 tons held in the United States, in order to verify the quality. The United States has negotiated to hand over this gold over a period of 7 years, which proves that their reserves of 8,000 tons are purely virtual.

Officially, in the early 2000's, Germany repatriated 930 tons of London to Frankfurt for analysis and certify the new standards. Last October, a member of the Bundesbank said: "With the end of the Cold War, there are now more compelling reason of storing gold in Paris." Paris is therefore going to have to show white paw and find nearly 400 tons of gold to give back to the Germans. Did the Bank of France "lease" this gold to the Bullion Banks?

This is probably one of the reasons for war in Libya and Mali, one of the largest gold producer in Africa.

Germany, claiming its gold, terminate interbank agreements and disrupts the game of the Cartel on the LBMA and COMEX. Bankers can sell 100 times the same ingot on markets but if a player asks for delivery, that creates a real panic.

Since then, some Austrian MP asked to repatriate the national gold and a petition with over 100,000 signatures puts pressure on the Swiss National Bank. A referendum should take place on this subject.

The SNB should hold 20% of its assets in gold, it is 2,000 tons. Switzerland will therefore have to buy nearly 1,000 tons of gold on the market, which will weigh on prices.

I would not be surprised to learn that the stocks of different Swiss Gold ETF be nationalized in order to find rapidly 300 or 350 tons.

The terms of this petition Swiss show what we already knew about the conditions to be imposed on G20's Central Banks by future monetary reform. Things are falling into place.

Germany was the first to destabilize London and New York. Its example will certainly be followed by all Northern Europe in the months that follow.

Here is evidence of that monetary change.

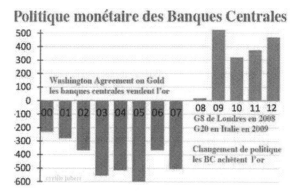

Major event on gold in early 2013

By studying the positions of the various players in the market of gold in the United States, we see that "commercials", ie the 4 major banks, which contain the price of precious metals by short selling, made sure to sell their positions to "large speculators", ie to the hedge funds.

Silver throughout History

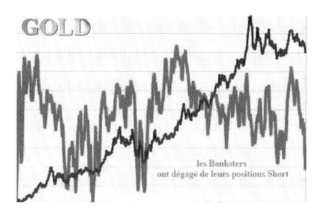

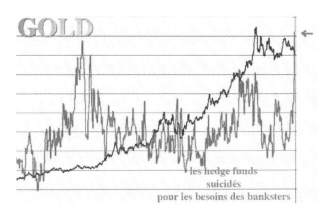

A GIGANTIC BEAR-TRAP

What conclusions can we draw?
The "commercials" are among the largest banks in the world. They are part of systemic banks, these "too big to fail" which, if they'd go bankrupt, would plunge all banks in complete chaos.

For hedge funds to accept this "status quo" American monetary authorities promised to drop the gold to $1,280, which corresponds to 38.20% of retracement for all the increase since 2001, may be by interest rate increase, which could cause a crash of the stock market and even bond, if the increase is rapid. HF hope therefore to make huge profits. It is much more likely that they were given a kamikaze role at their expense.

Hedge funds will be sacrificed in a historical Bear-Trap, a trap for those who lower their position. Their bankruptcy would not cause any systemic shock and the larger banks would be preserved.

To persuade hedge funds, numerous analysts and most of the media were asked to announce deep fall of gold in 2013.

Gold stocks available for sale fell to 2.99 tons on June 26th 2013, which is less than 100,000 ounces. With only 120 million dollars, China could cause the COMEX to default. Will she do it? Who will push the button?

Rates are rising in the markets. China is going through a cash crisis, passing the stage of credit freeze. A new crisis looms in Italy. Are we on the eve of a general crash to make precious metals fall even lower before the surge? It could be very fast and more violent than in 1979-1980. Some eve speak of an "overnight" increase. But when will it take place?

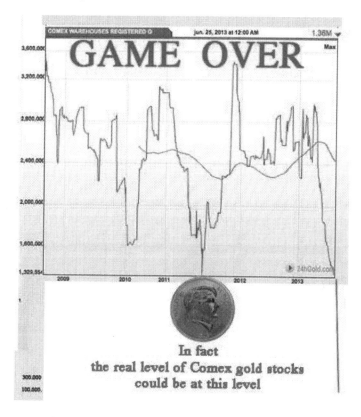

In fact the real level of Comex gold stocks could be at this level

All these are signs that a deep change of our monetary system approaches in the short term.

Do not sell today, because tomorrow when no one will be able to buy gold, yours will worth a fortune on the parallel market. France has experienced many similar periods when gold was "fixed-priced" that is to say at blocked value, not reflecting supply and demand. Every time, it has led to huge increases in trade between individuals.

CYRILLE JUBERT

ACUTE ECONOMIC DEPRESSION WHAT WILL SILVER BECOME?

Countries have to tighten all the bolts to try and balance their budgets to pay interests on their debts or start repaying them.

The first step is to put an end to the most easily manipulated secret tax havens (Switzerland, Luxembourg, Andorra...) According to information reaching us, this measure was effective in late May 2012, which explained the descent of the financial brigade in the French subsidiaries of Credit Suisse, UBS and other Swiss banks in early July.

States are now able to pressurize taxpayers who evaded taxes, unless they invested in metals which they put in anonymous safe. Insiders made bulk purchases and that's why the Swiss refineries are producing 3/8 now. Lots of gold is being put to safety in Asia.

In times of economic crises, the first sector to suffer is real estate. The crisis which started in 2007, was born out of loans granted to non-credit worthy people (subprime) to enable them to invest in real estate. There was overproduction in real estate in the United States, Western Europe (Spain, Ireland, Great Britain...), Central Europe and China with a huge bubble on the price of m². Housing stock for sale is huge whilst the demand dropped due to growing unemployment. Spanish banks are endangered by mortgages including 60% of bad loans. Santander, a leading systemic Spanish bank that acquired most of the mortgages in Great Britain, also went into depression. Evil is widespread.

Banks around the world were instructed to restrict credit, on one hand and increase their assets on the other. Demand is therefore going to fall at the very time when the supply is increasing. The construction of new real estate collapsed.

Morgan Stanley's barometer published on the 6th of March 2012, indicated that lead and tin were overproduced with large stocks. Demand for copper will decrease sharply due to the housing crisis.

In such a case, the copper, steel and tin mines will close their less profitable companies and keep a minimum staff to prevent their equipment from deteriorating. When the mines will idle, silver production coming from them as a byproduct, which represent 70% of the silver extracted in the world, will experience a sharp decline.

We saw in the study of the fundamentals that the main mines in the world experienced a dramatic decrease in density and a decline in silver production in recent years.

We also observed that some mines refused to sell their production when prices were too low… and that other mines, following Eric Sprott's advice, refused a double risk and decided to keep their cash in silver bullions instead of leaving them in paper money in the banks. **Therefore, silver supply should decrease more significantly.**

Joint IMF and GFMS study published in the first half of 2011, contemplated a growth of industrial demand for silver which alone could absorb almost all the mining production in 2012, leaving no room for the demand for coins, medals, investment silver, jewelry or others. However, the demand for physical silver to protect oneself from the monetary crisis has been growing for several years.

The acceleration of the economic, banking and monetary crisis in the second half of 2013 should strengthen this demand until the establishment of the first monetary reform.

The first reform, if there is any in 2013, will prove insufficient to solve long-term problems. The latter will resurface 18 months to two years later with greater magnitude. **Remember that the Federal Reserve committed to redeem all United States debt to 30 years and is now emitting debt to two years.** In late 2014 or early 2015, the United States will default on their debts or devalue the dollar massively. The monetary panic will then be total.

COMEX can collapse and the current markets may be closed temporarily, as in the case of Russia in August 2011. The remaining real tangible securities are the precious metals.

Don't chase rainbows. Don't play for money. Have confidence and as the English say, "keep your temper", keep your positions whatever happens in the short term.

Wait for the time that will reward your wisdom and intuition!

Finally, let's remember that Ron Paul, candidate for Republican nomination to face Obama in the US presidential elections, campaigned for the return of the gold standard which involved bimetallism, as defined in the 1776 US constitution.

In March 2012, during a debate on the audit of the Fed by the currency board of Congress, Ron Paul asked Bernanke why American citizens were not allowed to use the silver coins, Silver Eagle, as an alternative currency to the Federal Reserve fiat dollars although the Silver Eagles were enshrined in the US Constitution as legal tender.

Utah has already passed a law allowing the payment of taxes with gold or silver... it was followed by Colorado which is preparing to legalize alternative currencies to dethrone the Fed's dollar.

If Europe has inclinations to split, America could also being broken for monetary reasons. It happened in the 30s. Chicago's Fed refused drafts of NY Fed. There was no more trust between central bankers from one State to another.

Basics of Silver

1) SUPPLY

Mining production on the rise
Decrease in density of ores
Geographical distribution of production
North American silver mines
Silver reserves in the soil
Recovery of silver

2) DEMAND

Distribution of demand by sector
Elasticity of demand compared to the silver price
New Industrial Applications
Prospects for industrial demand
Silver investment ETF
SLV a means to control silver price

3) DEFICIT MARKET

4) PRICES

5) CYCLES

Silver throughout History

1) Mining production on the increase

60% to 70% of silver production is a by-product obtained during the refining of copper, lead, zinc or gold ores. Strictly speaking, there are very **few strictly silver mines**.

The "Cannington Mine" belonging to the mining giant, HP Billington, produced mainly lead and zinc, but incidentally, it also produced 7% of the world's silver. Did this represent the 38 million ounces of silver compared to the 8,552 million ounces of lead that came out of this mine?

In 2006, in terms of revenue, when silver was worth $10 an ounce, this production represented $400 million against $275 million for lead which stood at $0.50 a pound. Silver represented 68% of the revenue from the mine

The price of silver, kept very low for decades, did not help to make the extraction of this mineral profitable. Only the very high density veins could be exploited.

In 2002, the average cost for extracting silver was **$5 against $300** for gold. This explains the gold/silver ratio of the just ended decade.

Gold/silver ratio = number of ounces of silver needed to buy an ounce of gold.

The San Bartolomé mine in Bolivia, "Cœur d'Alene" Mines Corporation is one of the 3 largest pure silver mines in the world. In 2011, It produced 8 million ounces of silver at a production price of $7.87 an ounce.

Silver metal production In millions of ounces										
2000	2001	2002	2003	2004	2005	2006	2007	2008	2009
591.0	606.2	593.9	596.6	613.0	636.8	640.9	664.4	684.7	709.6
Prices in $ US										
4.953	4.370	4.599	4.879	6.658	7.312	11.549	13.384	14.989	14.674

Mineral production increased about 20% between 2004 and 2009. In 2011, it peaked at 761 million ounces.

The increase in silver price helped to intensify prospection and launch the exploitation of some sites in recent years.

The price of silver is not going up; it's rather the purchasing power of the currency that is declining.

To measure the relative increase in the price of silver, in addition to the gold/silver ratio, we can look at the price of energy which is included in the cost of extraction. One of the tools used in measuring the relativity of the silver price is the Silver-Oil Ratio. This ratio is now back to the average ratio obtained in 1975 at 0.36 ($41: $112).

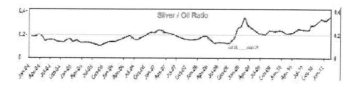

Silver Cost in Crude Oil: SCCO
With the barrel at $112 and an ounce of silver at $41, 2.73 ounces of silver is needed to purchase a barrel of oil.

To monitor the trend in the graph on a daily basis go to: http://stockcharts.com/freecharts/gallery.html?$wtic:$silver

An increase in a barrel eventually leads to a rise in gold and silver prices. Precious metals cannot be extracted at a loss.

2) Decrease in density of ores

A report on the lead market in 2011 indicated that lead and zinc production in the world is always increasing. Peak production of lead was expected towards the middle of the century.

On the other hand, the two graphs below clearly indicate that the density of lead and zinc deposits greatly deteriorated from 32 to 4 in 120 years for lead and reduction by half for zinc.

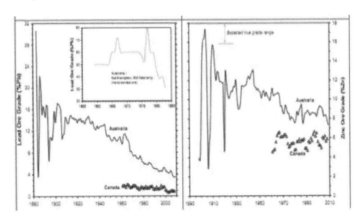

This means that the cost of producing a ton of lead to equal pay and stable energy prices increased by 8. Today, another criterion is to be taken into account.

This phenomenon is accelerating since 1997 nearly everywhere in the world. The weaker the density, the higher the damage to the environment. Expenses for this new item in the operating expenditures increased so much, that many mines were forced to close down.

Since silver is a byproduct of the lead or zinc mines representing 32% of its production, if the density of the lead or zinc in the base ore declines dramatically, there is high probability that the density of silver will also decrease and production costs will increase significantly in these mines.

The price of silver then can only rise.

On February 22 2012, Gavin Thomas, chairman of the Australian mining company "Kingsgate Consolidated" said on

CNBC that:

"Silver is a fantastic opportunity... there is a huge margin in rising silver prices due to lack of supply."

"The supply of silver is under pressure because the lead and zinc mines have become less prolific and silver is a byproduct of these mines. At the same time, demand is on the increase to respond to the new medical or industrial needs and the demand of silver for investment continue to grow in India and China. Both countries turn to silver as gold becomes expensive and more difficult to acquire."

This trend is also true in all the copper mines.

Silver is becoming more and more scarce

3) Geographical distribution of production

Peru is the world's leading producer of silver with a production capacity of 123.7 million ounces. The first silver mine in Peru produced 14.9 million ounces. "Antamina Copper-Zinc Mine" is a copper mine producing silver as a byproduct. This mine alone accounted for 12% of the production of silver in Peru. The second silver mine in Peru produces 10 million ounces (8%) and the third, 8.6 million ounces (7%). These first three mines produces a quarter of the country's silver and the rest is extracted by over 140 mines.

Mexico was the world's 2nd largest silver producer in 2010 with a declining production from 114 to 112.5 million ounces of silver. The first silver mine in Mexico "Fresnillo Silver Mine" produced 35.9 million ounces of silver in 2010, representing one third of the country's production and 5% of the world production of silver in 2010. It is the second silver mine in the world. This mine also produces gold, lead and zinc. Mexican Silver production seems to decline by 10% in 2013.

China is the world's 3rd largest silver producer with a growing silver production from 93.2 to 96.4 million ounces in 2010. The largest silver mine in China is a zinc and silver- lead mine. It represented only 4 to 5% of the national production and 0.6% of the world production. The lead and zinc mines in China were extremely old and on a small scale about 12 years ago. The government closed down many of the mines to modernize and structure the entire sector. China established joint-ventures with some Western professionals for the most promising sites.

Australia is the world's 4th silver producer with 54.6 million ounces. The country has the largest silver mine in the world. Cannington is a zinc and lead mine which also produced 2/3 of the country's silver and 5.2% of the world production.

Chili (n°1 copper producer), is the world's 5th silver producer with 48 million ounces of silver produced in 2010. Logically, the country's largest silver producer is the world's leading copper producer. It extracts a quarter of the silver production in Chili.

Russia is the world's 6th silver producer with 45 million ounces production in 2010. One third of this was from a single mine which produces gold with silver. Informations are difficult to gather.

Bolivia is the world's 7th silver producer with 43.7 million ounces in 2010. Its main silver mine, "San Cristobal", produced 19.4 million ounces of silver in 2010. The famous Potosi mine which made Spain's fortune from 1540 until the 17th Century was considered as Peru at the time. It is now in Bolivia. There are hundreds of small artisan mines in the exhausted mountain today where farmers' families without any means and security, continue to scrape the rock in search of white metal. On the other hand, Cœur d'Alene (CDE), one of the largest mining companies for almost pure silver in the world, successfully developed the San Bartolome site at the foot of Potosi. The company did not bother to dig the mountain whose veins were exhausted but it has been exploiting tons of tailings from this mine for 5 centuries. Current techniques are used to recover silver that the previous generations did not know how to separate from the base ore. Thus, San Bartolome is one of the most profitable silver mine in the world.

USA is the world's 8th silver producer with 41 million ounces. The leading silver mine in the USA, "Greens Creek Mine" in Alaska operated by Hecla, produces 8.9 million ounces, representing 17% of US production. The second is Lucky Friday, also operated by HECLA, with 3 million ounces. The world's 3rd largest zinc mine, "Red Dog Mine" also in Alaska, produced 2.4 million ounces. A large proportion of silver produced in the USA is from the copper mines.

Poland is the world's 9th silver producer with 38.5 million ounces. The silver production in Poland comes 100% from one mine, which is a copper mine. In 2012, HSBC bought most of Polish silver and have an similar agreement for 2013.

As we just observed, the largest silver mines in the world are primarily copper, zinc, lead or gold mines.

The six largest silver mines

Mine	Country	2010 Production
Cannington Silver/Lead/Zinc Mine	Australia	38.6 Moz
Fresnillo Silver Mine	Mexico	38.6 Moz
San Cristobal Polymetallic Mine	Bolivia	19.4 Moz
Antamina Copper/Zinc Mine	Peru	14.9 Moz
Rudna Copper Mine	Poland	14.9 Moz
Penasquito Gold/Silver Mine	Mexico	13.9 Moz

The production of the two largest silver mines in the world, Cannington and Fresnillo, fell sharply in 2011 compared to 2010.

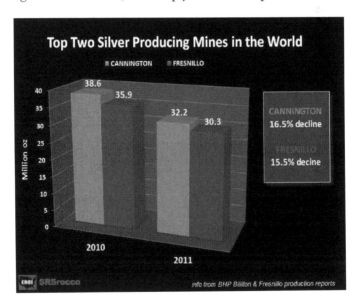

The first decreased from 38.6 Moz to 32.2 Moz (-19.8%) and the second dropped by 18.4% from 35.9 Moz to 30.3 Moz. The mining companies attributed this decline in production to the decrease in the density of the ore.

In 2011, the Polish copper mine, KGHM Polska Meidz, became the world's leading silver producer, increasing from 37.3 Moz in 2010 to 40.5 Moz in 2011. This was a total surprise on the market because BHP Billiton produced 2.5 times more copper than this Polish mine.

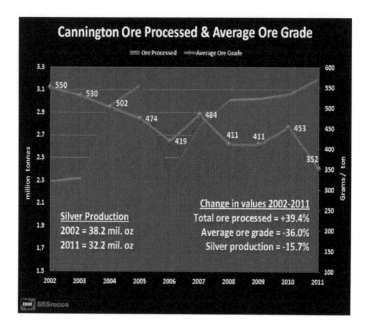

We see from this graph that in the last decade, Cannington, significantly increased the extraction and processing of ores from 2.3 to 3.1 million tons to produce less and less silver due to the constant lowering of the density.

Tajikistan: This country which is difficult to locate on a map is in Central Asia. It has 430 tons of gold reserves and one of the largest silver deposits on the planet, the "Bolchoï Koni Mansour" estimated at 50,000 tons by the Soviets in 1980. A call for tenders has been issued for its exploitation.

Companies that are currently best positioned are those with Chinese investment. We will soon hear about this rising value.

4) Silver Mines in the United States

The graph below shows the peak year for the extraction of silver from the US mines by each state. Most of these states had their peak production before 1937.

In other words, silver production in the United States have been declining since that time despite improved mining techniques.

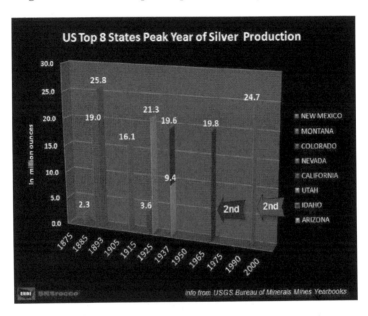

The most productive state today is Nevada, state next to California, whose production has been declining since the year 2000.

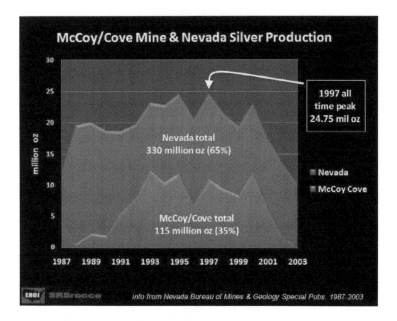

Global warming and snow melting in the far north of the American will certainly allow the discovery and exploitation of mines in Alaska, if environmentalists do not oppose it.

Today, domestic demand has exceeded American mining production by far.

According to the latest study conducted by USGS in early 2012, production of silver in the United States fell by 30% between October 2010 and October 2011. If the trend had continued till the end of the year, the United States would have produced only 35 Moz of silver while the demand for Silver Eagle exceeded 40 million ounces for two consecutive years.

Silver throughout History

	Nevada	Other States[2]	Total
2010:[p]			
October	21,900	95,300	117,000
November	17,200	73,700	91,000
December	18,100	82,400	101,000
January–December	217,000	1,050,000	1,270,000
2011:			
January	18,800	79,300 [r]	98,100 [r]
February	16,800	68,400 [r]	85,200 [r]
March	19,900	83,000 [r]	103,000
April	18,200 [r]	77,100	95,300 [r]
May	18,900 [r]	81,400 [r]	100,000
June[r]	19,700	72,800	92,500
July[r]	16,900	73,400	90,300
August[r]	17,200	72,700	89,900
September[r]	14,100	73,300	87,400
October	13,000	68,400	81,400
January–October	174,000	750,000	923,000

MINE PRODUCTION OF RECOVERABLE SILVER IN THE UNITED STATES, BY STATE[1] (Kilograms)

[p]Preliminary. [r]Revised.
[1]Data are rounded to no more than three significant digits; may not add to totals shown.
[2]Includes Alaska, Arizona, California, Colorado, Idaho, Missouri, Montana, New Mexico, South Dakota, and Utah.

October silver production falls 30% yoy

US production has declined by 50% since the peak of 70 million ounces in 1997, whereas the demand for Silver Eagle at that time was only 3.6 million ounces, barely 5% of domestic production of silver. Today, the demand accounts for 114% of mining production. For "Lucky Friday", one of HECLA Company's finest mines, the density of silver per ton of ore extracted from the ground was cut in half between 1965 and 2010. In other words, silver to energy cost and equal salaries became two times more expensive to produce.

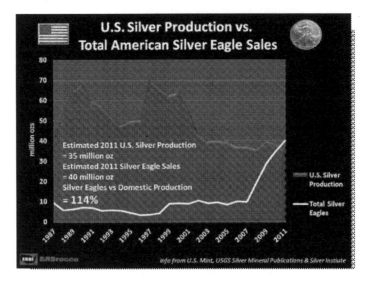

The US bureau of mines, USGS, published much more negative general statistics for all the American silver mines. It took 12 times more minerals to produce the same quantity of silver in 1993 than in 1935. The density of silver in the ore declined by almost 92%.

Hecla's Lucky Friday Mine	1965	2010	(+/-)
Tons of ore milled:	181,100	351,074	+94%
Silver Production:	3,223,580	3,359,379	+4.2%
Silver ore grades:	17.8 oz/t	10.25 oz/t	-42.4%
Lead ore grades:	11.3%	6.6%	-41.6%

info from 2010 Hecla 10-K & USGS Bureau of Mines Minerals Yearbook 1965

Meanwhile, silver production in Canada decreased by 57% from the highs of 2002 at 44 million ounces to only 18.6 million ounces in 2011. In 2002, the demand for Silver Maple Leaf was 576,196 million or 1.3% of production, while in 2011, 22.5 million of these an ounce coins were sold, representing a 30% increase compared to the two previous years.

United States Silver Mining Statistics 1935-1993

	1935	1970	1993	(+/-)
Tons of ore milled*:	36.1 million tons	252.5 million tons	483.7 million tons	+1240%
Silver production:	48.9 million oz	45.0 million oz	52.7 million oz	+7.8%
Silver ore grades:	1.35 oz/ton	0.77 oz/ton	0.11 oz/ton	-91.8%

*Includes total ore from gold, silver, copper, lead and zinc mining.

Info from USGS Bureau of Mines Minerals Yearbook

On this graph, we see that the Canadian demand for silver coins exceeded the mining production in Canada by far. If the trend had continued until 2011, sales of silver coins would have represented 121% of domestic production.

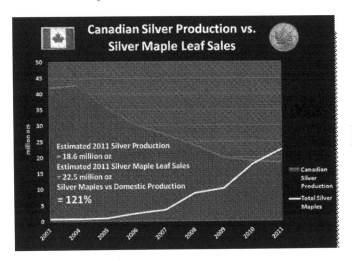

Personal Comments:

I consider these sharp declines in production in the United States and Canada extremely suspicious. Canada is an extremely vast and sparsely populated country whose huge mineral reserves are under-exploited. We can say the same for Alaska, which will be more easily exploitable due to the global warming.

Did the mines seek to keep their reserves under the ground,

especially since May 2011, in anticipation of a strong appreciation of silver? Or is it about broader guidelines of some oligarchy seeking to make silver more scarce on the markets to inflate a large bubble on the silver metal? That seems possible.

In January 2012, the US government closed HECLA's "Lucky Friday" Mine, one of the rare "pure silver" mines on the market. The decision was taken following an accident which caused minor injuries to seven mine workers on December 1.

The government requested that the shoring be replaced but that would take one year. HECLA securities lost 20% on the stock market the very day this decision was announced. This mine represents 30% of HECLA's silver production.

HECLA's decline in production by 3 million ounces of silver over one year represents almost a month's sale of Silver Eagle by the US Mint or 7.6% of US domestic production.

One more stone in the shoes of JPM on the CME but even more on the London Market.

GLENCORE-XSTRATA

The Swiss group Glencore first merchant of raw materials in the World, is trying to merge with the mining group Xstrata, which it already holds a controlling interest. The new group would control 60% of the zinc market and 50% of the copper market, not to mention its weight in the coal, aluminum, gold and especially silver. As 70% of silver comes from the mines of copper, lead, tin and zinc, Glencore is already able to control 35% of silver coming from the mines. An overwhelming position. Only China enjoy a greater position.

By studying the accounts and press releases of Rio Tinto, the mining company controlled by the Rothschild family, which is the fourth world producer copper, we find that its 698,000 tons of gross ore, give 321,000 tons of refined copper. *"The rest gives refining by-products, Gold, Silver, Molybdenum and sulfuric acid, which bring significant income to the company. Copper sales generated 8% of the company's revenue in 2008. Copper Revenues and its byproducts are recognized to be 16% of revenues in Rio Tinto."*

Xstrata operates among others but especially an Australian mine, Mount Isa Mines and a refinery: Britannia Refined Metals. This refinery, the largest lead producer in Europe, is located 40km from London in the estuary of the Thames, a perfect location to serve the British domestic market and the European market. It refines crude lead ore <u>from Mount Isa Mines since 1931.</u>

In 2005, the performance of MIM has been improved to provide 231,000 tons of zinc, 160,000 tons of refined lead and 11.36 Moz of silver (353 t). The Britannia Refined Metals (BRM) website present these improved results in 2011 of 180,000 tons of lead and 400 tons of silver.

At first glance, silver production is only the 450th of production of lead, so it is apparently small. If we do the accounts, that changes everything.

The lead hovered around $2,000 per ton. 180,000 tons of lead worth therefore $360 million, while 400 tons of silver are $400 million today. Silver represents half of the revenues of this refinery.

This dominance of Glencore on market allows this actor to have a key role in all the price manipulations of the white metal, even if his name was never heard of so far.

5) Silver Underground Reserves

The international reference for defining underground reserves is the USGS (United States Geological Survey). Every year, this US government agency publishes production figures of the various minerals and underground reserves.

Definitions
Reserves: Part of "basic reserves" that can be extracted or produced at the time of the study. The term "reserve" only requires an operating infrastructure already in place or operational.

Basic Reserves : identified, measured and quantified resource, meeting the minimum physical and chemical criteria used in the mining industry. This may include economically exploitable reserves at the planning of future productions, taking account of improved technologies, the "reserves" (see above) and non-economically exploitable reserves in a measurable future.

In this data compilation on silver, provided by the US government mines department, from the left, you have year by year, mining production, exploitable reserves and proven reserves in tons.

Mine production	Reserves¹	Reserve base¹	Mine production	Réserve de base	découvertes
1995ᵉ 14,000	280,000	420,000	1995ᵉ 14,000	420,000	0
1996ᵉ 14,800	280,000	420,000	1996ᵉ 14,800	406,000	0
1997ᵉ 15,300	280,000	420,000	1997ᵉ 15,300	391,200	0
1998ᵉ 16,200	280,000	420,000	1998ᵉ 16,200	375,900	0
1999ᵉ 15,900	280,000	420,000	1999ᵉ 15,900	359,700	0
2000ᵉ 17,900	280,000	420,000	2000ᵉ 17,900	341,800	0
2001ᵉ 18,300	280,000	430,000	2001ᵉ 18,300	323,500	10,000
2002 18,800	270,000	520,000	2002 18,800	304,700	90,000
2003ᵉ 19,000	270,000	570,000	2003ᵉ 19,000	285,700	50,000
2004ᵉ 19,500	270,000	570,000	2004ᵉ 19,500	266,200	0
2005ᵉ 20,300	270,000	570,000	2005ᵉ 20,300	245,900	0
2006ᵉ 19,500	270,000	570,000	2006ᵉ 19,500	226,400	0
2007ᵉ 20,500	270,000	570,000	2007ᵉ 20,500	205,900	0
2008ᵉ 20,900	270,000	570,000	2008ᵉ 20,900	185,000	0
2009ᵉ 21,400	400,000		2009ᵉ 21,400	163,600	0
2010ᵉ 22,200	510,000		2010ᵉ 22,200	141,400	150,000

After reading the compilation of the Mines Department (left table), the first observation is that the figures were not updated from year to year. Logically, the reserves should decrease each year depending on the production of the previous year.

I did all the calculations again by subtracting the previous year's production from the base reserves. Results: according to the new calculations, the official reserves have melted since 1995 from

Silver throughout History

420,000 to 141,400 tons.

Assuming the base reserves were identified manually in the 19th Century, without ever using satellite images, and supposing that they can suddenly become the object of sensational discoveries, doubling the proven reserves, the base reserves would increase at the most from 141,400 to **291,400** since 2001. **This is very far from the 510,000 tons figure announced.**

In 2009, the entire "base reserve" changed column and officially became technically and economically exploitable in their entirety. Isn't that amazing when oil prices have soared over the past three years?

141.4 thousand tons divided by 22 thousand tons of annual production = 6.42 years of production.
291,400 tons: 22 thousand tons of annual production = 13 years of production.

We are quickly approaching a serious silver shortage, until new techniques allow us to exploit hitherto unprofitable reserves or non-exploitable, like ocean floor. But to do this, the price of silver must be higher.

Please note that I have attached this document because it was part of the creed imposed by the government and it is useful to bear it in mind, but I think it is misleading as almost the entire official data nowadays.

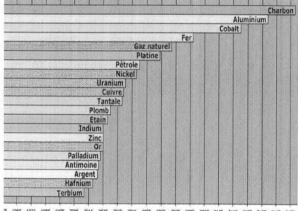

Depletion dates of the exploitable resources of our planet to the current consumption rate

I do not believe in the "peak oil" fable and thus even less in "peak gas", which are myths created by the Anglo-American oil cartel to ensure their domination.

The world's largest oil and gas producer is Russia. However, Russian experts claim that oil is abiotic, in other words, it is formed in the deep layers of the earth seeps to the surface through cracks. The tragedy of the Deepwater Horizon platform is due to the exploitation of abiotic oil in one of these deep BP cracks.

The huge deposits of oil and gas found in Eastern Mediterranean, Brazil and in all oceans globe, show that the data has been tampered with.

This map shows the gold mines in California. Geologists quickly realized that the gold found by the prospectors, first on the surface and then underground, came from a single and same vein of over 200 km long, with intertwined branches, the veins were between 30 cm and 3 meters wide. The cut in the map is purely administrative. To the right of this boundary, lies the state of Nevada, the richest state in silver of the USA.

mines d'or
mines de mercure

California is carved to the west by the famous cracks of San Andrea, which mark the recess between the Pacific tectonic plate and that of America. The movements of this plate formed the wrinkling rock of the Sierra Nevada, whose quartz is very rich in precious metals. These veins naturally continue to Mexico.

Chili, Bolivia, Peru, the richest states in copper and silver are located along the Pacific cracks, in the wrinkling mountains, the Andes, were shaped by the movement of tectonic plates.

The gold, silver and copper veins etc. were originally formed by lifting magnetic fluid towards the surface by the cracks. The cooling of these lava resulted in crystallizations of mineral particles at different temperatures and therefore different depths.

The configuration of cracks and mountainous folds exist under the surface of the oceans which cover 70% of the earth's surface. There are therefore richer gold and silver deposits than those in

California, Peru and Mexico together, which will be exploitable one day as oil from the great deeps exploited recently in Brazil. It will be more expensive, that's all.

The earth is alive.

For several years, there have been a warming of the magma, due to the tear from a heat shield of the earth, which allows a higher density of cosmic rays to pass. The warming of the magma making it more fluid causes different phenomena.

Tectonic plates slide faster on the earth's crust, causing more earthquakes of greater magnitude, more volcanic eruptions and new ruptures of cracks.

The same cause create the same effect. Metallic veins form again and, in the shorter term, breaks in the plates will update hitherto unknown veins because they plowed in great depth.

The pole moves. Territories that were not explored due to climatic conditions have already become and will become more accessible in the coming decades.

There is currently a gold rush in Alaska to "fish" gold from the Bering Sea. An American station even did a reality show about it, which turned out to be very successful.
www.akmining.com/mine/bering_sea_gold_the_nome_gold_rush.htm

In short, the end of all the earth's reserves is a myth in the long term. Since we are just men and we have to live under political, economic and monetary conditions in the short term, we need to think in terms of data in this time scale.

The USGS anticipates a 25% increase in silver production by 2020.

Silver throughout History

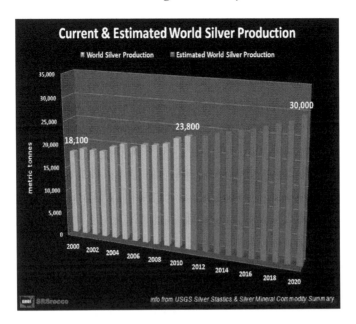

Rising oil prices should significantly impact silver in the coming years. The real reason is obviously the decrease of dollar's purchasing power.

CYRILLE JUBERT

GOLD RESERVES COMPARED TO SILVER RESERVES

1/10

"The gold/silver ratio is set according to the respective production costs of precious metals. (1/60). This ratio will suddenly change when the initial problems of shortages will appear."

Dany Chaize 2002

The latest report released by the USGS indicated 510,000 tons of silver and 51,000 tons of gold left to be extracted. You don't need to have attended Polytechnique to understand that there is **a ratio of 1 to 10.**

The figures provided by the USGS show a political will, a compromise value which is more monetary than industrial or geological.

"In politics, nothing ever happens by chance"
Franklin D. Roosevelt

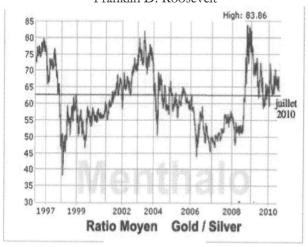

We can see in the graph above that the gold/silver ratio fluctuated a lot around of 65 from 1997 to 2013.

MINES NATIONALIZATION?

In the early summer of 2012, Bolivia announced that it would nationalize the Malku Khota Mine, reputed to be one of the largest silver reserves in the world, with 230 million ounces of silver, not to mention gold, indium or gallium. President Morales had already nationalized the tin and zinc of the Glencore Mining Group in June. Bolivia either compensated the mining companies or renegotiated the agreement on royalties.

Guatemala seems to have adopted the second option. The President wanted to impose 40% royalties by decree on all mining companies exploiting its underground reserves.

Currently, the gold and silver mines pay 4% royalties, the base metal mines, 3% and those who are solely interested in industrial minerals pay only 1% to the Guatemalan government. It is likely that these royalties were extremely undervalued until today, like those calculated by the Anglo-Persian Oil Company for Iran.

If the measure to impose a tenfold increase in the royalties on gold and silver was adopted and extended to all producing countries, it would be the equivalent of the oil shocks in the 70's on the prices of precious metals.

In September 2012, one of my sources told me of an oncoming nationalization of the purely Canadian gold mines. This nationalization would be the first sign of the confiscation of gold in the benefit of the banks in view of a return to the gold standard. It will be recalled that the Federal Reserve in its balance sheets speaks of "deep storage gold." The gold reserves of the U.S. mines could also be nationalized in the near future.

6) Silver from recycling

20% to 25% of Silver supply comes from recycling.

Argentic Photography
Part of recycling comes from the processing photographic films, radio or cinema. Recycling is achieved by electrolysis or precipitation.

Electronics
Every computer or electronic hardware contains 0.02 to 0.5% of silver that can be recovered on diodes, anodes, or cards and integrated or printed circuits. In 2000, this source represented 90 tons or 2.9 million ounces.

Jewelry
Worn out and broken jewelry are a constant source of recycling. The majority of silver jewelry is of poor quality alloys.

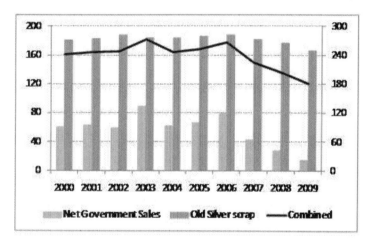

The higher the price of silver, the more profitable the recycling will become. Today, greater amount of the silver used in electrical or electronic gadgets is not recovered. In 10 years, the recovery remained stable from 190 million ounces/year with a peak in 2011 at 250 million ounces.

One of my friend working in one of the most renowned company in recycling, told me that they used to receive 500 kilos of bulk silver each day in 2011, but in the last year, they didn't receive such a quantity in a month. People hoard silver, if the price is too low.

CYRILLE JUBERT

Demand

CYRILLE JUBERT

Distribution of demand by sector

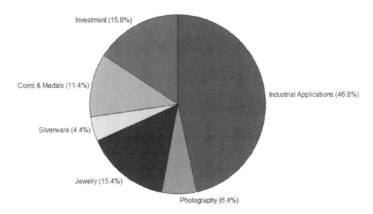

2011 Silver Demand

Photography
This sector declined from 218 million ounces in 2000 to 70 million ounces in 2011. It was divided by 3 as analog photography was gradually replaced by digital photography. Since the latter requires a computer or electronic equipment, the demand is only shifted in the table.

Silverware
Silverware seems to be less fashionable than in the late 90s. This sector has decreased by half from 100 million ounces to 50 million ounces.

Jewelry
Despite the fact that the price of silver multiplied by 5 in eleven years, demand remained relatively stable at 170 million ounces.

Coins and Medals
The demand for silver coins has been multiplied by 3.5 in the past eleven years, from 30 million ounces to 102 million ounces.

In 2011, silver coins, especially Silver eagle, the American one ounce coin, hit new record sales pace with 39,868,500 ounces, four times more than in 2006.

In 2012, the US Mint set a new sales record with 33 million of Silver Eagles.

In august 2013, 30.2 Millions of silver Eagles are already sold.

In Canada, the sale of coins has been virtually nonexistent for 10 years. In 2011, it accounted for 22 million ounces.

In China, the state minted a limited quantity of commemorative medals and it was forbidden to hoard silver metal until the summer of 2009. Since September 2009, Chinese investors are rushing on silver in all its forms. These figures did not seem to have been recognized by the American Silver Institute.

In Europe, quotas have been established to limit the export of silver coins by Germany. Figures are not public like in the US.

New applications

The antibacterial, virucidal and fungicidal properties of silver were known since the olden days. Today, products using colloids or nanoparticles of silver in medicine is on the increase. From the dressing base for the general public hospitals for burns, bedsores, or healing accelerator, silver is found everywhere.

For the same bactericidal reasons, silver is used in the treatment of air or water, both in hospital and hotel facilities as well as in water filters of individuals where silver particles are included in ceramics.

Colloidal silver which enables people to strengthen their immune system against microbial and viral attacks has become a common product for the American consumer nowadays.

Anecdotally, Eau Positive participated in vivo experiments with a group of oyster farmers and IFREMER to try to save the oysters at our coast, decimated by a killer bacterium, Vibrio Splendidus Biovar.

Photovoltaic

A new market. In 2004, this market consumed only 3 million ounces of silver. In 2011, PV required 73 million ounces and its growth prospects were huge in a world where fossil energy tended to become more scarce and increasingly expensive.

Photovoltaic accounted for 14% of industrial demand in 2011. It is believed that the annual demand for silver for PV will at least double by 2015. The progression is geometric.

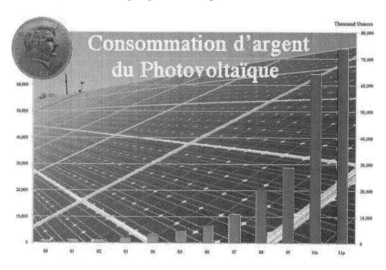

A photovoltaic cell contains only 0.15 to 0.25 grams of silver.

Fluctuations in the price of silver do not affect the selling price of the equipment. Even less since the price of silver remains in one way or the other correlated with the price of energy. The higher the price of oil, the greater the photovoltaic demand.

RFID Chips

Industrial race towards the miniaturization of RFID chips led the Japanese electronics industry to produce smaller chips. In 2004, the chips were the size of a grain of rice. Two years later, they were 0.15mm x 0.15mm to 7.5 microns thick.

Wal-Mart Company, leader in cheap clothing in the USA, equipped the entire subcontracted production in China with RFID chips.

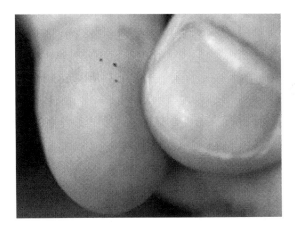

Today, all banknotes, identity documents and communication devices are fitted with RFID tags. This represents phenomenal quantities. In 2009, 30 billion items were chipped with RFID tags in France; the growth of this market is exceptional. All the chips contains an infinitesimal amount of silver but that represent a large and growing volume.

Prospects for Industrial Demand

A sharp increase in the demand for these new industrial applications is expected in the coming years.

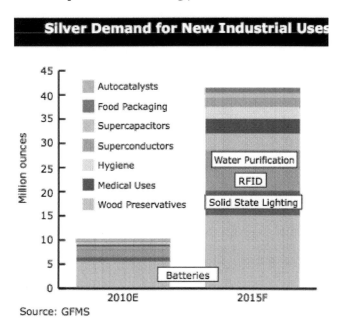

Source: GFMS

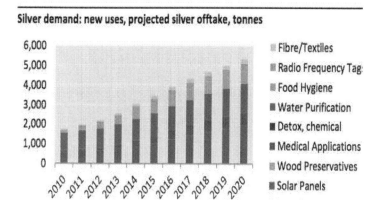

New Investment Fund

Through the ages, silver was used as a medium of exchange in the same way as gold. However, it was also a way of retaining part of one's capital by protecting it against economic, political and monetary hazards. Since 2001, the acceleration of monetary erosion in all fiat currencies has given a new meaning to the hoarding of precious metals.

In 2004, the bankers of the Anglo-American Oligarchy adopted the concept already developed by the Bank of Amsterdam in 1600 and modernized it. They created a financial product that was easy to buy or sell in a stock market as a company share, and had to bear the generic name of ETF for Exchange Traded Fund. This vehicle was supposed to allow the investor to buy gold and sell it without having to worry putting it in a safe or insuring it.

The customer, confident in the system, could only be surprised that contractually, he would be prohibited from requesting for the delivery of his bullion, which cannot get out of the secured warehouses of the issuing bank or the subcontracting company acting as a custodian. Suspicious customers are surely entitled to wonder.

In April 2006, after the success of ETF GLD, the bankers launched an equivalent product allowing investors to invest their cash in silver metal with ETF SLV.

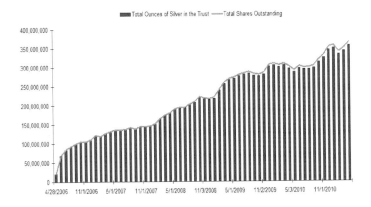

As you can see, this really pleased and SLV attracted a lot of capital to enable it invest massively in silver. Other financial groups

in Switzerland, Canada and elsewhere and recently China followed the example of SLV as we will see later.

In a lecture given in 2011, Eric Sprott, manager of a Canadian investment fund that created ETF Silver (PSLV), displayed the proven silver reserves around the world. Ishare SLV (circled in red) claimed to have about 340 million ounces of silver or nearly half of the proven stock.

SILVER :: DEPOSITORIES : ETFS

Name	Fund	Storage	Total Weight
COMEX	Registered	Depository	44,839,053 oz
COMEX	Eligible	Depository	59,575,472 oz
COMEX	Total	Depository	104,414,525 oz
TOCOM	Total	Depository	473,584 oz
Brompton	PBU-UN.TO	ETF	1,033,556 oz
Claymore	SVR.UN	ETF	2,915,000 oz
Deutsche Bank	XAD6	ETF	6,850,000 oz
ETF Securities	PHAG/SIVR	ETF	51,515,439 oz
iShares	SLV	ETF	340,004,314 oz
Japan	Physical	ETF	13,216 oz
Julius Baer	JBSI	ETF	9,411,000 oz
SilverBullion	SBT.U	ETF	3,143,830 oz
Sprott	PSLV	ETF	22,298,540 oz
UBS	SVCHA	ETF	250,000 oz
ZKB	ZSIL	ETF	77,034,712 oz
BMG Bullion	BMG	FUND	4,960,697 oz
Central Fund	CEF	FUND	75,209,103 oz
BullionVault		EFUND	4,243,969 oz
eGold		EFUND	85,244 oz
GoldMoney		EFUND	22,590,211 oz
	TOTAL	STOCKS	726,446,940 oz

Eric Sprott made ironic comments on the stock since many analysts who know this market are aware that a substantial part of the stock is totally fictitious. No independent body has ever been able to control the actual bullions that SLV supposedly hold.

Two banks, JPM and HSBC banks, massively dominate the gold and silver market. One is the official custodian of the stocks of GLD, while the other take custody of the stocks of SLV... but both banks sell gold and silver in huge quantities on the market. What these two banks sell on the market is not the actual metal. It is "paper money". In practical terms, they sell silver bullions that will not come out of the warehouse where nobody has the right to enter to check if the warehouse is full. They also sell metal bars on the futures, that is, they sell metals that they commit to deliver 3 or 6 months after the purchase date. However, on the delivery day, they "roll their positions" by delaying delivery from 3 months to 3 months.

Ubiquity & Triple Accounting

A common view shared among analysts is that there is triple accounting. The same silver bullions are recorded three times:
- in COMEX warehouses in the New York market
- in LBMA warehouses, the London market
- in SLV warehouses, on horseback between London and NY

But, the official guards of the different warehouses are the same two complicit banks: JPM and HSBC. A simplistic mind could tax these accusations with the catch-all term, "conspiracy theory", but this would ignore the warnings of the market authorities including the American CFTC. This recently strengthened agency should implement all the new laws passed in July 2010 to regulate this market. But, they have the powerful US Wall Street Banks in front of them.

On his website, the CFTC warns against fraud on the precious metals market.

(Quote)
NOTICE AGAINST CONSUMER FRAUD

Beware of companies that sell investments in precious metals that make promises of easy profits to be made from rising prices in gold, silver, platinum, palladium and other precious metals.

Be especially alert to companies that sell investments in precious metals, claiming that you can make a lot of money with little risk by purchasing metal through a financing agreement with only a small payment upfront.

The CFTC has seen an increase in the number of companies that offer customers the opportunity to buy or invest in precious metals. However, many of these companies do not actually purchase or store any metals for their customers.

This precious metals consumer fraud advisory describes how some precious metals companies may use fraudulent tactics to induce customers to invest, how these companies actually operate and provides warning signs to help you identify a potential precious metals scam.

The CFTC's experience is that precious metals companies, making such sales often, do not purchase any precious metals for the customers at any time. Yet charge phony investment, insurance and storage fees.

Do not store any metal with an independent bank or storage facility, but charge phony storage fees.

WARNING SIGNS

Beware of precious metals companies that:
- Expressly state that their precious metals transactions are not regulated by the Commodity Futures Trading Commission (CFTC) or the National Futures Association (NFA). Such statements are common in account agreements associated with precious metals scams.
- Do not identify where the physical metal is located, or claim to deliver the physical metal to a foreign bank or foreign storage facility.

USE EXTRA CARE WHEN DEALING WITH U.S. COMPANIES CLAIMING TO USE OVERSEAS STORAGE FACILITIES

Sometimes, U.S. companies that solicit customer investments in precious metals claim that the metals will be delivered to a facility located outside the United States.

If you place your funds in U.S. companies that make such claims, it may be difficult or impossible for you to verify your investment or recover your money.

Therefore, ask where your funds will be deposited and kept, where the metal will be stored and, if possible, call the overseas storage facility. **(End of quote from CFTC website)**

If we compare this official warning with the SLV ETF prospectus: from the 1st paragraph of the 1st page, there is a sign, CROOKS.

"The trust is not a commodity pool for purposes of the Commodity Exchange Act, and its sponsor is not subject to regulation by the Commodity Futures Trading Commission as a commodity pool operator, or a commodity trading advisor."

The CFTC warned you above, beware of companies, that *"expressly state, that their precious metals transactions are not regulated by the CFTC or the NFA."*

"Neither the Securities and Exchange Commission (SEC) nor any state securities commission has approved or disapproved of the securities offered in this prospectus, or determined if this prospectus is truthful or complete. Any representation to the contrary is a criminal offense."

SLV is warning you that neither the S.E.C. (Stock Exchange Authorities) nor any other government agency has approved or disapproved of the terms of this prospectus, nor even indicated it was telling the truth or a plot (understand if it lied by omission). In other words, this document has no legal value in the United States.

"Silver owned by the trust will be held by the custodian in England, and other locations that may be authorized in the future."

The CFTC has warned you against *"U.S. companies that solicit customer investments in precious metals and claim that the metals will be delivered to a storage facility located outside of the United States."*

In short, the GLD and SLV ETF correspond point by point to these scams described by the CFTC. SLV largely uses cash from customers, not to buy silver, but to control the price, by short selling on the silver futures that they do not have or no longer have. Note that if JPM and HSBC and their accomplices are crooks, protected by their financial powers and their multiple accomplices in the American plutocracy, are there honest and serious ETFs ?

The Zurich Kantonal Bank (ZKB) was theoretically guaranteed by the Swiss state. In June 2012 Jim Willie published the misadventures of a ZKB customer who requested for the delivery of his metal (gold and silver). He received a motion to dismiss from the bank. Despite all the previous claims by the bank, he was only the owner of certificates. Finally, ZKB issued a check for the customer who then went to buy precious metals from other places. In 2013, officially, ZKB tells you, that you cannot ask for delivery. You buy a tracker on gold or silver. That's it.

Sprott Management is supposed to be exemplary but its ETF might be too prominent to forfeit easily. His Gold and Silver could be easily nationalized.

CYRILLE JUBERT

A MARKET IN PERPETUAL DEFICIT

3000 AC - 1492   1493 - 1930   1931 - 2011
procuction minière en milliards d'onces

The discovery of deposits in the Americas and Japan as well as the improved extraction and refining techniques allowed a sharp growth in silver production from the 16th Century to the end of the 19th Century.

The combustion engine, electricity, new mining prospection and exploration techniques accelerated production exponentially throughout the 20th Century especially from 1970.

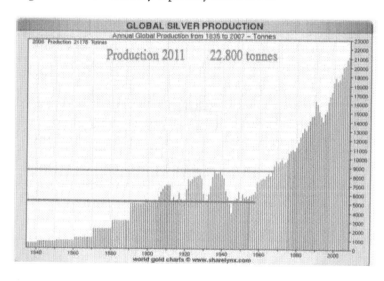

Silver throughout History

In the aftermath of the Second World War, the consumer society brought a proliferation of more sophisticated household appliances essential for "modern comfort".

The invention of electronics, then integrated circuits and microprocessors in the late 60s led to an extremely high demand for silver, essential material for its intrinsic conductibility.

Silver is the best conductor among the elements.

From 1950, the U.S. Treasury alone held 2 billion ounces of silver. He had to arbitrate this market in deficit by selling the metal to prevent silver to exceed the rate of its monetary value.

From 1960 to 1965, 342 million ounces were sold for the same purpose and 814 million ounces were still used to mint coins. In 1965, Lyndon Johnson was forced to admit that industrial demand is such that it would become impossible for the U.S. Treasury to continue to mint silver coins.

Silver was replaced by coins made up of different cupro-nickel alloys. Most countries followed the American example and demonetized silver. Governments had a fabulous silver stock estimated at 10 billion ounces that they sold on the market Their objective was twofold:
- Control the precious metals market to prevent speculation against the fiat currencies, at a time when the dollar was under attack due to the U. S. budget deficits (1963-1973)
- Sell their useless stocks in the best conditions.

From 1966 to November 1970, the U.S. government alone sold 674 million ounces. The government stock melted with only 170 million remaining in 1971. The Hunt brother raised the price and were fleeced by the U.S. government who put in place structures to better control prices.

The development of information technology in the past 3 decades, and the generalization of a society of communication (PC and phones) resulted in high industrial demand, since all the electronic connections required a small amount of silver.

Demand always precedes Production.

CYRILLE JUBERT

The deficit accumulates.

Année	Prod	Cons
1942	249	280
1943	217	370
1944	186	285
1945	157	300
1946	129	220
1947	157	250
1948	173	260
1949	174	230
1950	203	275
1951	199	270
1952	216	260
1953	216	270
1954	214	230
1955	223	217
1956	222	260
1957	231	296
1958	239	270
1959	222	301
1960	240	325
1961	231	352
1962	242	366
1963	251	409
1964	249	550
1965	251	708
1966	253	484
1967	266	452
1968	275	438
1970	301	397

Année	Prod	Cons
1971	294	379
1972	301	427
1973	308	495
1974	295	459
1975	294	390
1976	316	467
1977	340	457
1978	344	478
1979	346	447
1980	341	355
1981	361	353
1982	383	364
1983	392	349
1984	415	363
1985	418	446
1986	418	495
1987	445	496
1988	460	536
1989	474	546
1991	485	544
1992	503	602
1993	473	620
1994	446	636
1995	483	600
1996	491	742
1997	520	771
1998	544	812
1999	548	838

Année	Prod	Cons
2000	587	904
2001	611	867
2002	607	838
2003	611	853
2004	634	836

Un Déficit
chaque année
depuis 71 ans

Silver throughout History

Since the beginning of mankind, man has refined almost 4.4 billion ounces of gold and 48 billion ounces of silver. Ten times more.

Nearly 95% of gold was retained in the form of coins or bullions.

Nearly 85% of silver was finally destroyed by the industry. *

In 1900, the global stock was 12 billion ounces of silver.*
In 1933, the global monetary stock was 4.94 billion ounces.*
In 1990, there were only 2.2 billion ounces of silver .*
In 2011, there was less than 1 billion ounces.
The rest has been destroyed by the industry.*

(*) These figures do not include the silver transformed into jewelry

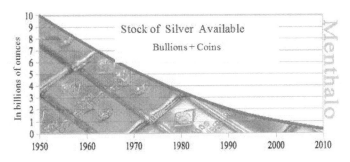

Government stocks were completely sold.

In 2011 there was nearly 800 million ounces of silver in coins or bullions in private hands, or ETFs… plus strategic or monetary reserves of China and perhaps India, as we shall see in the pages ahead. In theory, these 800 million alone should only cover two or three years of deficit which could cause a panic in the West.

Individuals who stocked silver are waiting for the price to be released so the price of silver finally reflect this shortage.

CYRILLE JUBERT

THE REFERENCE MARKETS

Two major international markets set the price of gold and silver followed by the secondary markets, Zurich and Tokyo (Tocom).

The Shanghai Gold Exchange is expected to play an essential role in the coming years. It seems to be already a good challenger for the LME

The **London Bullion Market** is the oldest and largest of the gold and silver « futures » markets. 18 million ounces of gold and 107 million ounces of silver are traded daily on this market. In other words, total annual gold production are exchanged every 4.4 days and the total silver production every 6 days.

GATA (Gold Anti-Trust Association) said that these figures are reduced and that the total annual gold production is traded every day in London. The same applies to silver.

If there are accounts allocated where the dealers keep the bars numbered and referenced for any customer, most of the trade is done with non-allocated metal. The actual metal reserves is supposed to cover 15% of metal traded daily.

It suffices for 1 out of 6 customers to request for the delivery of the metal purchased to empty the stocks and lead to a systemic crash. On the London market, customers may request for delivery of their metal two days after purchase. This rule has been changed in august 2013 for 5 days. It is therefore a physical market even if it is the biggest electronic metals or "paper" market.

New York COMEX operates in the same way as the LBM but delivery can be requested for only at the end of the month. Some months (March, June, September, December) are more important than others.

A silver contract on COMEX is 5,000 ounces. A law passed since 2008 allows COMEX traders to replace physical delivery with SLV or GLD shares. COMEX is now a very provincial market beside of Shanghai.

The market regulator is the CFTC (Commodity Futures Trading Commission) which has practically no authority today due to the presence of the dominant banks.

CYRILLE JUBERT

Silver throughout History

The Price of Silver

Price Elasticity of Demand

Generally, when the price of certain products increases, demand weakens. This is known as price elasticity of demand compare to price.

In the case of silver, the elasticity is zero, meaning, industrial demand does not decrease when the price increases. Why?

A mobile phone contains only 0.250 grams of silver or about 18 euro cents. Even if the price of silver increased tenfold, it would not change the demand for 5 billion mobile telephones in the world (2010 sales).

In a desktop computer or laptop, there is only one gram of silver, or €0.72. The price of silver will not affect demand.

Your car has between 10 and 30 grams of silver depending on the model. This is not what affects the selling price of cars.
The automobile market absorbs 36 million ounces of silver or 5% of mining production. Market growth in emerging countries, China and India in mind, is expected to increase demand in the coming years.

Manufacturers cannot replace silver with ersatz due to its unique qualities. **Silver metal is a pure element and the best conductor of electricity at room temperature.**

Price Control

At the time when silver was the currency, we saw that an influx of too much metal (from 1550 to 1650) had led to high inflation in the prices of goods and commodities. The purchasing power of silver fell.

Governments therefore controlled the price of silver metal so that it does not exceed the face value of coins. To do this, they lowered the silver content in coins before removing all silver coins except the collectibles.

From 1934, the united States monopolized the mass of silver money on the planet to control its price and let its intrinsic monetary value be forgotten. The U.S. government and allied central banks sought to control the price of gold and by extension, that of silver to maintain the illusion about the strength of the U.S. dollar, the currency required for international trade.

The control of gold was done by agreements between central banks which sold large quantities of gold to each other to control prices. These formal agreements were called Washington Agreement on Gold (WAG). The latest to date authorized the sale of only 500 tons.

The control of the price of silver was done by the sale of government stock of bullions. This stock of silver money was exhausted in the early 2000's. Since 2006, various complementary techniques have been used by the banks and organizations supposed to regulate the markets.

COMEX raised the margins and custodian fees, forcing speculators to sell part of their contracts when the speculation sparks.

Partners of the Anglo American banking cartel used subtle maneuvers to sell above certain key levels to cause automatic traders robots sales and thus drop the price from one level to the other.

SLV allowed the cartel to control the cash invested in the metal as well as a large quantity of silver metal which can be introduced abruptly on the market to bring down the prices.

Silver throughout History

The banking cartel also borrowed (lease) some amount of metal either from Bullion Banks, investment funds (ETF), states and oil companies, to sell it on the futures market. When they had to return the metal borrowed, the banking cartels offered SLV shares, therefore paper money instead of hard metal. If lenders refused, they were repaid in dollars with a high premium on the value of the silver.

The losses generated tooth and nail to defend the apparent value of the dollar cost the banking cartels nothing. The Federal Reserve, not accountable to anyone, refilled the accounts of the defenders from the generous transfers of billions of dollars, as was recently demonstrated by the audit of the U.S. Congress.

When short vendors found themselves in a tight corner, unable to deliver, they did not hesitate to bankrupt a bank whose "long" position disturbed their maneuvers, as was the case with Bear Stearns or make a Broker fall, as was done in October 2011 to MF Global, swiping the customers' metals at the same time.

Therefore, the price of silver has always been controlled but different forces caused the increase of the base price by TEN in a decade. Prices shot up from **$5 to $50 from 2002 to 2011.**

Recent history appears to suggest that the price could increase significantly in the coming months and years.

The fact that this metal is essential in many key technologies, that its production was lower than demand for 70 years in a row, as well as its scarcity, call for increased advocacy in this direction.

Current negotiations between the various factions of the oligarchy, include among others, the role of silver compared to gold and oil in a potential basket of commodities. Nothing has been decided today but we know that this subject is on the table.

CYRILLE JUBERT

Future Price

In 2013, we see a decrease in the effects of financial leverage which would cause a deflation in all the markets. The price of silver could fall at the first stage.

At the second stage, currencies will seek to devalue competitively to continue to monetize the debts of the states. Prices of commodities in general, and those of precious metals in particular, will then increase significantly.

According to our analysis on one hand, and information from other sources, on the other, the price of gold is expected to reach a value around $3,450 an ounce (in session) The price of silver could then take a sharp upward trend which could bring it between $145 and $175.

From 2014 to 2016, the inflation born from massive injections of liquidity by the central banks since 2008, should lead to a sharp rise in the prices of precious metals but also in everything.

Silver prices could exceed unreasonable limits for various reasons that we will see later. I think its price should stabilize between 900 and 3,000 today's dollars.

SILVER CYCLES
Annual Cycle

Silver also goes through an annual cycle. The lowest point is traditionally in late June before it starts increasing again. The highest point is linked to deliveries to COMEX in December and March.

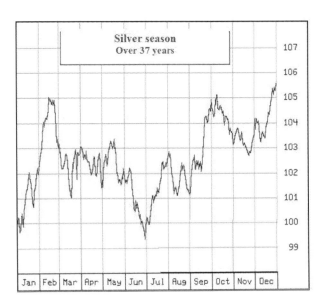

This statistical truth is not verified every year.

According to a study by Gertrude Shirk, who predicted the highest point dates in 1980, the price of silver undergo cycles of 31 years, 15.36 years, 9.26 years and 5.58 years.
Highest point **1980 + 31 years = 2011**
Highest point Late April 2011 + 5.58 = **December 2016?**

The price of silver is also closely linked to that of gold. One pulls the other upward or downward. In 1979-80, it was mainly the price of silver that pulled that of gold.

I am convinced that in the short term, Gold will follow the same pattern as in 1979-1980 and 2008.

It appears that silver has had the same long term support for 100 years. We would have bounced over in 2002. This long term support is around $9 actually.

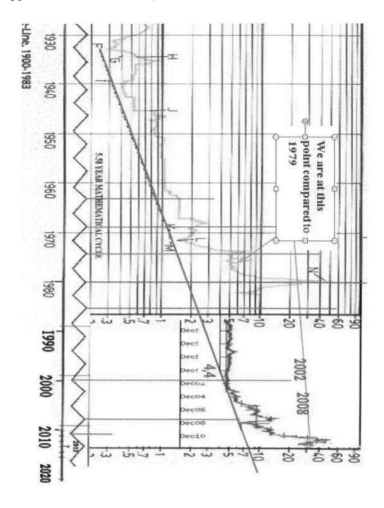

Silver throughout History

According to this study by Gertrude Shirk
Highest point late April 2011 + 5.58 = **December 2016?**

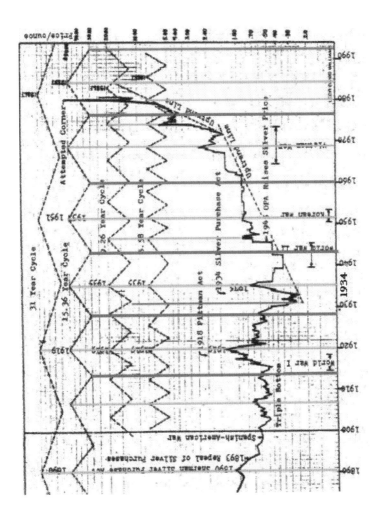

Figure from 1979-1980

The rebound in the price of gold led to the rebound in that of silver with perhaps a time lag. If the price of silver decreased sharply, it rose again even more sharply.

Since 2001, prices have been fluctuating in the channel drawn below. The subprime crisis and the collapse of Lehman Brothers caused a financial tsunami in 2008 forcing hedge funds to sell the securities that resisted best including gold and silver.

When current prices rise above the upper limit of the channel COMEX changed 5 times the trading rules in 8 days, resulting in a strong consolidation of the prices. Recovery of higher silver price should resume at the end of the summer.

We will see later, in the news section, why I expect the price to be around $200 first, then at a minimum level of $1,000 in the coming years. You just have to be patient and not stress yourself out because of the news.

Silver is a long term investment.

The Future Bubble of the Century

Silver throughout History

We are experiencing a change in cycle.

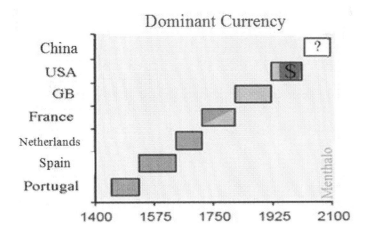

The peso of the Spanish Empire gave way to the florin of Amsterdam, which also gave way to the Germinal Franc. The bimetallism in France collapsed before the gold standard of the British Empire at the peak of its power. The Second World War established the dollar, first exchangeable against gold, and then as a fiat currency. The American Empire is buried in corruption and failure at the end of the reign. The barons of the regime, the WS and the City bankers, defend the fiat money tooth and nail, using any means in defiance of all laws.

China has become the world's second economic power and is taking control. By establishing the bilateral monetary swaps with Russia, Japan, India, Brazil, Iran, United Arab Emirates, South Africa and recently Chili and excluding the use of the dollar, the Chinese are weakening the declining international money.

The Anglo-American banks which required that these capital flows passed through their clearing companies could collapse due to the loss of their prerogatives.

Simultaneously, the highly innovative and sophisticated financial products created by WS in the 1990s, have become death traps. Like viruses, these products increased in the heart of the financial institutions making the banking system totally interdependent. The bankruptcy of some of them will inevitably lead to the bankruptcy of the others in a systemic chain crash.

The governments and the central banks are trying to save the banking system by printing currency endlessly. It is like trying to save a drowned person by forcing him to drink. Now, by creating currency in trillions of dollars, pounds, euros or yens, the bankers are destroying the fiat currencies. If this system manages to last for a year or at most 18 months, all the nations will experience Argentina or Weimar hyperinflation. The German Republic saw its currency destroyed due to excessive debts. Our nation states are in the same situation.

I do not think that the people in the world will be enslaved by debt in the disenchanted future. This is the situation today, but it could be shattered at the end of this cycle. These upheavals will probably involve difficult and chaotic transition phases. But I am confident in the future, once the storms pass.

Silver metal is more likely to help you to pass through this course of monetary destruction, than gold. Silver will remain an essential metal for the industry, as well as for monetary authorities. The market deficit for over 70 years, hidden for monetary and political reasons, will worsen over the years. All the banks who worked to prevent the price increase went bankrupt one after the other. The central banks who led this policy covertly are at the brink of bankruptcy today.

I KNOW that gold will be remonetized at the Central Bank's level.

Silver should be... do we ever know?

But for several reasons, as we have seen, its price will soar.

Silver throughout History

I think a "tulip mania" will develop on silver in the coming years. For now, we are very far from it. The Tulip mania in 1647 saw an increase of 5,900%. eDigital' bubble topped the list with 45,400% but if you look again at Weimar prices, everything is possible, when the lack of confidence in the money drives the hyperinflation.

Date:	German Marks needed to buy one ounce of gold
Jan 1919	170.00
Sept 1919	499.00
Jan 1920	1,340.00
Sept 1920	1,201.00
Jan 1921	1,349.00
Sept 1921	2,175.00
Jan 1922	3,976.00
Sept 1922	30,381.00
Jan 1923	372,477.00
Sept 1923	269,439,000.00
Oct 2, 1923	6,631,749,000.00
Oct 9, 1923	24,868,950,000.00
Oct 16, 1923	84,969,072,000.00
Oct 23, 1923	1,160,552,882,000.00
Oct 30, 1923	1,347,070,000,000.00
Nov 5, 1923	8,700,000,000,000.00
Nov 30, 1923	87,000,000,000,000.00

For nearly a century, the price of silver was held in check by the U.S. Treasury and then crashed by the banking cartel in 1971. The situation is still the same today. We are going to witness a swing back with an excess in the opposite direction, which we should be wary of one day.

Bix Weir - Road-to-Roota Theory, developed a 20-point analysis, a surge in silver price at **$204,964 an ounce**. I consider Bix

Weir's analysis as a sheer folly, unless it is a Zimbabwean hyperinflation, that is, a destruction of the fiat money. In that case, there won't be any limit.

The Silver Mania

We may wonder what events could trigger a maniac phase in the increase of silver price. For now, there is absolute peace and quiet. The press has not yet spoken about the white metal, nor its significant increase from 2010-2011, nor for its current consolidation.

When the rise in gold price will exceed $1,920, silver could be at its lowest price due to the recent manipulation of banksters on COMEX silver paper. Will the peculiar speed at which silver prices increase bring it back to its unavoidable stages and settle at $50 and then shoot up suddenly to $72 before widening its horizons...?

Rising Oil Prices

A conflict in the Persian Gulf which would threatened oil supplies of the West, causing oil prices to increase rapidly to $250. With wage costs, the price of energy, is the second budget of the expenses of the mining industry. Rising oil prices would lead to a rise in that of gold and silver, otherwise all the mining companies would go bankrupt. If the latter are in bankruptcy, the supply would decrease while the demand would continue to increased thus raising the price of physical silver.

Shortage and Delivery Times

Delivery time will extend, due to the continued shortage. The manufacturers of electronic, photovoltaic, computer, photography and medical equipment will want to stock white metal in order not to experience technical unemployment, when they finally became aware of the shortage in the market. Therefore the industrial demand for physical silver will increase abruptly. The huge orders for silver by an Asian buyer in June has currently monopolized several refineries that can start delivery only after two months. There is very few stock available today. The situation may come under significant pressure very quickly.

Derivatives Tsunami

For the record, JPM and partners still have about 6.5 years of production that was short sold through derivatives. When the

Silver throughout History

reprisals against JPM resume, it will have to cover all its positions in disaster upwards. In other words, there will be a sort of public auction where JPM will offer higher and higher purchase price until the vendors agree to release their treasures. This can be very brutal, much more brutal than the gold or silver graph for 1979-80, when prices multiplied by 10 within 12 months.

GOLD CONFISCATION
2013, 2014 OR 2015?

Remember John Law's bankruptcy under the Regency!
Remember what the state did during the collapse of the assignats!

So many times during the century, the state sought to recover gold from individual as in the case of Roosevelt in 1934.

Now imagine the price of gold soaring as expected and rising within a few weeks or months to $3,450. Assuming that at this stage, in one way or the other, western governments have blocked prices and confiscated gold. The physical stocks of Gold ETF and other Bullion Banks and gold in "metal accounts" in the banks will be nationalized.

We know through an insider that such an opportunity has already been the subject of an agreement between bankers in Switzerland. This process will be triggered if the national currency falls in danger.

All individuals and institutions will then be required to deliver their gold to the government as it happened in 1934, or other sad periods in history, in a more or less motivating or coercive way. Silver, in history, has also been confiscated. Today, the elites are trying to make us believe that it is just a base industrial metal. They are not going to change a policy that they implemented since the Mexican War of Independence which led to the demonetization of silver in 1873 and the pure fiat money in 1971.

Today, silver is already confiscated due to its price.

Investors who relied on gold will have to fall back on an alternative investment. Having suddenly received huge sums of money after being paid by the government in brand new bank notes they will then rush on silver as the second safe investment.
The microscopic silver market cannot support such acceleration in demand for physical silver. Prices could then resemble those of Weimar by soaring high.

And especially after a few days or weeks at the expiry of the ultimatum to return gold, the central banks, with one accord, could massively devalue fiat currencies by reducing the price of gold to 10 times its previous value around $32,000. This devaluation could spread over several months or during a long week-end.

2014-2015

Once again, this event seems to have been programmed by the Federal Reserve, which bought debt payable in 30 years and debts with 2 years maturity on the market. At that time, the U.S. economy will be in deeper crisis than today: tax revenues will not be sufficient to repay the debts and the United States will massively devalue the dollar after gold confiscation, in order not to default on debt payment.

Silver could reach its peak in 5.58 years after that of 2011, around the middle of December 2016.

In the 70s, an American pastor, David Wilkinson, revealed his prophetic visions many of which have already been fulfilled:
"Holders of gold will lose everything one day."
"Silver price will reach an astronomical value."

Silver has always experienced chaotic and violent times. It will be fun to surf this gigantic bubble by keeping a cool head and trying to make the best out of this mafia system.

It is certain that we should invest heavily in silver before gold gets confiscated and before the U.S. Treasury Bonds expire in 2015.

Watch the movie, "Le Sucre". This bubble can inflate for months or even years for silver to reach unimaginable values if the "exogenous events" allow the bankers to get to their end. The trick of course will be to transform this wealth in time by diversifying one's capital in the best timing possible, by monitoring the gold/silver ratio but also the prices of real estate, cereals and acres of agricultural land which have already gone up.

Prepare a refuge in the countryside so that you will not be in the city when the disturbances related to the economic and monetary collapse will begin. **Take your treasure out of the cities**, because in case of social unrest, you cannot do that safely because it is always difficult to travel with kilos of silver. Put it where you think you can run to and take refuge in times of unrest.

If you have a place to store it, don't hesitate to diversify your investments. Gold and silver are not edible. If you can, store grains and non-perishable food items which will allow you to feed your family or barter.

The Hammurabi Code
€900 an ounce

In the historical part at the beginning, I told you about the first code of laws of humanity, that of Judge Hammurabi who reigned in Mesopotamia in 1750 BC. At the gate of each city, a monument recalling the legislation in force was erected so that no one claimed to be unaware of the laws. Among them was the salary of a worker, expressed in grams of silver.

A laborer earned between 1.88 and 2.1 grams of silver per day.

At the current price of $32, 2 grams are worth about €1.60
The net daily minimum wage in 2012 is €57.84
2 grams should be worth €57.84
So an ounce of silver should be worth 28.92 x 31.10 = €899

Silver should today be 37 times more expensive.

The Hammurabi Code is surprisingly referred to often, either by the freemasons or those who are supposed to be their opponents on the other side of the mirror. On 31 March, he was again cited by Drake who was interviewed by David Wilcox about the impending American Revolution. According to them, these laws were dictated by the gods. It appears that for most people in the oligarchy, this first phase of the history of mankind is essential.

The tablets found on many archaeological sites provided evidence that Hammurabi conducted four general cancellations of debts (in -1792, -1780, -1771 and -1762 B.C.). To ensure social peace, the powers that be canceled periodically all debts of the population, thus avoiding free men to become enslaved by their debts and limiting the constitution of too large private properties. There is evidence of debt cancellation by judges before and after Hammurabi from -2400 to -1400 B.C. The famous Rosetta Stone, translated by Champollion mention these debt cancellations in both Mesopotamia and Egypt.

Our leaders would do well to imitate the wisdom of the ancients in the cancellation of debts, before they face uncontrollable uprisings.

CONCLUSIONS

This book has been written backwards. Fully aware of the current manipulations of bankers following orders of the financial oligarchy, I dug backwards in History. The more I learned, the more new stories enriched the picture. Even today, informations are still flooding in: about the reasons why Julius Caesar was assassinated, or the actual reasons for the Cromwell Revolution or the slaughter of the Templar. I refrained from adding chapters on the huge gold scams put in place since the 60s by the world leaders. There should be a complete book on that subject. This one is already quite heavy.

Retain the most essential:
The enormity of the debt bubble involves monetization, ie devaluation of currencies against the tangible values, including gold and silver. Gold could reach a value between $32,000 and $53,000 by 2020. After a first plateau around $3,450. Gold will probably be reserved for the central banks, as it was the case in the U.S.A in 1934.

When will this confiscation take place? We do not know it. My reference timing is the peak of $3,450.

Remember also that two hundred 20F gold coins were enough to support a family during the last war and a world war could be close.

You won't see silver coins in the street in the world of tomorrow. There is not enough metal for that and silver is essential to many industries. Nevertheless, silver will experience a phase of panic buying from investors when gold will be confiscated and it will not be possible to give a limit to the final price during this bubble.

Israel Friedman wrote that one day silver will become more expensive than gold. That will not be difficult if the price for the public is blocked at $3,500. Silver in a bubble can do a lot more.

In 2013, it has been difficult to find silver in large quantities in France. Those who have any doesn't want to sell it at the current price. That is why you should purchase when you have the opportunity, even if you have to pay a premium on the official price. You will congratulate yourself in the coming years.

We know that very large national and international funds are in cash today, not knowing the value or the currency which will collapse the least in the coming months.

When the "deleveraging" tsunami will be over, these funds will be engulfed in the bullish wave of precious metals, accelerating its speed of surge, whose violence will be proportional to the QE of central banks.

It is recalled that in June 2012, the largest banks in the world had to fill a very detailed document called their "living wills" so that in case of bankruptcy, the authorities can untangle their most secret operations. The shadow-banking, guarantees that banks give to each other for every operation have formed a very close mesh.

Today where small bankruptcies are increasing, these guarantees are called daily, giving headaches to the authorities and putting all the majors in danger.

When banks and states go bankrupt, chaos sets in very quickly. Argentines have experienced it from 1998 to 2002; as well as the Russians, during the same period. We pass very quickly from the comfort to the most precarious life.

This will also happen to us, probably as soon as 2014. An insider told us in July, that we will see new banks falling.

Your silver metal is the best insurance in adversity.

Nobody knows at the time of this writing, if the bail-in will not capture the contents of your safe, be they in France, Canada, Belgium, Luxembourg or Switzerland. Prudence is the mother of Surety. Get out your precious metals from bank vaults.

Some Disaster Scenarios

Silver throughout History

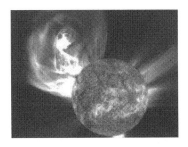

The "exogenous event" mentioned above refer to an electromagnetic shock which may have two origins.

An EMP (Electro Magnetic Pulse) is a high altitude explosion which causes an electromagnetic wave. The EMP technology was born out of American nuclear experiments on the Bimini Atoll. The shock wave cause electrical problems in Hawai at thousands of kilometers from there. The present currency war between the USA and the BRICAD could lead to the use of EMP weapons to destroy, in an instant, a large part of the Western electronics and reduce the U.S. financial power instantly to nothing.

The movie, *Ocean's Eleven* shows the use of an EMP.

An ELM is an electromagnetic storm coming from a natural source. It could be caused by a solar CME (Coronal Mass Ejection), due to a peak in solar activity, such as photographed on June 13 2011 (photo above). If such CME is directed towards the earth, it will cause a major electromagnetic storm, and destroy all the electrical and electronic installations in its path. Such an event occurred several times with greater or lesser intensity. In 1859, a violent electromagnetic storm destroyed all the telegraph networks in North America and Europe.

Background of the state of the world in 1859.
In 1832, Samuel Morse invented an electric telegraph in the laboratory.
In 1838, the first electric telegraph was built by Wheatstone and operated between London and Birmingham.
In 1859, the telegraphic networks were certainly booming though they were still in their very early stages.
In 1879, Thomas Edison introduced his first incandescent light bulb.
In 1859, there were no networks for electrical lighting and fewer

high tension lines, microchips, computers, purely electronic bank accounts, etc.

In 1989, a solar storm deprived 6 million people of electricity.

The NASA heliophysicians announced in the press on several occasions in 2011, that a very violent ELM storm was expected in the coming months and years with absolute certainty. The peak of the probability would be between 2012 and 2015. They announced that the solar storm could put an end to the current electronic civilization.

Where appropriate, the electronic payment systems would become inoperative and all commercial food and energy distribution channels will be blocked to create total economic, political and social chaos. No more drinkable water at the tap, no more natural gaz or gasoline, no more electricity for months, no more credit cards and not a cent left on your bank account.

People with their capital in gold or silver coins will instantly have an immeasurable increase in their relative purchasing power.

It is likely that the public will never know if this electromagnetic storm was of human or solar origin.

Disturbing Coincidences

US-AF Study

A "US-AF research" paper, written in 1996, trying to determine the role of US-AF in 2025, described a scenario of possible futures. Originally classified document, it has remained classified since. This paper discusses a global H1N1 pandemic in 2009 (which actually took place, at least in the media) and **destruction of WS and U.S. finance by electromagnetic weapons in 2012.**

You can check this information for yourself
http://csat.au.af.mil/2025/a_f.pdf
By shortening the link, http://csat.au.af.mil

CSAT= center for Strategy and Technology
AU=Air University
AF=Air Forces
.mil= indicates a military site

Obviously, this is only a possible scenario. However, it should be emphasized that we are at the heart of a global monetary and financial war which has lasted for several years. Tensions have risen between China, Russia, the U.S. and NATO, with a dangerous fixation point around Iran. Iran is only a terrorist country, because it threatens the stability of the dollar, this is the worst crime in the Anglo American oligarchy.

Lindsey Williams regularly reveals part of the timing of the cartel on order from them. It has so far turned out to be relatively accurate and reliable.

In 2008, when oil price soared to $150 and GS announced a surge to $200, LW declared during a radio show that oil prices would not go up but rather fall under $50 per barrel. This was verified in the following months.

In October 2010, he announced that certain events would take place on February 15 in the MENA and a war will be launched on March 15. These events are now referred to as the "Arab Spring" since that time. The war in Libya was triggered on march 15. These two pieces of information were perfectly accurate and the timing could not be more precise.

In mid-October 2011, he announced that *"before the end of 2012, all the fortunes in paper values (i.e. electronic) will be totally wiped out."* He did not give any explanation as to why or how.

Of course, you already know that the timing was false, but this event has just been delayed. We know that the oligarchs changed their timings at least 3 times in the 7 last years. This alert could correspond to an EMP of human origin which will destroy the wealth of the middle classes and also reduce most of the US financial power to nothing in view of a New monetary World Order later.

However, the wire-pullers of the oligarchy have the talent to STICK to natural events, amplify them or even create some that seem natural, but are totally caused by weapons such as HAARP or seismic weapons. It has always been very difficult to distinguish between what is natural and what is artificial, an if so, in what proportions.

If this EMP attack occurs, be sure it will be under false flag, they will accuse North Korea or Al Qaida. It will be an inside job of the financial oligarchy.

Prophecies

Marie Julie Jahenny lived in France between 1881 and 1942. She announced many events that already occurred. She described a terrible period of 3 years and a half, when France will have to face a serial of dramatic events, which would occur more or less in this order:
- Economic collapse, massive unemployment
- Opening of the doors of jails and asylums
- Social unrest, revolution and civil war
- Invasion wars from East and South
- Earthquakes, volcanic eruptions
- A three days and nights electromagnetic storm
- Famine and pandemia

There is obviously no maturity dates for these prophecies, except that the events will be linked to each other, then with great intensity for three and a half years. The economic collapse is already here. The French government do not send anymore thieves and offenders in jail. Social unrest is growing and an insider of the oligarchy told to a close friend of mine early august 2013, that we have to be prepared for 4 years of total Chaos.

These various events were also described by Father Pel and Padre Pio in the 50s. You will also find them in the prophecies of La Salette at the end of the 19th Century, in the revelations of Fatima in 1914 and in more than hundred different prophecies.

I really believe that we are about to live this in the months and years to come. Therefore, I don't think about gold and silver in financial terms but in terms of barter. I am not trying to stock more precious metal right now, but food to share with people that will be so poor tomorrow.

Connecting the dots

Now, if we look at what is natural but totally overshadowed by the media, you could fear the effects of the twelfth planet that the Assyrians called Nibiru and the Greeks named Nemesis. Its cycle is supposed to be about 3600 years. It is back and close to our solar system and disrupting its global balance.

It is a brown dwarf, which is 4 times the mass of Jupiter. Depending on its composition, its diameter could be at least 6 times or 37 times that of the earth. When this brown dwarf will get closer to the sun, in perihelion, it will cause a major electromagnetic storm. This ELM storm might destroy all the electronic financial values and the bulk of our modern comfort entirely driven by electronics, or a portion of the planet in its entirety. This will depend on the duration of the storm.

The prophecies describe a magnetic storm which will last for three nights and two days. This means the whole world will be affected.

In earlier civilizations, the passages of Nibiru and Nemesis were associated with disasters, such as flood and violent movements of tectonic plates, like the one that wiped out the Atlantis.

Personally, I believe in the existence of this brown dwarf, after a thorough investigation for several months about it. NASA closed the information to public consultation but many more tools, many huge information sites, have confirmed the existence of a celestial body which is putting us in danger. There also, what are the deadlines?

In May 2012, the British Daily Mail wrote an article about the presence of a Brown Dwarf near Pluto. We already had this information five years ago.

I consider the destruction of electronics by an ELM shock as a future fact with a very high probability, which can happen at any time between the end of 2013 and 2017. If all the electronics is destroyed, there will be no more bank accounts and people will no longer have any means of payment. Instantly, gold and silver will be worth an absolute fortune.

Silver throughout History

Nobody can hope such chaos. With no means of communication or information, without possibility to travel, buy or sell, trapped in cities which will receive no more supplies, with power cuts, random water distribution, society will quickly turn into a barbaric state.

You are probably doubting whether this could happen and yet, the European Union opened the Ark Green Norway with pomp and pageantry, an underground bunker which houses all the grains which form the wealth and diversity of this planet.

And yet, civilian and military underground cities have been rehabilitated and modernized in recent years in the United States, Russia, China or Europe. They are now fully operational. What are they going to be used for and when?

Why do FEMA organizes its "shake out" nationwide exercises?

Why these numerous FEMA camps all around the United States?

Why did the NASA asked is employees and contractors to "be prepared" for an emergency?

http://www.nasa.gov/centers/hq/emergency/personalPreparedness/index.html#.UgTKYxb0PzI

The government cannot create a panic by telling what will happen when this travelling brown dwarf will cross our solar system. You have better to search by yourself and be ready.

Even without this ELM storm, when banks go bankrupt, states are in default because of their debts, economic and social chaos can happen within a few days.

Simone Wapler, French editor in chief of the media group, Agora, also announced a total economic chaos. The subtitle of her letter particularly speaks for itself:

"You have the choice between famine or migration out of the cities."

Simone Wapler has always been very conservative in her analysis. These words have more weight under her pen.

It is time to look outside of your financial planet to find what is coming on in our societies.

For further information, visit:

www.eaupositive.com/contact.php

www.omniaveritas.org

August 2012

ABOUT THE AUTHOR

The unpretentious author claims to be a mere philistine, watchdog in a very complex market.

After studying economics and political science, Cyrille Jubert pursued a postgraduate degree in marketing. After passing through advertising agencies, he successfully created his company surfing the wave of telematics in France, the ancestor of internet.

Company founder, designer, journalist, he also developed his artistic talents to become "The" European portraitist of Gotha's kennels. Since 2008, putting away his brush to take up the pen, Cyrille Jubert scrutinized again the economics and politics, writing under the guise of Menthalo. Discovering the deliquescence of society and the dark monetary perspective, he focused on gold before exploring the niche market of silver. Early 2011, collecting 3 years of his analysis and chronicles, he first launched a 40 pages dossier about silver. Digging deeper and deeper through History to understand the real causes of today's events, Cyrille Jubert ended with a real book focusing on the role of Silver in geopolitics, drawing an exciting and colorful story.

Made in the USA
Lexington, KY
16 January 2014